THE LOEB CLASSICAL LIBRARY

FOUNDED BY JAMES LOEB, LL.D.

MINOR LATIN POETS

I

284

MINOR LATIN POETS

IN TWO VOLUMES

I

WITH AN ENGLISH TRANSLATION BY

J. WIGHT DUFF

EMERITUS PROFESSOR OF CLASSICS; DURHAM
FELLOW OF THE BRITISH ACADEMY

AND

ARNOLD M. DUFF

ASSISTANT LECTURER IN CLASSICS, UNIVERSITY COLLEGE
OF WALES, ABERYSTWYTH

CAMBRIDGE, MASSACHUSETTS
HARVARD UNIVERSITY PRESS

LONDON
WILLIAM HEINEMANN LTD

MCMLXXXII

American ISBN 0-674-99314-4
British ISBN 0 434 99284 4

First edition 1934
Revised edition 1935
Reprinted 1954, 1961, 1968, 1978, 1982

Printed in Great Britain
by Fletcher & Son Ltd, Norwich

CONTENTS

Volume I

CONTENTS
Volume II

CONTENTS

PREFACE TO NEW EDITION

The original edition of *Minor Latin Poets* (1934: revised edition 1935) was, for a series based on the principle of uniformity, disproportionately large; and it has now become necessary to divide the work into two volumes to conform with the size and price of other volumes in the Loeb Classical Library.

The material embraced in these two volumes provides some of the most difficult problems in editing Latin texts, and it is evident that for their solution much still remains to be done. Against the day when a definitive revision of the Loeb Minor Latin Poets becomes a feasible proposition I have noted at the appropriate places details of relevant work produced in recent years.

March 1982 G.P.G.

PREFACE TO FIRST EDITION

To select for inclusion in a single volume of the Loeb Library a series of works representing the minor poetry of Rome has been a task of much interest but of no little difficulty. The mere choice of poets and poems could hardly be thought easy by anyone acquainted with the massive volumes issued in turn by Burman senior and his nephew, the *Poetae Latini Minores* by the former (1731) and the *Anthologia Latina* by the latter (1759—1773). But a more serious difficulty confronted the editors; for, in spite of the labours of scholars since the days of Scaliger and Pithou on the minor poems collected from various sources, the text of many of them continues to present troublesome and sometimes irremediable *cruces*. This is notably true of *Aetna* and of Grattius; but even for the majority of the poems there cannot be said to be a *textus receptus* to be taken over for translation without more ado. Consequently the editors have had in most cases to decide upon their own text and to supply a fuller *apparatus criticus* than is needful for authors with a text better established. Certainly, the texts given by Baehrens in his *Poetae Latini Minores* could not be adopted wholesale; for his *scripsi* is usually ominous of alterations so arbitrary as to amount to a rewriting of the Latin.

At the same time, a great debt is due to Baehrens in his five volumes and to those who before him, like the Burmans and Wernsdorf, or after him, like

Vollmer, have devoted scholarly study to the *poetae Latini minores*. Two excellent reminders of the labours of the past in this field can be found in Burman's own elaborate account of his predecessors in the *Epistola Dedicatoria* prefixed to his *Anthologia*, and in the businesslike sketch which Baehrens' *Praefatio* contains. The editors' main obligations in connection with many problems of authorship and date may be gauged from the bibliographies prefixed to the various authors.

In making this selection it had to be borne in mind that considerable portions of Baehrens' work had been already included in earlier Loeb volumes—*e.g.* the *Appendix Vergiliana* (apart from *Aetna*) and the poems ascribed to Petronius. Also, the *Consolatio ad Liviam* and the *Nux*, both of which some scholars pronounce to be by Ovid, were translated in the Loeb volume containing *The Art of Love*. Other parts such as the *Aratea* of Germanicus were considered but rejected, inasmuch as an English translation of a Latin translation from the Greek would appear to be a scarcely suitable illustration of the genuine minor poetry of Rome. It was felt appropriate, besides accepting a few short poems from Buecheler and Riese, to add one considerable author excluded by Baehrens as dramatic, the mime-writer Publilius Syrus. He is the earliest of those here represented, so that the range in time runs from the days of Caesar's dictatorship up to the early part of the fifth century A.D., when Rutilius had realised, and can still make readers realise, the destructive powers of the Goths as levelled against Italy and Rome in their invasions. This anthology, therefore, may be regarded as one of minor imperial poetry extending over four and a half centuries. The arrangement is broadly chronological, though some poems, like the *Aetna*, remain of unsettled date and authorship.

While, then, the range in time is considerable, a correspondingly wide variety of theme lends interest to the poems. There is the didactic element—always typical of Roman genius—pervading not only the crisp moral saws of Publilius Syrus and the *Dicta Catonis*, but also the inquiry into volcanic action by the author of *Aetna* and the expositions of hunting-craft by Grattius and by Nemesianus; there is polished eulogy in the *Laus Pisonis*, and eulogy coupled with a plaintive note in the elegies on Maecenas; there is a lyric ring in such shorter pieces as those on roses ascribed to Florus. A taste for the description of nature colours the *Phoenix* and some of the brief poems by Tiberianus, while a pleasant play of fancy animates the work of Reposianus, Modestinus and Pentadius and the vignette by an unknown writer on *Cupid in Love*. Religious paganism appears in two *Precationes* and in the fourth poem of Tiberianus. Pastoral poetry under Virgil's influence is represented by Calpurnius Siculus, by the Einsiedeln Eclogues and by Nemesianus, the fable by Avianus, and autobiographic experiences on a coastal voyage by the elegiacs of Rutilius Namatianus. Although Rutilius is legitimately reckoned the last of the pagan classic poets and bears an obvious grudge against Judaism and Christianity alike, it should be noted, as symptomatic of the fourth century, that already among his predecessors traces of Christian thought and feeling tinge the sayings of the so-called "Cato" and the allegorical teaching of the *Phoenix* on immortality.

PREFACE

The English versions composed by the editors for this volume are mostly in prose; but verse translations have been written for the poems of Florus and Hadrian, for two of Tiberianus and one of Pentadius. Cato's *Disticha* have been rendered into heroic couplets and the *Monosticha* into the English iambic pentameter, while continuous blank verse has been employed for the pieces on the actor Vitalis and the two on the nine Muses, as well as for the *Cupid Asleep* of Modestinus. A lyric measure has been used for the lines by Servasius on *The Work of Time*. Some of the poems have not, so far as the editors are aware, ever before been translated into English.

The comparative unfamiliarity of certain of the contents in the miscellany ought to exercise the appeal of novelty. While *Aetna* fortunately engaged the interest of both H. A. J. Munro and Robinson Ellis, while the latter also did excellent service to the text of Avianus' *Fables*, and while there are competent editions in English of Publilius Syrus, Calpurnius Siculus and Rutilius Namatianus, there are yet left openings for scholarly work on the minor poetry of Rome. It possesses at least the merit of being unhackneyed: and the hope may be expressed that the present collection will direct closer attention towards the interesting problems involved.

Both editors are deeply grateful for the valuable help in copying and typing rendered by Mrs. Wight Duff.

July, 1934.

J. W. D.
A. M. D.

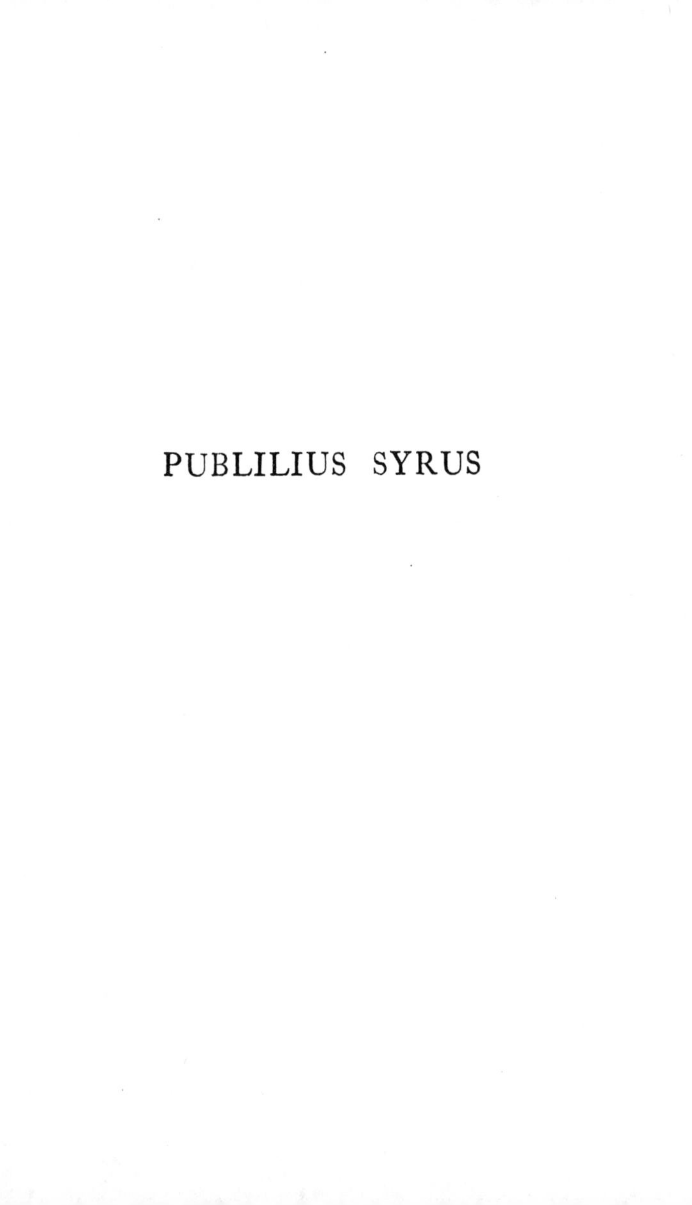

PUBLILIUS SYRUS

INTRODUCTION

TO PUBLILIUS SYRUS

To the Caesarian age belonged two prominent writers of mimes with both of whom the great Julius came into contact—Decimus Laberius (105–43 B.C.) and Publilius Syrus. Publilius reached Rome, we are told by the elder Pliny,[a] in the same ship as Manilius, the astronomical poet, and Staberius Eros, the grammarian. As a dramatic performance the mime[b] had imported from the Greek cities of Southern Italy a tradition of ridiculing social life in tones of outspoken mockery; it represented or travestied domestic scandals with ribald language and coarse gestures. At times it made excursions into mythological subjects: at times it threw out allusions which bore or seemed to bear audaciously on politics. Audiences who were tiring of more regular comedy found its free-and-easy licence vastly amusing, though Cicero's critical taste made it hard for him to sit through a performance of pieces by Laberius and Publilius.[c]

[a] Plin. *N.H.* xxxv. 58 (199). The correct form of his name, instead of the erroneous "Publius," was established by Woelfflin, *Phil.* 22 (1865), 439.

[b] See Hermann Reich, *Der Mimus, ein litterarentwickelungsgeschichtlicher Versuch*, Berlin, 1903. For brief account, J. Wight Duff, *Lit. Hist. of Rome*, 1909, pp. 222–23; Klotz, *Gesch. der röm. Lit.*, 1930, p. 77.

[c] *Ad Fam.* XII. 18. 2.

There came a day in 45 B.C. when Caesar forced the veteran knight Laberius—he was then sixty—to play in one of his own mimes as a competitor against the alien Publilius, who had thrown down a dramatic challenge to all comers. The dictator, while he awarded the prize to the foreigner, restored to the Roman, with ostentatious condescension, the ring which outwardly confirmed the equestrian rank sullied by his appearance on the stage. This eclipse of Laberius marked for Publilius an opportunity which he knew how to use. Some fresh invention, some originality in treatment capable of catching the popular favour, may be conjectured as the reason why the elder Pliny calls him " the founder of the mimic stage." Of Syrian origin, he had come to Rome as a slave, most likely from Antioch.[a] His wit secured his manumission, and the gift of understanding Roman psychology was a factor in his dramatic success. And yet, in contrast with forty-four known titles of plays by his vanquished rival Laberius, only two of Publilius' titles have come down to us in uncertain form—" The Pruners," *Putatores* (or, it has even been suggested, *Potatores*, " The Tipplers "), and one conjecturally amended to *Murmidon*.[b] Perhaps his improvisations were too precariously entrusted to actors' copies to guarantee literary immortality; and, in any case, though pieces of his were still staged under Nero, the mime gradually lost its vogue in favour of pantomime. The didactic element in him, however, was destined to survive. The elder Seneca praises him for

[a] Plin. *N.H. loc. cit. Publilium* † *lochium* (*Antiochium*, O. Jahn, *Phil.* 26, 11) *mimicae scenae conditorem*.

[b] Nonius, 2, p. 133; Priscian, *Gramm. Lat.* (Keil), 2, 532, 25.

putting some thoughts better than any dramatist, Greek or Roman; Petronius gives a specimen of his style in a passage sixteen lines long, and in the second century Gellius recognises the neatness and quotability of his moral maxims, of which he cites fourteen examples, all but one to be found in our extant collections.[a] Roman educators soon saw practical advantage in excerpting from his mimes, for use in school, wise saws and modern instances, the inherited experience of human conduct brought up to date in pithy Latin. Similar anthologies had already been made from Menander in Greek and very possibly from Ennius in Latin.[b] Such a text-book had been available for generations before Jerome[c] as a schoolboy learned the line "aegre reprendas quod sinas consuescere." But if the earliest collection of the maxims in the first century A.D. was purely Publilian, it is now hard to decide how much proverbial philosophy has been foisted into later collections by free paraphrase of genuine verses and by insertion of thoughts from Seneca (or Pseudo-Seneca) and others. It is equally hard to decide how much has been spoiled or lost by such misreading and distortion of genuine verses (iambic senarii or trochaic septenarii) as led copyists to mistake them for prose. There is, however, good authority for the acceptance of over 700 lines as genuine survivals of what was once a considerably larger selection.

It will be appreciated that Publilius' lines, originally

[a] Sen. *Controv.* VII. 3. 8; Petron. *Sat.* 55; Gell. *N.A.* xvii. 14.

[b] Phaedrus, III. *Epil.* 33–35.

[c] Hieron. *Epist.* 107, 8 (I. 679, Vallarsi): cited again *Epist.* 128, 4: see F. A. Wright, *Select Letters of St. Jerome* (Loeb Cl. Lib.), pp. 356, 478.

spoken by different dramatic characters, could not constitute a uniform ethical standard. In contrast, therefore, with generous sentiments we meet such self-regarding maxims as "It mayn't be right, but if it pays think it so" (quamvis non rectum quod iuvat rectum putes), or the pernicious morality of "The end justifies the means" (honesta turpitudo est pro causa bona). As in the proverbs of all nations, there are contradictory ways of looking at the same thing: while "Deliberation teaches wisdom" (deliberando discitur sapientia), it is also true that "Deliberation often loses a good chance" (deliberando saepe perit occasio); for the sagacity of the ages has always to reckon with both the impetuous and the over-cautious.

Further, if not necessarily either moral or consistent, proverbs are not necessarily profound. So if a few aphorisms dare to be paradoxical, some are the sheerest of platitudes. But, though shallow sayings take us nowhere, the reader meets with pleasure even familiar thoughts in Latin guise like "Honour among thieves" (etiam in peccato recte praestatur fides); "Least said, soonest mended" or *Qui s'excuse s'accuse* (male dictum interpretando facias acrius); "No man is a hero to his valet" (inferior rescit quicquid peccat superior); and "Touch wood!" (irritare est calamitatem cum te felicem voces).

A few remarks on the manuscript collections are needed to indicate how the text is composed.[a] To

[a] Cf. Schanz-Hosius, *Gesch. der röm. Lit.* ed. 4, 1927, pp. 261–62; W. Meyer, *Die Sammlungen der Spruchverse des Publilius Syrus*, Leipzig, 1877, and the introd. to his edition of the *Sententiae*, Leipzig, 1880. Friedrich (ed. 1880) testifies to Woelfflin's full discussion of Publilian MSS. in the Prolegomena to his edition of 1869, II. pp. 15–23.

the so-called " Seneca Collection," of which the best manuscripts go back to the ninth or tenth century, and are classed under Σ in the Sigla, belong 265 verses arranged in sequence by their initials from A to N. Of these, 159 are preserved in that collection alone. By the ninth century the latter half of the verse-sayings from O to V had disappeared, and the collection was filled up with 149 prose *sententiae* from the so-called Senecan work *De Moribus*. The title then imposed on the collection was *Senecae sententiae* or *Senecae proverbia*: and in some manuscripts these proverbs, wherein Publilius lay embedded but unnamed, were combined with works of Augustine. This is true of the codex Dunelmensis, brought early in the fourteenth century to Durham, which has been inspected during the preparation of the present volume, and is described in a subsequent note. In the tenth century the latter half of the verse-sayings had reappeared: and the Π collection, now represented by lines A to I, in the Palatino-Vaticanus (formerly Heidelbergensis), supplied 325 additional verses. It was when Π still contained the second half of the sayings that a scribe in the eleventh century combined the texts of a Π and a Σ manuscript into Ψ, inserting any new verses from Π after the prose sentences under each alphabetical letter, so that his manuscript, F, the Frisingensis, is the most complete corpus of Publilian *sententiae* extant. To the 265 verse *sententiae* of Σ it added 384, making a total of 649. Gretser's Ingolstadt edition of 1600, four years before Gruter, made use of the Frisingensis. The Zürich Collection, Z, contains 132 sayings, including 50 not found elsewhere: it is represented by Turicensis C. 78 (tenth century), giving a set of *sententiae* C to V;

and Monacensis 6369 (eleventh century), giving a set of *sententiae* A to D. The Verona excerpts, O (fourteenth century), entitled *Flores moralium autoritatum*, give 60 verses (16 of them new), indicating their Publilian origin under the incorrect names of " Publius," " Publius Syrus " or " Publius mimus."

EDITIONS

(A full list is given in Bickford-Smith's bibliography.)

D. Erasmus. *Disticha moralia titulo Catonis . . . Mimi Publiani (cum scholiis Erasmi)*, . . . London. 1514.

Jos. Scaliger. *P. Syri Sentent. et Dion. Catonis Disticha graece redd.* Leyden. 1598.

J. Gretser. Ingolstadt. 1600.

J. Gruter. *Senecae et Syri Mimi forsan etiam aliorum singulares Sententiae centum aliquot versibus ex codd. Pall. et Frising. auctae* (Ed. i. 1604). Leyden. 1708. [Contains 771 iambics and 81 " trochaici quasi."]

R. Bentley: at end of his edition of Terence and Phaedrus. Cambridge. 1726. [238 iambics and 27 trochaics.]

J. Konrad Orelli. *Publii Syri Mimi et aliorum Sententiae . . .* Leipzig. 1822. [791 iambics and 83 trochaics, with Scaliger's Greek verse renderings.]

—— *Supplementum editionis Lipsiensis . . .* Leipzig. 1824.

J. Kaspar Orelli (with *Phaedri fabulae novae*). *Publii Syri Codd. Basil. et Turic. antiquissimi.* Zürich. 1832. [216 verses from the *Basiliensis*, and others from the *Turicensis*.]

O. Ribbeck. *P. Publilius Lochius* (*sic*) *Syrus* in *Comicorum Latinorum Reliquiae*. Leipzig. 1855. [857 *sententiae*, including 269 " minus probatae " and 43 from the *Turicensis*.]

E. Woelfflin. *Publilii Syri Sententiae*. Leipzig. 1869. [693 verses, including 40 from the *Turicensis*. Woelfflin rejected many spurious verses.]

A. Spengel. *Publilii Syri Sententiae*. Berlin. 1874. [721, including 71 from Zürich and Munich MSS., some in prose.]

W. Meyer. *Publilii Syri Sententiae*. Leipzig. 1880. [733 lines.]

O. Friedrich. *Publilii Syri Mimi Sententiae*. Berlin. 1880. [761 lines besides others under the headings of " Caecilii Balbi Sententiae," " Pseudo-Seneca," " Proverbia " and 390 " Sententiae falso inter Publilianas receptae."]

R. A. H. Bickford-Smith. *Publilii Syri Sententiae*. London. 1895. [722 lines.]

SIGLA

O = Collectio Veronensis: codex Capituli Veron. 168 (155): a. 1329.

Σ = Collectio Senecae.
P = P^a et P^b.
P^a: Paris. 2676: saec. x–xi.
P^b: Paris. 7641: saec. x.
R = Rheinaugiensis 95: saec. x.
B = Basiliensis A.N. iv. 11 (K. III. 34): saec. x.
A = Vindobonensis 969: saec. x.
F et V: *cf. infra.*
C = Paris. 8049: saec. xiv.
S = Monac. 484 chart.: saec. xv.

Z = Monac. 23474: saec. xiv.
Dun. = Dunelmensis B II. 20: saec. xiv.
Inc. = editiones ante editionem Erasmi (a. 1514) impressae.

Π = Collectio Palatina.
H = Palatino-Vatic. 239 (olim Heidelbergensis): saec. x–xi. (A–I).

Ψ = Collectio Frisingensis.
F = Monac. 6292 (olim Frisingensis): saec. xi.
V = Vindobon. 299: saec. xii. (circ. cxx. versus).
ψ = Monac. 17210: saec. xiii.
Dresd. = Dresdensis J. 44: saec. xiii (contulit M. Manitius, *Hermes* xli, 1906, pp. 294–99).
Bart : = Giunta ad librum Bartholomaei da San Concordio " Ammaestramenti degli Antichi."
π = Vatic. Regin. 1896: saec. xiii.
α = Albertani Brixiensis libri.
κ = Monac. 7977: saec. xiii.
σ = Monac. 17210: saec. xiii.
par. = Paris. 8027: saec. xiv.

Z = Collectio Turicensis.
M = Monac. 6369: saec. xi. (A–D).
T = Turic. C. 78: saec. x. (C–V).

Φ = Caecilii Balbi quae vocatur collectio maior: φ minor.

A Note on the Dunelmensis

The Durham manuscript, examined in preparing the text of this work, may be briefly described as an example of the Σ group. This codex of the *Sententiae* forms, under the significant misnomer of " Proverbia Senec(a)e," part of a folio volume of

212 double-columned vellum sheets, of which the main contents are tractates, genuine or doubtful, bearing the name of Augustine. Immediately preceding the "Proverbia" there is a page given to "Sententiae quorumdam philosophorum" and over two pages to excerpts from Cicero's *De Divinatione*. In a note near the end of the volume it is described as "liber Sti. Cuthberti de Dunelm. ex procuratione fr̃is Robti. de Graystan." Robert de Graystan was "electus" as bishop of Durham in 1333, but was not admitted to the episcopate. The manuscript cannot be said to possess independent value with regard to Publilius. Though written in well-formed letters with decorated initials, it has not a few imperfections apart from unscannable lines and its mixture of prose and verse. Within the first 30 lines there occur blunders like the haplography of *aut* (6), *a deo* for *deo* (22), *actus sñ dũ* for *aetas cinaedum* (24), and *crinem* for *crimen* (29). Of its total of over 450 *sententiae*, the letters A to N have 313 sayings which are mainly verse (though of the 45 under N about four-fifths are prose). For the remainder, O to V, beginning "Omne peccatum actio est," material is drawn entirely in prose from a work of uncertain authorship, *De Moribus*. After the V *sententiae* there follows a moral poem of about 120 hexameters by a Christian poet, beginning

Quisquis vult vere Domino per cuncta placere,
Hunc fugiens mundum totum cor vertat ad illum.

The text of Publilius is in this volume largely based on Meyer's valuable edition of 1880: the main alterations are noted. Lines accepted by Meyer at the close of each letter-section under the formula " Publilii esse videtur " are given in brackets: also l. 145, which, though not in any manuscript of Publilius, is entitled to the same heading, because it is quoted by Gellius and Macrobius.

For the significance of the Greek letters on the left of the Latin text, readers are referred to the table of *Sigla* and to the remarks on the manuscript collections earlier in the Introduction. Meyer's obelus (†) has been retained only where the text printed remains unsatisfactory in respect of metre or meaning.

Bibliographical addendum (1982)

Die Sprüche des Publilius Syrus (Latin with German translation), ed. H. Beckby (Tusculum series), Munich 1969.

Σ Alienum est omne quicquid optando evenit.
Ab alio exspectes alteri quod feceris.
Animus vereri qui scit, scit tuto ingredi.
Auxilia humilia firma consensus facit.
Amor animi arbitrio sumitur, non ponitur.
Aut amat aut odit mulier: nihil est tertium.
Ad tristem partem strenua est suspicio.
Ames parentem si aequus est: si aliter, feras.
Adspicere oportet quicquid possis perdere.
Amici vitia si feras, facias tua.

Alienum aes homini ingenuo acerba est servitus.
Absentem laedit cum ebrio qui litigat.

Amans iratus multa mentitur sibi.

[3] tuto *m* 2 in B et P^a : tuta PRAFVS : tutus C *Incun.*
[10] *sic* M : si B *m* 1 *in rasura,* C : nisi *ceteri.* facis *plerique codd.* : facias *Ribbeck.*

PUBLILIUS SYRUS

WHAT comes by wishing is never truly ours.[a]

As you treat a neighbour, expect another to treat you.

Courage that can fear can take the road with safety.

United feeling makes strength out of humble aids.

Love starts but is not dropped at will.

Woman either loves or hates: there is no third thing.

Suspicion is ever active on the gloomy side.[b]

Love your parent, if he is just: if not, bear with him.

You ought to watch whatever you can lose.

Tolerate a friend's faults, and you make them your own.

For the freeborn, debt is bitter slavery.

Wrangling with a drunk man is hurting one who is off the scene.

The lover in anger tells himself many a lie.

[a] Quoted by Seneca, *Epist.* viii. 9.

[b] A long exegetical account is given in Gruter's *notae postumae* (1708 ed.). There is no need to change with Friedrich to *attritam in partem*.

Avarus ipse miseriae causa est suae.
Amans quid cupiat scit, quid sapiat non videt.
Amans quod suspicatur vigilans somniat.

Ad calamitatem quilibet rumor valet.
Amor extorqueri non pote, elabi potest.
Ab amante lacrimis redimas iracundiam.
Aperte mala cum est mulier, tum demum est bona
Avarum facile capias ubi non sis item.

Amare et sapere vix deo conceditur.
Avarus nisi cum moritur nihil recte facit.
Aetas cinaedum celat, aetas indicat.
Avarus damno potius quam sapiens dolet.
Avaro quid mali optes nisi: " vivat diu! "
Animo dolenti nihil oportet credere.
Aliena nobis, nostra plus aliis placent.
Amare iuveni fructus est, crimen seni.

18 *sic Spengel, Meyer*: potest . . . potest *pler. codd.*: pote . . . pote V. elabi HC: sed elabi PRAFVSZ: sed labi B.

21 item *Bothe*: idem *codd.*

22 deo H *Erasmus*: adeo *ceteri*.

24 aetas *Pithoeus*: aestate P^b P^a *corr.* BRA: aestatem P^a: astute FVCS: astus *Woelfflin* cinae dum A: cinedum B: cenae dum P^a: crines dum FVCS: caelat P^bA: actus sñ dũ

The miser is himself the cause of his misery.

A lover knows his desire: his wisdom is out of sight.

Even when awake, the lover has dreams of his suspicions.

To accredit disaster any tale has power.

Love can't be wrested from one, but may slip away.

Tears may buy off a lover's wrath.

A woman is good at last, when she's openly bad.

The miser may be your easy prey, when you're not a miser too.

Wisdom with love is scarcely granted to a god.

The one right thing a miser does is to die.

Time conceals and time reveals the reprobate.

It's the miser, not the wise man, whom a loss pains.

What ill could you wish a miser save long life?

One must not trust at all a mind in pain.

We fancy the lot of others; others fancy ours more.

Love is the young man's enjoyment, the old man's reproach.

Dunelm. etas te celat, etas te iudicat *Dresd.* astute dum celatur aetas se indicat *Erasmus*: astu crimen celatur, aetas indicat *Zwinger cit. apud Gruterum*: astus cinaedum celat, aestus indicat *Friedrich.*

26 *sic* M H: nisi ut *pler. codd.*

Anus cum ludit morti delicias facit.
Amoris vulnus idem sanat qui facit.
Ad paenitendum properat, cito qui iudicat.
Aleator quanto in arte est, tanto est nequior.
Amor otiosae causa est sollicitudinis.
Π Avidum esse oportet neminem, minime senem.
Animo virum pudicae, non oculo eligunt.
Amantis ius iurandum poenam non habet.
Amans ita ut fax agitando ardescit magis.
Amor ut lacrima ab oculo oritur in pectus cadit.

Animo imperabit sapiens, stultus serviet.

Amicum an nomen habeas aperit calamitas.

Amori finem tempus, non animus, facit.
Z Audendo virtus crescit, tardando timor.
Auxilium profligatis contumelia est.
Affatim aequa cui fortuna est interitum longe effugit.

34 otioso C *Inc.*

39 oculis H *Meyer*: ab oculis FVακ: ab oculo *Woelfflin*: amoris lacrima ab oculis in p.c. *Spengel*: ámor ut lacrima obóritur oculis, óculis in pectús cadit *Friedrich.*

The old woman in skittish mood is Death's darling toy.

The one who causes also cures the wound of love.

Hasty judgement means speedy repentance.

The cleverer the gamester, the greater his knavery.

Love causes worry in the leisure hour.

None should be greedy, least of all the old.

Modest women choose a man by mind, not eye.

A lover's oath involves no penalty.

A lover is like a torch—blazes the more he's moved.

Love, like a tear, rises in the eye and falls on the breast.

The sage will rule his feelings, the fool will be their slave.

Misfortune reveals whether you have a friend or only one in name.

'Tis time, not the mind, that puts an end to love.

Courage grows by daring, fear by delay.

Help wounds the pride of those whose cause is lost.

The man whose luck is fair enough gives ruin a wide berth.

---

45 *sic Wight Duff*: Affatim inqua fortuna longe non habet interitum M: affatim si cui fortuna *Christ*. affatim si quoi fortunast *Ribbeck*: affatim aequa si fortuna *Meyer*.

Avaro acerba poena natura est sua.
Avaro non est vita sed mors longior.
Alienam qui orat causam se culpat reum.
Adsidua ei sunt tormenta qui se ipsum timet.
Animo imperato ne tibi animus imperet.
Animo ventrique imperare debet qui frugi esse vult.
O Aegre reprendas quod sinas consuescere.
Amico firmo nihil emi melius potest.

ϕ (Amicis ita prodesto ne noceas tibi.)
(Avarus animus nullo satiatur lucro.)
(Amici mores noveris non oderis.)
Σ Bis fiet gratum quod opus est si ultro offeras.
Bonarum rerum consuetudo pessima est.
Beneficium dare qui nescit iniuste petit.

Bonum est fugienda adspicere in alieno malo.

Beneficium accipere libertatem est vendere.

[48] *sic Meiser* : Alienam qui suscipit causam semet criminat esse rerum M.

For the miser his own nature is bitter punishment.

The miser has no life save death delayed.

The pleader of another's cause arraigns himself.

He who dreads himself has torment without end.

Rule your feelings lest your feelings rule you.

He who would be discreet must rule his mind and appetite.

Reproof comes ill for a habit you countenance.[a]

There's nothing better in the market than a staunch friend.

Benefit friends without hurt to yourself.

No gain satisfies a greedy mind.[b]

Study but do not hate a friend's character.

Twice welcome the needed gift if offered unasked.

Constant acquaintance with prosperity is a curse.

He who can't do a good turn has no right to ask one.

In another's misfortune it is good to observe what to avoid.

To accept a benefit is to sell one's freedom.

[a] St. Jerome records his reading this maxim when at school: *Epist.* 107, 8 (*legi quondam in scholis puer: aegre,* etc.). He quotes it also in *Epist.* 128, 4: see Introduction.

[b] Quoted by Seneca, *Epist.* xciv. 43.

Bona nemini hora est ut non alicui sit mala.

Bis emori est alterius arbitrio mori.
Beneficia plura recipit qui scit reddere.

Bis peccas cum peccanti obsequium commodas.
Bonus animus laesus gravius multo irascitur.

Bona mors est homini vitae quae exstinguit mala.
Beneficium dando accepit qui digno dedit.
Blanditia non imperio fit dulcis venus.
Bonus animus numquam erranti obsequium commodat.

Beneficium qui dedisse se dicit petit.
Benivoli coniunctio animi maxima est cognatio.
Beneficium saepe dare docere est reddere.
Bonitatis verba imitari maior malitia est.

Bona opinio hominum tutior pecunia est.

Nobody has a good time without its being bad for someone.

To die at another's bidding is to die a double death.

He receives more benefits who knows how to return them.

65 You sin doubly when you humour a sinner.[a]

When a good disposition is wounded, it is much more seriously incensed.

Good for man is death when it ends life's miseries.

The giver of a gift deserved gets benefit by giving.

Coaxing, not ordering, makes love sweet.

70 Good judgement never humours one who is going wrong.

Claiming to have done a good turn is asking for one.

The alliance of a well-wisher's mind is truest kinship.

To confer repeated kindness is tuition in repayment.

Aping the words of goodness is the greater wickedness.

75 There is more safety in men's good opinion than in money.

[a] It is difficult to grasp the meaning of some of the sayings, as the original dramatic context is unknown. The double sin here may imply a sin twice as bad: *cf.* the expression *bis emori*, 63, and the sentiment in 10.

Bonum quod est supprimitur, numquam exstinguitur.

Bis vincit qui se vincit in victoria.

Benignus etiam causam dandi cogitat.
Bis interimitur qui suis armis perit.
Bene dormit qui non sentit quam male dormiat.
Bonorum crimen est officiosus miser.

Bona quae veniunt nisi sustineantur opprimunt.

Bona fama in tenebris proprium splendorem tenet.
Bene cogitata si excidunt non occidunt.
Bene perdit nummos iudici cum dat nocens.

Bona imperante animo bono est pecunia.

Bonum ad virum cito moritur iracundia.
Brevissima esto memoria iracundiae.

82 *sic Gruter*: b.q. eminent nisi sustineantur obprimunt *Buecheler*: n. s. cadunt ut opprimant *pler. codd.*

86 *sic Bickford-Smith*: bona imperante animo est pecunia S: bono PRA: in parente anima *nonnulli codd.*: bona imperante bono animo est pecunia *Meyer in not.*

A good thing may be trampled on but never annihilated.

Twice is he conqueror who in the hour of conquest conquers himself.

Generosity seeks to invent even a cause for giving.

Doubly destroyed is he who perishes by his own arms.

He sleeps well who feels not how ill he sleeps.

The dutiful man reduced to misery is a reproach to the good.

Prosperity must be sensibly sustained or it crushes you.

A good name keeps its own brightness in dark days.

Good ideas may fail but are not lost.

When the culprit bribes the judge, he loses coin to some purpose.

When the mind issues good orders, money is a blessing.

With the good man anger is quick to die.

Let the harbouring of angry thoughts be of the briefest.

---

88 *sic Gruter in notis postumis* (*om.* Dunelmensis): breve mens BRP^{b}AP^{a} *corr.*: breviens P^{a}: brevis mens S: breve amans FV. est ipsa FVS.

Bona turpitudo est quae periclum vindicat.
Bona comparat praesidia misericordia.
Beneficium dignis ubi des omnes obliges.

Π Brevis ipsa vita est sed malis fit longior.
Beneficia donari aut mali aut stulti putant.

Bene perdis gaudium ubi dolor pariter perit.
Bene vixit is qui potuit cum voluit mori.

† Bene audire alterum patrimonium est.
Boni est viri etiam in morte nullum fallere.

Z Bona causa nullum iudicem verebitur.
Bonus vir nemo est nisi qui bonus est omnibus.
Σ Consueta vitia ferimus, nova reprendimus.
101 Crudelis est in re adversa obiurgatio.
Cavendi nulla est dimittenda occasio.
Cui semper dederis ubi neges rapere imperes.

[96] *sic* FVH : bene vulgo audire *Gruter* : bene e patre audire *Friedrich.*

[100] nova *Bentley, Meyer* : inconsueta Z : non *ceteri codd., Woelfflin, Spengel, Friedrich.*

Foul is fair if it punishes the menace of a foe.

90 Pity provides good defences.

Whenever you benefit the deserving, you put the world in your debt.

Life, short itself, grows longer for its ills.

They are either rogues or fools who think benefits are merely gifts.

You are content to miss joy when pain is also lost.

95 Well has he lived who has been able to die when he willed.

To have a good name is a second patrimony.

It is the mark of a good man to disappoint no one even in his death.[a]

A good case will fear no judge.

No one is a good man unless he is good to all.

100 We tolerate the usual vices but blame new ones.

Rebuke is cruel in adversity.

No opportunity for caution should be let slip.

By perpetual giving you would invite robbery when you say " no."

[a] *i.e.* his manner of dying must equal the standard of his life.

Crudelem medicum intemperans aeger facit.
Cuius mortem amici exspectant vitam cives oderunt.

Cum inimico nemo in gratiam tuto redit.
Citius venit periclum cum contemnitur.
Casta ad virum matrona parendo imperat.

Cito ignominia fit superbi gloria.
Consilio melius vincas quam iracundia.
Cuivis dolori remedium est patientia.
Cotidie damnatur qui semper timet.
Cum vitia prosunt, peccat qui recte facit.
Contumeliam nec fortis pote nec ingenuus pati.

Conscientia animi nullas invenit linguae preces.
Comes facundus in via pro vehiculo est.
Cito improborum laeta ad perniciem cadunt.
Contemni ⟨sapienti⟩ gravius est quam stulto percuti.

Cotidie est deterior posterior dies.

[115] nullas PA : nullus RB : nullius FVC : nimias *Friedrich.*
[118] sapienti *addidit Gruter in notis* : contemni est * gravius quam stultitiae percuti *Meyer.*

The intemperate patient makes the doctor cruel.

He for whose death his friends are waiting lives a life his fellows hate.

No one is safe to be reconciled to a foe.

Danger comes more quickly when under-estimated.

The chaste matron of her husband's home rules through obedience.

The boast of arrogance soon turns to shame.

Policy is a better means of conquest than anger.

Endurance is the cure for any pain.

The man in constant fear is every day condemned.

When vices pay, the doer of the right is at fault.

Insult is what neither bravery nor free birth can brook.

A good conscience invents no glib entreaties.[a]

A chatty road-mate is as good as a carriage.

The joys of rascals soon collapse in ruin.

Contempt hurts the wise man more than a scourge does the fool.

Daily the following day is worse (*i.e.* for prompt action).

[a] Friedrich takes *conscientia* as " a bad conscience " and reads *nimias*.

Crimen relinquit vitae qui mortem appetit.
Π Cogas amantem irasci amare si velis.
Contra imprudentem stulta est nimia ingenuitas.

Crudelis est non fortis qui infantem necat.
Consilium inveniunt multi sed docti explicant.

Cave quicquam incipias quod paeniteat postea.
Cui omnes bene dicunt possidet populi bona.

Cui nolis saepe irasci irascaris semel.

Crudelis lacrimis pascitur non frangitur.
Caeci sunt oculi cum animus alias res agit.

Caret periclo qui etiam cum est tutus cavet.

Cum ames non sapias aut cum sapias non ames.

Cicatrix conscientiae pro vulnere est.
Cunctis potest accidere quod cuivis potest.

122 imprudentem *codd.* : impudentem *Gruter, Meyer.*
124 consiliis iuniorum multi se docti explicant FV : *alii alia.*

120 Eagerness for death bequeaths an indictment of life

Force a lover to anger if you wish him to love.

To counter ignorance, too much breadth of mind is fatuous.

Barbarous, not brave, is he who kills a child.

Many can hit on a plan, but the experienced find the way out.

125 Beware of starting what you may later regret.

The man of whom all speak well earns the people's favours.

Lose your temper once for all with the man with whom you don't want to lose it often.

Cruelty is fed, not broken, by tears.

The eyes are blind when the mind is otherwise occupied.

130 He's free from danger who even in safety takes precaution.

Love means you can't be wise: wisdom means you can't be in love.

The scar of conscience is as bad as a wound.

What can happen to any can happen to all.

---

133 Cunctis . . . cuivis FV: cuivis . . . cuiquam *cit. apud Senecam, de Tranq.* xi. 8: cf. *Consol. ad Marciam* ix. 5.

Cave amicum credas nisi si quem probaveris.

Contra felicem vix deus vires habet.

Cum das avaro praemium ut noceat rogas.

Z Cum se ipse vincit sapiens minime vincitur.

Contra hostem aut fortem oportet esse aut supplicem.

Cito culpam effugias si incurrisse paenitet.

Cum periclo inferior quaerit quod superior occulit.

Consilium in dubiis remedium prudentis est.

† Cum inimico ignoscis amicos gratis complures acquiris.

Contubernia sunt lacrimarum ubi misericors miserum adspicit.

O Crebro ignoscendo facies de stulto improbum.

(Cui plus licet quam par est plus vult quam licet.)

139 *sic Orelli* : culpa effugiri T : potest MT : si T : culpam penitet incurrisse MT : cito culpam effugere pote quem culpae paenitet *Meyer*.

141 *sic Meyer* : in adversis medicinae remedium MT.

142 *alii alia*.

Mind you think no man a friend save him you have tried.

135 Against the lucky one scarcely a god has strength.

In rewarding the avaricious you ask for harm.

When the sage conquers himself, he is least conquered.

Facing a foe, one must be either brave or suppliant.

You could soon avoid a fault, if you repent having run into it.

140 At his peril does an inferior search for what a superior hides.

The prudent man's remedy at a crisis is counsel.

When you forgive an enemy, you win several friends at no cost.

When pity sees misery, there comes the comradeship of tears.

Frequent pardons will turn a fool into a knave.

145 He who is allowed more than is right wants more than is allowed.[a]

[a] This *sententia* (*cf.* "give an inch and he takes an ell") is quoted by Gellius, *N.A.* xvii. 14, and Macrob. *Saturn.* ii. 7, but omitted by MSS. of Publilius.

Σ Discipulus est prioris posterior dies.
Damnare est obiurgare cum auxilio est opus.

Diu apparandum est bellum ut vincas celerius.

Dixeris male dicta cuncta cum ingratum hominem dixeris.
De inimico non loquaris male sed cogites.

Deliberare utilia mora tutissima est.
Dolor decrescit ubi quo crescat non habet.
Didicere flere feminae in mendacium.
Discordia fit carior concordia.
Deliberandum est saepe: statuendum est semel.
Difficilem habere oportet aurem ad crimina.
Dum est vita grata, mortis conditio optima est.
Damnum appellandum est cum mala fama lucrum.
Ducis in consilio posita est virtus militum.
Dies quod donat timeas: cito raptum venit.

155 quicquid PBRA: diu quicquid CSZ: saepe quicquid F: saepe *Woelfflin*: diu del. st. est semel *Bothe*: del. est decies *Friedrich*.

Next day is pupil of the day before.

When there's need of help, reproach is to make things worse.

War needs long preparation to make you win the sooner.

Call a man ungrateful and you have no words of abuse left.

Devise evil against your enemy, but speak none of him.

To think out useful plans is the safest delay.

Pain lessens when it has no means of growth.

Woman has learned the use of tears to deceive.

Harmony is the sweeter for a quarrel.

Think things out often: decide once.

One should not lend a ready ear to accusations.

When life is pleasant, the state of death is best.[a]

Ill-famed gain should be called loss.

Soldiers' valour hangs on their general's strategy.

Fear what a day gives: soon it comes to rob.

[a] The *sententia* means that the best time for death is while (*dum* temporal) life is pleasant: *i.e.* before sorrows come, one might die, in Tacitus' words, *felix opportunitate mortis*. Joseph Scaliger's translation of the line is εὐημεροῦσιν αἵρεσις θανάτου καλή.

Dimissum quod nescitur non amittitur.
II Deliberando discitur sapientia.
Deliberando saepe perit occasio.
Duplex fit bonitas simul accessit celeritas.
165 Damnati lingua vocem habet, vim non habet.

Dolor animi ⟨nimio⟩ gravior est quam corporis.
Dulce etiam fugias fieri quod amarum potest.
Difficile est dolori convenire cum patientia.
Deos ridere credo cum felix vovet.

Z Durum est negare superior cum supplicat.
171 Dissolvitur lex cum fit iudex misericors.
Dominari ex parte est cum superior supplicat.
Decima hora amicos plures quam prima invenit.
Σ Etiam innocentes cogit mentiri dolor.
175 Etiam in peccato recte praestatur fides.

166 nimio *add. Bothe*: quam corporis dolor *Gruter, Orelli.* 168 difficilius cum dolore convenit sapientiae *Friedrich.* 169 fovet H: vocet F: infelix vovet *Meyer in notis*: deo se credere credit cum felix vovet *Friedrich.*

The loss that is not known is no loss.

Deliberation teaches wisdom.

Deliberation often means a chance is lost.

Bounty is doubled so soon as speed is added.[a]

The condemned man's tongue has utterance, not force.

Pain of mind is far more severe than bodily pain.

Shun even a sweet that can grow bitter.

'Tis hard for pain to agree with patience.

I trow the gods smile when the lucky man makes his vow.[b]

Refusal is difficult when your better entreats.[c]

Law is weakened when a judge yields to compassion.

One is half master when one's better entreats.

Evening discovers more friends than the dawn does.[d]

Pain forces even the innocent to lie.

Even in crime loyalty is rightly displayed.

[a] *Cf. bis dat qui cito dat* and l. 274.

[b] If the reading is right, it implies that the gods rejoice in their prospect of gain: the lucky man's vow is a sure debt.

[c] *Cf.* use of *superior* in 172.

[d] It is a cynical thought that friends are more likely to gather round a man late in the day. They can then be social and convivial without any need to help him in his daily task. There might even be a hint that morning tempers are often unsociable.

Etiam celeritas in desiderio mora est.
Ex vitio alterius sapiens emendat suum.
Et deest et superest miseris cogitatio.
Etiam oblivisci quid sis interdum expedit.
Ex hominum questu facta Fortuna est dea.
Effugere cupiditatem regnum est vincere.
Exsul ubi ei nusquam domus est sine sepulcro est mortuus.
Etiam qui faciunt oderunt iniuriam.
Eripere telum non dare irato decet.
Exsilium patitur patriae qui se denegat.
Etiam capillus unus habet umbram suam.
Eheu quam miserum est fieri metuendo senem!
Etiam hosti est aequus qui habet in consilio fidem.

Excelsis multo facilius casus nocet.

II Extrema semper de ante factis iudicant.

191 Ex lite multa gratia fit formosior.

Etiam bonis malum saepe est adsuescere.

Desire finds even quickness slow.

From a neighbour's fault a wise man corrects his own.

The wretched have too little and too much of thought.

Sometimes 'tis fitting even to forget what you are.

180 The grumbling of men made Fortune a goddess.

To shun desire is to conquer a kingdom.

The exile with no home anywhere is a corpse without a grave.

Even those who do an injustice hate it.

Anger is rightly robbed of a weapon, not given one.

185 He suffers exile who denies himself to his country.

Even one hair has a shadow of its own.

Alas, how wretched to be aged by fear!

He who has confidence in his policy is fair even to an enemy.

The exalted are much more readily hurt by misfortune.

190 The end always passes judgement on what has preceded.

After much strife reconciliation becomes more beautiful.

It is often bad to grow used even to good things.

Z † Est utique profunda ignorantia nescire quod pecces.

194 Etiam sine lege poena est conscientia.
O Errat datum qui sibi quod extortum est putat.

Σ Fidem qui perdit quo rem servat relicuam?

Fortuna cum blanditur captatum venit.
Fortunam citius reperias quam retineas.
Formosa facies muta commendatio est.
200 Frustra rogatur qui misereri non potest.
Fortuna unde aliquid fregit cassumst ⟨reficere⟩.

Fraus est accipere quod non possis reddere.
Fortuna nimium quem fovet stultum facit.
Fatetur facinus is qui iudicium fugit.
205 Felix improbitas optimorum est calamitas.
Feras non culpes quod mutari non potest.
Futura pugnant ne se superari sinant.
Furor fit laesa saepius patientia.
Fidem qui perdit nihil pote ultra perdere.

[196] *sic Friedrich*: se servet FB*m*l: se servat PBAC: reservat R. reliquum PBRA: relicuo *Bentley, Meyer.*
[201] *sic Spengel*: cassum est F: quassum est PBRACS: cassum est non perit *Ribbeck*: quassat omnia *Friedrich.*

It is surely the depth of ignorance not to know your fault.

Even without a law conscience works as punishment.

195 It is a mistake to think one is given what has been extorted.

With credit lost, what means are there of saving what remains?

When Fortune flatters, she comes to ensnare.

It is easier to strike luck than to keep it.

A handsome appearance is an unspoken testimonial.

200 Vain is the appeal to him who cannot pity.

That from which Fortune breaks off something, 'tis vain to repair.

It's cheating to take what you could not restore.

Fortune turns her spoiled darling into a fool.

A man owns guilt by avoiding trial.

205 Successful wickedness means good folk's disaster.

What can't be changed you should bear, not blame.

The future struggles not to let itself be mastered.

Patience too often wounded turns to frenzy.

Lose credit and one can lose no more.[a]

[a] *Cf.* 196.

Facilitas animi ad partem stultitiae rapit.
Fides in animum unde abiit ⟨vix⟩ umquam redit.
Fidem nemo umquam perdit nisi qui non habet.
Fortuna obesse nulli contenta est semel.
Fulmen est ubi cum potestate habitat iracundia.

Frustra, cum ad senectam ventum est, repetas adulescentiam.
Falsum maledictum malevolum mendacium est.
Feminae naturam regere desperare est otium.

Feras difficilia ut facilia perferas.
Fortuna vitrea est: tum cum splendet frangitur.
Feras quod laedit ut quod prodest perferas.
Facit gradum Fortuna quem nemo videt.
Fortuna plus homini quam consilium valet.
Π Frugalitas miseria est rumoris boni.
Z Famulatur dominus ubi timet quibus imperat.

210 animi *codd.*: nimia *Woelfflin*: ad partem *codd.*: sapit PBRA: rapit FCS: f. nimia partem stultitiae sapit *Spengel, Meyer*.

211 *sic Spengel.*

221 gratum *codd.* (gatum R): gradum *Nauck*: Facit Fortuna quem non remoreris gradum *Friedrich, cuius praefationem vide.*

222 homini $\mathrm{P^a}$RFCZ: in homine *Spengel, Meyer*.

Complaisance is a rapid road in the direction of folly.

Honour scarce ever revisits the mind it has quitted.

None ever loses honour save him who has it not.

Fortune is not content with hurting anyone once.

'Tis thunder and lightning when anger dwells with power.

It is no good asking for youth again when age is reached.

The ill-grounded curse is an ill-intentioned lie.[a]

To control woman's nature is to abandon the hope of a quiet life.

Endure what's hard so as to stand the test of the easy.

Luck is like glass—just when it glitters, it smashes.

Bear what hurts so as to stand the test of success.

Luck takes the step that no one sees.

Luck avails a man more than policy.

Frugality is wretchedness with a good name.

The master is valet when he fears those he orders.

[a] "Frigida omnino sententia" is Orelli's criticism. "Sententia nimium quantum languet," Ribbeck.

Facile invenies qui bene faciant cum qui fecerunt coles.
Frenos imponit linguae conscientia.
O Felicitatem in dubiis virtus impetrat.
Falsum etiam est verum quod constituit superior.
Σ Grave praeiudicium est quod iudicium non habet.

Gravissima est probi hominis iracundia.
Gravis animi poena est quem post facti paenitet.

Gravis animus dubiam non habet sententiam.
Gravius malum omne est quod sub adspectu latet.
Gravius nocet quodcumque inexpertum accidit.
Gravis est inimicus is qui latet in pectore.

Gravissimum est imperium consuetudinis.
Grave crimen, etiam leviter cum est dictum, nocet.
Z Grave est quod laetus dederis tristem recipere.

ϕ (Geminat peccatum quem delicti non pudet.)

227 *sic Baehrens*: facilitatem . . . imperat *codd.*
238 *sic Woelfflin in notis*, p. 115: quod fronte laeta des tristi accipi *Meyer*.

225 You'll easily find folk to do kindnesses by cultivating those who have done them.

Conscience sets a bridle on the tongue.

Valour secures success in hazards.

Even false becomes true when a superior so decides.

Where there is no judgement, there is grave pre-judging.[a]

230 Most potent is the anger of an upright man.

Heavy the penalty on the mind which afterwards regrets a deed.

The steadfast mind admits no halting opinion.

It is always a more serious evil that lurks out of sight.

A novel disaster always works the graver mischief.

235 The foe that lurks in the heart is one to be reckoned with.

Most tyrannous is the sway of custom.

A serious charge, even lightly made, does harm.

'Tis hard getting back in sadness what you gave in joy.

He who is unashamed of his offence doubles his sin.

[a] *E.g.* hanging without trial might be called the worst "prejudice."

Σ Heu quam difficilis gloriae custodia est!

241 Homo extra corpus est suum cum irascitur.

Heu quam est timendus qui mori tutum putat!

Homo qui in homine calamitoso est misericors meminit sui.

Honesta turpitudo est pro causa bona.

245 Habet in adversis auxilia qui in secundis commodat.

Heu quam miserum est ab eo laedi de quo non possis queri!

Hominem experiri multa paupertas iubet.

Heu dolor quam miser est qui in tormento vocem non habet!

Heu quam multa paenitenda incurrunt vivendo diu!

250 Heu quam miserum est discere servire † ubi sis doctus dominari!

Habet suum venenum blanda oratio.

Homo totiens moritur quotiens amittit suos.

Homo semper aliud, Fortuna aliud cogitat.

Honestus rumor alterum est patrimonium.

255 Homo ne sit sine dolore fortunam invenit.

Alas, how hard the maintenance of fame!

A man when angry is outside himself.

Ah, how formidable is he who thinks it safe to die!

Pity for a stricken fellow-man is to remember one's own lot.

Foul is fair when the cause is good.

Aid lent in weal brings aid in woe.

Ah, how ghastly is a hurt from one of whom you daren't complain!

Poverty orders many an experiment.

How pitiful the pain that has no voice amid torture!

Ah, how many regrets does length of life incur!

Ah, how wretched to learn to be a servant when you have been trained to be master!

The wheedling speech contains its special poison.

One dies as often as one loses loved ones.

Man's plans and Fortune's are ever at variance.

An honourable reputation is a second patrimony.[a]

Man meets with fortune that pain may dog him still.[b]

[a] *Cf.* the sentiment in 96.

[b] Nisard's rendering is "L'homme serait sans douleur s'il ne trouvait la fortune."

Honeste servit qui succumbit tempori.

Homo vitae commodatus non donatus est.
Heredis fletus sub persona risus est.
Heredem ferre utilius est quam quaerere.

Habent locum maledicti crebrae nuptiae.
Π Honeste parcas improbo ut parcas probo.
Humanitatis optima est certatio.
Honos honestum decorat, inhonestum notat.

Heu, conscientia animi gravis est servitus!
Hominem etiam frugi flectit saepe occasio.
Homini tum deest consilium cum multa invenit.

Z Humilis nec alte cadere nec graviter potest.
Honestum laedis cum pro indigno intervenis.

Σ Inferior rescit quicquid peccat superior.
Inimicum ulcisci vitam accipere est alteram.

264 haec (c *in rasura*) F : heu quam *Gruter* : heu *Woelfflin, Meyer*.

269 rescit PA : nestit R : orrescit B : horrescit FCSZ : reus est *Ribbeck*.

To yield to the need of the time is honourable service.

Man is only lent to life, not given.

Beneath the mask an heir's weeping is a smile.

It's of more use to tolerate an heir than seek one out.

Frequent re-marriage gives room for the evil tongue.

To spare the good you may fairly spare the bad.

The finest rivalry is in humanity.

Honour adorns the honourable; the dishonourable it brands.

Ah, conscience doth make bondsmen of us all!

Opportunity often sways even an honest man.

When you discover many openings, you are gravelled for a plan.

The humble can fall neither far nor heavily.

You hurt the honourable by intervening for the unworthy.

Any fault in a superior is found out by his inferior.[a]

Revenge on an enemy is to get a new lease of life.

[a] The usual form is *resciscere*, but for the simple verb *rescire* see Gell. *N. A.* ii. 19. 2.

Invitum cum retineas, exire incites.

Ingenuitatem laedas cum indignum roges.

In nullum avarus bonus est, in se pessimus.
Inopi beneficium bis dat qui dat celeriter.

Inopiae desunt multa, avaritiae omnia.
Instructa inopia est in divitiis cupiditas.
Invitat culpam qui peccatum praeterit.
Iucundum nihil est nisi quod reficit varietas.
Ingenuitas non recipit contumeliam.
Irritare est calamitatem cum te felicem voces.
Impune pecces in eum qui peccat prior.
Ingratus unus omnibus miseris nocet.

In miseria vita etiam contumelia est.
Ita amicum habeas, posse ut facile fieri hunc inimicum putes.
Invidiam ferre aut fortis aut felix potest.

In amore semper mendax iracundia est.

Hold back a man against his will, and you might as well urge him to go.

An appeal to the unworthy is an insult to the noble mind.

The miser treats none well—himself the worst.

To do a kindness to the needy at once is to give twice.

Beggary lacks much, but greed lacks everything.

In riches greed is but poverty well furnished.

He who passes over a sin invites wrong-doing.

There's nothing pleasant save what variety freshens.

The noble mind does not take an insult.

To call yourself " happy " is to provoke disaster.

You may safely offend against him who offends first.

One ungrateful person does harm to all the unfortunate.

In misery even life is an insult.

Treat a friend without forgetting that he may easily become a foe.

It's either the brave man or the lucky that can stand unpopularity.

In love anger is always untruthful.

Invidia tacite sed inimice irascitur.
Iratum breviter vites, inimicum diu.

Iniuriarum remedium est oblivio.
Iracundiam qui vincit hostem superat maximum.
Iactum tacendo crimen facias acrius.

In malis sperare bene nisi innocens nemo solet.
In iudicando criminosa est celeritas.
Inimicum quamvis humilem docti est metuere.
In calamitoso risus etiam iniuria est.
Iudex damnatur cum nocens absolvitur.
Ignoscere hominum est nisi pudet cui ignoscitur.

In rebus dubiis plurimi est audacia.
Illo nocens se damnat quo peccat die.

Ita crede amico ne sit inimico locus.
Iratus etiam facinus consilium putat.

291 iáctum in te tacéndo acumen crímen facias ácrius (*trochaicus*) *Friedrich.*
293 *sic* HBCF : vindicando PRAS.
297 nisi *codd.* : ubi *Incun.*, *Meyer.*

Silent but unfriendly is the anger of envy.

Avoid an angry man for a little, but an enemy for long.

For wrongs the cure lies in forgetfulness.[a]

Who quells his wrath o'ercomes the mightiest foe.

You aggravate a charge thrown at you, if you meet it with silence.

None but the guiltless can nurse bright hopes in woe.

In judgement rapidity is criminal.

Experience dreads an enemy however humble.

When a man is ruined, even a laugh is a wrong.

Acquittal of the guilty damns the judge.[b]

It is for men to pardon, unless the pardoned puts one to the blush.

In a tight corner boldness counts for most.

The culprit condemns himself on the day of his offence.

So trust a friend as to give no room for an enemy.

The angry man takes (hostile) intention as an actual deed.

[a] Quoted by Seneca, *Epist.* xciv. 28.

[b] This line, chosen as the motto for *The Edinburgh Review*, founded 1802, marked its tendency to severity in criticism.

Invidia id loquitur quod videt non quod subest.

Π Iniuriam aures facilius quam oculi ferunt.
Iacet omnis virtus fama nisi late patet.

Ignis calorem suum etiam in ferro tenet.
In venere semper certat dolor et gaudium.
In amore forma plus valet quam auctoritas.
Ingrata sunt beneficia quibus comes est metus.
Imprudens peccat quem peccati paenitet.
Inertia indicatur cum fugitur labor.
Iratus cum ad se rediit sibi tum irascitur.

In amore saepe causa damni quaeritur.

Iucunda macula est ex inimici sanguine.

In venere semper dulcis est dementia.
In misero facile fit potens iniuria.
Interdum habet stultitiae partem facilitas.

306 certant ψ *Spengel.*

Envy speaks of what she sees, not of what is beneath the surface.

The ear tolerates a wrong more readily than the eye.

Every virtue is depressed unless it gains wide recognition.

305 Fire keeps its own heat even in steel.

In love, pain is ever at war with joy.

In love, beauty counts for more than advice does.

Unwelcome are the favours whose attendant is fear.

He who regrets his offence offends without foresight.

310 Work shunned is an index of laziness.

It is on returning to his senses that the angry man is angry with himself.

In love, an opportunity for suffering loss is often sought.[a]

It's a pleasant stain that comes from an enemy's blood.

To lose your wits in love is always sweet.

315 Over the wretched unfairness easily gets power.

Compliance is sometimes half folly.

[a] Possibly of a lover's lavish expenditure on a lady-love which may eventually be a serious loss to him; but it probably means that lovers are so foolish that they are continually devising something which really does them harm.

Inertia est laboris excusatio.
Iniuriam facilius facias quam feras.
Iratus nihil non criminis loquitur loco.
Incertus animus dimidium est sapientiae.
In turpi re peccare bis delinquere est.
Ingenuus animus non fert vocis verbera.
Iniuriam ipse facias ubi non vindices.
Is minimum eget mortalis qui minimum cupit.
Inimici ad animum nullae conveniunt preces.
Inimico exstincto exitium lacrimae non habent.
Ibi semper est victoria ubi concordia est.
Iter est quacumque dat prior vestigium.

Ibi pote valere populus ubi leges valent.
Z Insanae vocis numquam libertas tacet.
331 Improbe Neptunum accusat qui iterum naufragium facit.

Σ Loco ignominiae est apud indignum dignitas.

320 remedium *codd.*: dimidium *Bothe*: incertis animis r. e. sapientia *Meyer in appar. crit.*
324 minimo *Seneca, Epist.* cviii. 11.
326 exitum H ψ: exitium (*antiquo sensu usurpatum*) *ceteri codd.*
330 † invectibe T: insanae *Friedrich*: invectae *Bickford-Smith.*

Excusing oneself from work is laziness.

A wrong is easier done than stood.

An angry man has nothing but accusations to utter.

320 The hesitant mind is the half of wisdom.[a]

An offence in base circumstances is a double fault.

A noble mind brooks not the lashes of the tongue.

You yourself do wrong when you do not punish.

The man with least desires is least in want.

325 No entreaties are fitted to reach an unfriendly mind.

When an enemy is destroyed, tears have no outlet.

Victory is ever there where union of hearts is.[b]

The road runs wheresoever a predecessor leaves his footprint.

Where laws prevail, there can the people prevail.

330 The outspokenness of wild invective is never hushed.

It is an outrage in a man twice shipwrecked to blame the God of Sea.

To stand high with the unworthy is tantamount to shame.

[a] *Cf.* 162.

[b] The saying means that victory in a conflict lies with the thoroughly united side.

Laus nova nisi oritur, etiam vetus amittitur.
Laeso doloris remedium inimici est dolor.
Levis est Fortuna: cito reposcit quod dedit.

Lex universa est quae iubet nasci et mori.
Lucrum sine damno alterius fieri non potest.
Lascivia et laus numquam habent concordiam.
Legem nocens veretur, Fortunam innocens.
Libido, non iudicium est, quod levitas sapit.
Libido cunctos etiam sub vultu domat.
Π Longum est quodcumque flagitavit cupiditas.
Ψ Lapsus ubi semel sis, sit tua culpa, si iterum cecideris.
Lex videt iratum, iratus legem non videt.

Legem solet obliviscier iracundia.
Locis remotis qui latet lex est sibi.
Late ignis lucere, ut nihil urat, non potest.

[341] cunctos *codd.*: cinctos (= strenuos) *Salmasius.*
[342] *sic Friedrich*: † longum est quod flagitat cup. FH, *Meyer*: longinquum est omne quod cup. fl. *Gruter.*
[345] oblivisci *codd.*: obliviscier *Gruter.*
[347] *alii alia.*

Unless fresh praise is won, even the old is lost.

The injured man's cure for pain is his enemy's pain.

335 Fickle is Fortune: she soon demands back what she gave.

'Tis a universal law that ordains birth and death.

Gain cannot be made without another's loss.

Wantonness and honour are never in harmony.

The guilty fear the law, the guiltless Fortune.

340 Flippancy's taste is caprice, not judgement.

The wanton will subdues all under its very glance.[a]

Tedious the tale of greed's demands.

When you've slipped once, be it your fault if you fall again.

The law sees the angry man, the angry man doesn't see the law.

345 Anger usually forgets the law.

He who lurks in remote places is a law unto himself.

Fire cannot throw its light afar without burning anything.

[a] Gruter explains "eam esse vim libidinis ut homines superet ipso aspectu": according to his second explanation *sub vultu* implies "beneath their apparently grave countenance."

Licentiam des linguae cum verum petas.

Z Lucrum est dolorem posse damno exstinguere.

Σ Malignos fieri maxime ingrati docent.

351 Multis minatur qui uni facit iniuriam.
Mora omnis odio est sed facit sapientiam.
Mala causa est quae requirit misericordiam.
Mori est felicis antequam mortem invoces.
Miserum est tacere cogi quod cupias loqui.

Miserrima est fortuna quae inimico caret.
Malus est vocandus qui sua est causa bonus.

Malus bonum ubi se simulat tunc est pessimus.

Metus cum venit, rarum habet somnus locum.
Mori necesse est, sed non quotiens volueris.

Male geritur quicquid geritur fortunae fide.

You must give licence to the tongue when you ask for the truth.

It is gain to be able to extinguish pain at the cost of a loss.

It is especially the ungrateful who teach folk to become niggardly.

A wrong done to one means a threat to many.

All delay is hateful, but it makes wisdom.

It's a poor case that seeks pity.

Lucky to die before having to invoke death.

It's wretched to be forced to conceal what you'd like to reveal.

It's a very poor fortune that has no enemy.

He must be called bad who is good only in his own interest.

When the villain pretends to be good, he is most villain.

When fear has come, sleep has scanty place.

You needs must die, but not as often as you have wished.[a]

The business that trusts to luck is a bad business.

[a] *Cf.* "Cowards die many times before their death: The valiant never taste of death but once" (*Jul. Caes.* ii. 2).

Mortuo qui mittit munus, nil dat illi, adimit sibi.

Minus est quam servus dominus qui servos timet.
Magis fidus heres nascitur quam scribitur.

Malo in consilio feminae vincunt viros.
Mala est voluntas ad alienam adsuescere.

Maximo periclo custoditur quod multis placet.
Mala est medicina, ubi aliquid naturae perit.
Malae naturae numquam doctore indigent.
† Misereri scire sine periclo est vivere.
Male vivunt qui se semper victuros putant.
Male dictum interpretando facias acrius.
Male secum agit aeger medicum qui heredem facit.

Minus decipitur cui negatur celeriter.
Mutat se bonitas irritata iniuria.
Mulier cum sola cogitat male cogitat.
Male facere qui vult numquam non causam invenit.

366 ad alienum consuescere *codd.*: adsuescere *Erasmus*: alienam ads. *Meyer* (*in apparatu*).
370 misereri R *Dresd.*: miseri PA: miseriam FS *Inc.*

A gift sent to a dead man is nothing to him, but means less for oneself.

A master who fears his slaves is lower than a slave.

One can trust the heir by birth more than the heir by will.[a]

365 In an ill design woman beats man.

'Tis poor will-power to get used to another's beck and call.

What many like is very perilous to guard.

It's a bad cure when a bit of nature is lost.

Bad natures never lack an instructor.

370 To know how to pity is to live without danger.[b]

Theirs is a bad life who think they are to live for ever.

Explain an ill saying and you make it worse.

The patient who makes an heir of his doctor treats himself badly.

There is less mistake when one says " no " at once.

375 Kindness alters when provoked by wrong.

A woman when she thinks alone thinks ill.

The intention to injure can always find a reason.

[a] *Cf*. 259.

[b] The Dresdensis alone shares with R the likeliest reading.

Malivolus semper sua natura vescitur.
Multos timere debet quem multi timent.
Male imperando summum imperium amittitur.
Mulier quae multis nubit multis non placet.
Ψ Malivolus animus abditos dentes habet.
Medicina calamitatis est aequanimitas.
Muliebris lacrima condimentum est malitiae.
Metum respicere non solet quicquid iuvat.
Malo etiam parcas, si una periturus bonus.

Magnum secum affert crimen indignatio.
Malus etsi obesse non potest tamen cogitat.

Mage valet qui nescit quod calamitas valet.

Mora cogitationis diligentia est.
Multa ignoscendo fit potens potentior.
Multis placere quae cupit culpam cupit.
Minimum eripit Fortuna cum minimum dedit.
Meretrix est instrumentum contumeliae.

389 † magis F, *Meyer* : mage *Gruter, J. C. Orelli, Woelfflin.*
393 cum F : cui σ, *Bentley, Meyer.*

The spiteful man ever battens on his own nature.

Many must he fear whom many fear.[a]

380 By bad ruling the most exalted rule is lost.

The woman who marries many is disliked by many.

The spiteful mind has hidden teeth.

The medicine for disaster is equanimity.

A woman's tear is the sauce of mischief.

385 It's pleasure's way to take but small account of fear.

You may spare even the bad, if the good is to perish along with him.[b]

Indignation brings with her some serious charge.

A villain, even though he cannot do a hurt, yet thinks of it.

He has the more power who knows not the power of calamity.

390 Slow deliberation is but carefulness.

By forgiving much, power grows more powerful.

She who would fain please many would fain be frail.

Fortune robs least when she has given least.

A harlot is an instrument of shame.

[a] *Cf.* Laberius' *Necesse est multos timeat quem multi timent.* For Laberius see Introduction.

[b] *Cf.* 261.

Malus bonum ad se numquam consilium refert.
Manifesta causa secum habet sententiam.
Multorum calamitate vir moritur bonus.
Metus improbos compescit non clementia.
Muneribus est, non lacrimis, meretrix misericors.
Metuendum est semper, esse cum tutus velis.
Mors infanti felix, iuveni acerba, nimis sera est seni.

Malam rem cum velis honestare improbes.

Malum est consilium quod mutari non potest.
Malitia unius cito fit male dictum omnium.
Mortem ubi contemnas viceris omnes metus.
Misera est voluptas ubi pericli memoria est.
Male vincit ⟨is⟩ quem paenitet victoriae.
Misericors civis patriae est consolatio.
Malitia ut peior veniat se simulat bonam.
Malus animus in secreto peius cogitat.
Mutare quod non possis, ut natum est, feras.
Multa ante temptes quam virum invenias bonum.

402 honestatem F ψ: honestare *Meyer*.

395 The villain never lays a good plan before his mind.

A clear case brings the right verdict with it.

The affliction of many is death for the good man.

Fear, not clemency, restrains the wicked.

Not tears but gifts can touch a courtesan.

400 You must always fear when you would be safe.

Death is luck for childhood, bitter for youth, too late for age.

In wishing to give fair colour to a bad case, you condemn it.

It's an ill plan that can't be changed.

The malice of one soon becomes the curse of all.

405 Despise death and you've conquered every fear.

It's but sorry pleasure when danger is remembered.

He's a poor victor who regrets his victory.

A merciful citizen is the solace of his country.

To make her onset worse, malice pretends to be good.

410 The evil mind thinks worse evil in secret.

What you cannot change, you should bear as it comes.

You may make many attempts before finding a good man.

Miserrimum est arbitrio alterius vivere.
Mansueta tutiora sunt sed serviunt.

Mala mors necessitatis contumelia est.
Minus saepe pecces si scias quid nescias.

Malus quicumque in poena est praesidium est bonis.

Z Mala est inopia ex copia quae nascitur.
O Monere non punire stultitiam decet.
Multo turpius damnatur cui in delicto ignoscitur.

φ (Malum ne alienum feceris tuum gaudium.)
Σ Nihil agere semper infelici est optimum.
Nihil peccant oculi, si animus oculis imperat.

Nihil proprium ducas quicquid mutari potest.
Non cito ruina obteritur qui rimam timet.

416 quod F ψ : quid *Gruter, Meyer.*

420 *sic* O, *Meyer* : cuius delictum (*vel* delicto) agnoscitur φ : cui delictum ignoscitur *Friedrich, Bickford-Smith.*

425 perit ruina *a Meyer* : ruina perit CS : r. peritur P^b : r. perituir P^aRAF : r. opteritur *Woelfflin* : rimam P^b : ruinam TFCSZ *Dunelm.*

The height of misery is life at another's will.

The tame way is safer, but it's the way of slaves.

A dishonourable death is fate's insolence.

You'd go wrong less often if you knew your ignorance.

Any evil-doer under punishment is a protection to the good.

It's an ill want that springs from plenty.

Advice, not punishment, is what fits folly.

He who is pardoned in his wrong-doing is far more shamefully condemned.[a]

Make not another's misfortune your joy.

For the unlucky it's always best to do nothing.

The eyes commit no wrong, if the mind controls the eyes.

Think nothing your own that can change.

It's long before the downfall overwhelms him who fears a crack.

[a] *i.e.* a man who has such a bad character that no one pays attention to his misdeed is, in fact, wholly out of court. To treat his misdeed so lightly shows what is thought of the offender.

Nullus est tam tutus quaestus quam quod habeas parcere.
Nescias quid optes aut quid fugias: ita ludit dies.

Numquam periclum sine periclo vincitur.
Nulla tam bona est fortuna de qua nihil possis queri.

Nusquam melius morimur homines quam ubi libenter viximus.
Negandi causa avaro numquam deficit.
Ψ Naturam abscondit cum improbus recte facit.

Non turpis est cicatrix quam virtus parit.
Numquam ubi diu fuit ignis defecit vapor.

Necesse est minima maximorum esse initia.
Non corrigit, sed laedit, qui invitum regit.

Nimia concedendo interdum fit stultitia ⟨stultior⟩.

Nihil magis amat cupiditas quam quod non licet.

426 tantus *codd.*: tam tutus *Woelfflin*: parcere *Ingolst.*: carcere R: arcere PFC *Dunelm.*: carere A *Inc.*
437 stultior *supplevit Meyer.*

There's no gain so safe as saving what you've got.

You never can tell what to wish for or what to avoid: such is the day's jest.

A risk is never mastered save by risk.

There's no luck so good but you could make some complaint about it.

Nowhere do we men die better than where we have lived to our liking.

The miser never lacks a reason for saying "no." [a]

When a rascal does right, he is concealing his character.

Never ugly is the scar which bravery begets.

Where there has been fire for long, there's never a lack of smoke.

Very big things must have very small beginnings.

He who controls the unwilling hurts rather than corrects.

By excessive yielding, folly sometimes grows more foolish still.

Greed likes nothing better than what is not allowed.

[a] This is the last of the verses in Σ, the rest of whose *sententiae* are in prose.

Nisi vindices delicta, improbitatem adiuves.
Nulli facilius quam malo invenies parem.
Nihil non acerbum prius quam maturum fuit.
Nocere posse et nolle laus amplissima est.

Non vincitur, sed vincit, qui cedit suis.

Necessitas dat legem, non ipsa accipit.

Nescio quid agitat, cum bonum imitatur malus.

Nulla hominum maior poena est quam infelicitas.
Non novit virtus calamitati cedere.
Necessitas ab homine quae vult impetrat.
Necessitati quodlibet telum utile est.
Nocere casus non solet constantiae.
Non pote non sapere qui se stultum intellegit.
Necessitas egentem mendacem facit.
Non facile solus serves quod multis placet.

Necessitas quod poscit nisi des eripit.
Nocens precatur, innocens irascitur.

If you didn't punish offences, you'd help roguery.

It's the bad man whose like you'll find most easily.

Everything ripe was once sour.

Power to harm without the will is the most ample fame.

He who yields to his own people is conqueror, not conquered.

Necessity prescribes law: she does not bow to it herself.

When the rogue copies good folk, he has something in mind.

Man meets no worse punishment than misfortune.

Bravery knows no yielding to calamity.

Necessity wins what she wants from man.

Necessity finds any weapon serviceable.

Misfortune seldom hurts steadfastness.

He must have wit who understands he is a fool.

Necessity makes beggars liars.

Single-handed, you'd find it hard to keep what many want.

Necessity snatches what she asks, unless you give it.

Guilt entreats where innocence feels indignant.

Nec vita nec fortuna hominibus perpes est.
Non semper aurem facilem habet felicitas.
Numquam non miser est qui quod timeat cogitat.

Ni qui scit facere insidias nescit metuere.

Negat sibi ipse qui quod difficile est petit.

Nimium altercando veritas amittitur.
Nullo in loco male audit misericordia.
Necessitas quod celat frustra quaeritur.
Necessitas quam pertinax regnum tenet!
Nemo immature moritur qui moritur miser.
Nocentem qui defendit sibi crimen parit.

Nihil non aut lenit aut domat diuturnitas.

Nihil turpe ducas pro salutis remedio.
Noli contemnere ea quae summos sublevant.
Nihil aliud scit necessitas quam vincere.
Nemo timendo ad summum pervenit locum.

456 *sic Gruter*: propria est hominibus *Spengel, Meyer*: perpetua est F *a*.

Neither life nor luck is lasting[a] for man.

Success has not always the ready ear.

Misery never quits him whose thoughts run on something to dread.

Everyone fails to fear an ambush except him who can set one.

He who begs for what is difficult says " no " to himself.

In excessive wrangling truth gets lost.

Pity gets a bad name nowhere.

What necessity hides is sought for in vain.

How firm the hold of Necessity upon her throne!

None dies untimely who dies in misery.

The champion of the guilty begets a charge against himself.

There's naught that time does not either soothe or quell.

To cure bad health, think nothing unclean.

Do not despise the steps which raise to greatness.

Necessity knows naught else but victory.

Fear never brought one to the top.

[a] *perpes* is a Plautine as well as a late Latin word: *perpetem pro perpetuo dixerunt poetae*, Fest. 217, Müll.

Nisi per te sapias, frustra sapientem audias.

Necessitati sapiens nihil umquam negat.
Non facile de innocente crimen fingitur.
Nimium boni est in morte cum nihil est mali.
Ni gradus servetur, nulli tutus est summus locus.

Nihil est miserius quam ubi pudet quod feceris.

Nec mortem effugere quisquam nec amorem potest.
Necessitatem ferre non flere addecet.
Nusquam facilius culpa quam in turba latet.

Z Non leve beneficium praestat qui breviter negat.
(Non est beatus esse se qui non putat.)
Ψ Omnis voluptas quemcumque arrisit nocet.
Officium benivoli animi finem non habet.
O vita misero longa, felici brevis!
Obiurgari in calamitate gravius est quam calamitas.

480 numquam F ψ : nusquam *Woelfflin*.
483 *sic* F : qu(a)ecunque ψ.
484 officium F : obsequium *a* ψ, *Meyer*.
485 *sic citat. apud Senecam, Contr.* vii. 18.

Without mother-wit of your own, it's no good listening to the wise.

A wise man never refuses anything to necessity.

A charge is not easily framed against the guiltless.

Death is too much a boon when it has no bane.

Unless one's step be guarded, the summit is safe for none.[a]

There's nothing more wretched than being ashamed of what you've done.

There's no one can escape either death or love.

'Tis fitting to bear and not bemoan necessity.

Crime is nowhere more easily hidden than in a crowd.

To say " no " at once is to confer no slight kindness.

He's not happy who does not think himself so.[b]

All pleasure harms whomso it charms.

The services of a benevolent mind have no end.

O life, long for woe but brief for joy!

To be scolded in misfortune is harder than misfortune's self.

[a] *i.e.* a slip in the highest positions is ruin.
[b] The Latin comes from Sen. *Ep.* ix. 21.

O dulce tormentum ubi reprimitur gaudium!
Omnes aequo animo parent ubi digni imperant.
Occidi est pulchrum, ignominiose ubi servias.

O tacitum tormentum animi conscientia!
Optime positum est beneficium ⟨bene⟩ ubi meminit qui accipit.
Obsequio nuptae cito fit odium paelicis.

Occasio receptus difficiles habet.
O pessimum periclum quod opertum latet!
Omnes cum occulte peccant, peccant ocius.
Occasio aegre offertur, facile amittitur.
O Oculi ⟨occulte⟩ amorem incipiunt, consuetudo perficit.
Ψ Probus libertus sine natura est filius.

Prodesse qui vult nec potest, aeque est miser.

Pericla timidus etiam quae non sunt videt.
Pudor doceri non potest, nasci potest.

491 *sic Spengel*: ubi eius *Gruter*.
495 *sic Woelfflin*: o. c. peccant occulte pacantur citius F.

'Tis sweet torture when joy is held in.

When worth holds sway, all cheerfully obey.

It is noble to be slain, when your servitude is shameful.

O conscience, silent torture of the mind!

A benefit is best bestowed when the recipient has a good memory.

The bride's complaisance soon brings loathing for a harlot.

The favourable moment is hard to recover.

O worst of dangers that lurks unseen!

Sinners in secret are always quicker to sin.

Opportunity is slow to offer, easy to miss.

The eyes start love secretly: intimacy perfects it.

An upright freedman is a son without the tie of blood.

The wish to help without the power means sharing misery.[a]

Cravens see even dangers which do not exist.

Modesty is born, not taught.

[a] Meyer punctuates " nec potest aeque, est miser."

Plus est quam poena sinere miserum vivere.

Pudorem alienum qui eripit perdit suum.
Patientia animi occultas divitias habet.
Peiora multo cogitat mutus dolor.
Pecunia ⟨una⟩ regimen est rerum omnium.
Pudor dimissus numquam redit in gratiam.
Perdendi finem nemo nisi egestas facit.
Poena ad malum serpens iam cum properat venit.

Plus est quam poena iniuriae succumbere.
Pro medicina est dolor dolorem qui necat.
Patiens et fortis se ipsum felicem facit.

Prospicere in pace oportet quod bellum iuvet.
Parens iratus in se est crudelissimus.
Perdit non donat qui dat nisi sit memoria.

Probi delicta neglegens, leges teras.

[502] sine rem F : sinere *Spengel* : sine spe *Woelfflin* (*in not.*), *Meyer*.
[505] multa *codd.* : multo *Tzschucke*, *Meyer*.
[509] serpentia F : serpendo *Bothe* : serpens, iam *Bickford-Smith*.

It is more than punishment to let one live in misery.

Who steals another's modesty loses his own.

Patience of mind has secret wealth.

Dumb grief thinks of much worse to come.

Money alone is the ruling principle of the world.

Modesty, once dismissed, never returns to favour.

Only want sets a limit to waste.

Punishment with creeping pace comes on the offender in the moment of his haste.

'Tis more than punishment to yield to wrong.

The pain that kills pain acts as medicine.

The man who unites patience and courage secures his own happiness.

In peace one must forecast the sinews of war.

The parent enraged is most cruel to himself.

A gift is lost, not presented, unless there be recollection of it.

In overlooking even a good man's offences, you would impair the laws.

---

[516] † probe delicta cum legas deteras *codd.*, *Meyer*: probi *Ingol.*: cum tegas *Spengel*: cum neglegas (? nĕglĕgās), leges teras *Woelfflin.*

Pars benefici est quod petitur si belle neges.
Properare in iudicando est crimen quaerere.
Populi est mancipium quisquis patriae est utilis.

Per quae sis tutus illa semper cogites.
Perfugere ad inferiorem se ipsum est tradere.
Peccatum amici veluti tuum recte putes.

Potens misericors publica est felicitas.
Praesens est semper absens qui se ulciscitur.

Perfacile quod vota imperant felix facit.

Poenam moratur improbus, non praeterit.

Perdidisse ad assem mallem quam accepisse turpiter.

Paucorum est intellegere quid donet deus.
Perenne coniugium animus, non corpus, facit.
Pereundi scire tempus adsidue est mori.

527 ad assem *add. Friedrich*: honeste *Woelfflin*: *om. codd.*
528 † det F, *Meyer*: celet *Ribbeck*: dicat *Buecheler*: donet dies *Woelfflin*: doceat dies *Meiser.*

A nice refusal of a request is half a kindness done.

Haste in judgement is to look for guilt.

Whoever is useful to his country is the nation's slave.

Always bethink yourself of means of safety.

To take refuge with an inferior is self-betrayal.

You would do right to consider your friend's fault as if it were your own.

Mercy in power is good fortune for a people.

He who avenges himself though absent is ever present.[a]

It's very easy for the lucky man to do what his wishes command.

The villain delays his punishment—he does not escape it.

I'd rather lose to the last farthing than get dishonourably.

It is granted to few to comprehend what God gives.

Mind, not body, makes lasting wedlock.

To know the hour of doom is continual death.

[a] *E.g.* a tyrant through a system of espionage might be called ubiquitous: *cf.* the "eyes and ears" of the Persian king, Xen. *Cyrop.* viii. 2, 9–10 (τίς δ' ἄλλος ἐδυνάσθη ἐχθροὺς ἀπέχοντας πολλῶν μηνῶν ὁδὸν τιμωρεῖσθαι ὡς Περσῶν βασιλεύς;)

Potenti irasci sibi periclum est quaerere.

Peccare pauci nolunt, nulli nesciunt.
Paucorum improbitas est multorum calamitas.
Pro dominis peccare etiam virtutis loco est.
Patiendo multa venient quae nequeas pati.
Paratae lacrimae insidias non fletum indicant.
Peccatum extenuat qui celeriter corrigit.
Pudorem habere servitus quodammodo est.
Potest uti adversis numquam felicitas.

Prudentis vultus etiam sermonis loco est.
Probo beneficium qui dat ex parte accipit.

Pudor si quem non flectit, non frangit timor.
Poena allevatur ubi relaxatur dolor.
Plures tegit Fortuna quam tutos facit.
Post calamitatem memoria alia est calamitas.

Probo bona fama maxima est hereditas.

533 est multorum *Buecheler* : universis est F.
539 *sic Bickford-Smith* : potest ultus in F.

To be angry with the powerful is seeking danger for oneself.

Few are unwilling to sin—none but know the way.

The wickedness of a few is widespread calamity.

To do wrong for one's master even passes for merit.

Sufferance will bring much you could not suffer.

The ready tear means treachery, not grief.

The quick corrector weakens sin.

To feel qualms is in a measure slavery.

The lucky man never knows how to deal with adversity.

The wise man's looks are as good as a discourse.

The giver of a benefit to the good is in part the receiver.

If honour sways one not, fear cannot quell.

The punishment is lightened when the pain slackens.

Fortune shields more people than she makes safe.

After misfortune, remembrance is misfortune renewed.

For the upright a good name is the greatest inheritance.

Pericla qui audet ante vincit quam accipit.

Perpetuo vincit qui utitur clementia.

Z Plures amicos mensa quam mens concipit.

O Prudentis est irascier sero et semel.

551 Per quem sis clarus illi quod sis imputes.

Poenae sat est qui laesit cum supplex venit.

Ψ Quamvis non rectum quod iuvat rectum putes.

Quisquis nocere didicit meminit cum potest.

555 Qui metuit calamitatem rarius accipit.

Quam miserum est mortem cupere nec posse emori!

Qui pro innocente dicit satis est eloquens.

Qui cum dolet blanditur post tempus sapit.

Quod timeas citius quam quod speres evenit.

560 Quod vult cupiditas cogitat, non quod decet.

550 *sic Friedrich*: irasci et sero et semel O: nec sero et semel *Halm, Meyer.*

The bold defeat danger before meeting it.

He is for ever victor who employs clemency.

One's table receives more friends than one's heart does.

550 It is wisdom to lose one's temper late and then once for all.

To the man who made you famous give the credit of what you are.

'Tis penalty enough when the offender comes on his knees.

Think right what helps, though right it may not be.

Power to harm once learned is remembered when the chance comes.

555 He who dreads disaster rarely meets it.

How wretched to long for death yet fail to die!

The pleader for innocence is eloquent enough.

If a man takes to coaxing when he feels the smart, it is wisdom learned too late.

The dreaded thing happens sooner than you might expect

560 Greed contemplates what it wishes, not what befits.

---

554 quicquid *Meyer.*
555 contumeliam raro *Spengel, Meyer.*

Quicquid conaris, quo pervenias cogites.

Qui bene dissimulat citius inimico nocet.

Quod semper est paratum non semper iuvat.

Quodcumque celes ipse tibi fias timor.

Qui ius iurandum servat quovis pervenit.

Quod aetas vitium posuit aetas auferet.

Quemcumque quaerit calamitas facile invenit.

Quod periit quaeri pote, reprendi non potest.

Quam miserum officium est quod successum non habet!

Quam miser est cui est ingrata misericordia!

Quam miserum est cogi opprimere quem salvum velis!

Quem fama semel oppressit vix restituitur.

Quod vix contingit ut voluptatem parit!

Quam miserum est id quod pauci habent amittere!

573 vix . . . vix *Gruter*: vi . . . vix *Woelfflin*: quidvis . . . ut (*velut sententia ex Epicureorum disciplina profecta*) *Friedrich*.

In your every endeavour contemplate your goal.

An apt dissembler sooner hurts his foe.

What is always at hand does not always help.

Your guarded secret means you grow a terror to yourself.

565 He who observes his oath reaches any goal.

The fault which time has set up time will take away.

Disaster easily finds whomsoever it seeks.

What is destroyed can be looked for but never recovered.

How sorry the service that has no success!

570 How wretched he to whom pity is against the grain!

How wretched to be forced to crush him you fain would save!

It is hard restoring him whom ill report has once crushed.

What pleasure is produced by what is won with difficulty!

How pitiable it is to lose what few possess!

Qui in vero dubitat male agit cum deliberat.

Qui timet amicum, amicus ut timeat, docet.

Quicquid vindicandum est, ⟨omnis⟩ optima est occasio.

Quam miserum auxilium est ubi nocet quod sustinet!

Qui pote consilium fugere sapere idem potest.

Qui ulcisci dubitat improbos plures facit.

Qui obesse cum potest non vult prodest ⟨tibi⟩.

Quicquid bono concedas, des partem tibi.

Quod nescias cui serves stultum est parcere.

Quae vult videri bella nimis, nulli negat.

Qui debet limen creditoris non amat.

Qui pote transferre amorem pote deponere.

Qui culpae ignoscit uni suadet pluribus.

579 potest F: pote *Gruter*. capere *Gruter* (*in not. post.*), *Spengel*: rapere *Woelfflin*.

581 tibi *add. Halm*.

584 † nimium illi negat F, *Meyer*: nimis, nulli negat *Gruter*, *Orelli*: nimium litigat *Spengel*.

He who hesitates in the case of truth acts ill when he deliberates.[a]

Who fears a friend teaches a friend to fear.

When aught has to be punished, every opportunity is best.

A sorry help when support hurts!

The man who can shun advice may yet be wise.[b]

A hesitating avenger makes rascals increase.

He who will not hurt when he may is your benefactor.

Whatever you may grant to the good, you give partly to yourself.

It's silly to be sparing, if you don't know for whom you're saving.

She who is over fain to be thought pretty, refuses none.

The debtor loves not his creditor's threshold.

If one can transfer affection, one can put it aside.

To pardon one offence is to prompt more offenders.

[a] *i.e.* he who hesitates when facts are plain commits a crime by his very deliberation.

[b] *i.e.* there is advice which it is wise not to take. This is pithier than the truism involved in the change to *capere*.

Quod improbis eripitur donatur probis.
Qui sibi non vivit aliis merito est mortuus.

Quicquid fit cum virtute fit cum gloria.
Qui exspectat ut rogetur officium levat.
Qui timet amicum vim non novit nominis.

Qui ⟨non⟩ potest celare vitium non facit.

Qui omnes insidias timet in nullas incidit.
Quam malus est culpam qui suam alterius facit!

Qui docte servit partem dominatus tenet.
Qui se ipse laudat cito derisorem invenit.

[589] sibi non F: sibi minime T: sibimet *Ribbeck, Spengel*: sibi modo *Gruter* (*not. post.*), *Bothe*.

[593] *sic Meyer in not*: qui potest zelare non facit vitium ψ: qui pote celare vitium, vitium non facit *Gruter* (fugit *Ribbeck*).

What is snatched from the bad is a gift to the good.

He who does not live a busy life of his own is as good as dead for others.[a]

A deed of valour is a deed of fame.

He who waits to be asked lessens his service.

He who fears a friend doesn't know the meaning of the word.

He who cannot conceal a vicious act does not commit it.[b]

He who fears every ambush falls into none.[c]

What a rascal he is who throws his own guilt upon another!

The skilled servant holds part of his master's power.

The self-praiser soon finds a mocker.

[a] The man who cannot attend to his own affairs with competence is no good to others. *Sibi vivere* is not here "to live only for oneself": it does not, as Orelli takes it, imply a miser who spends neither on himself nor on others. Friedrich aptly illustrates the sense from Sen. *Ep.* lv. 4–5, where the phrase is used of one who rises above slothful retirement or an animal-like existence of self-indulgence to a strenuous and full life in which through serving others he will serve his highest self (cf. *ibid. non continuo sibi vivit, qui nemini*).

[b] A criminal is usually inspired with the hope of eluding detection: so a character in a mime might be imagined to say, "He who can't get away with it, doesn't do it." The text is, however, uncertain (see appar. crit.).

[c] *Cf.* sentiment in 400.

Quam miserum est bene quod feceris factum queri!

Quam est felix vita quae sine odiis transiit!
Quicquid futurum est summum ab imo nascitur.
Quam miserum est ubi consilium casu vincitur!
Quicquid fortuna exornat cito contemnitur.
Quicquid plus quam necesse est possideas premit.
Qui pote nocere timetur cum etiam non adest.

Quem bono tenere non potueris, contineas malo.

Quod senior loquitur omnes consilium putant.
Quam miserum est, ubi te captant, qui defenderent!

Quod quisque amat laudando commendat sibi.

Quem diligas etiam † queri de ipso malum est.

Qui venit ut noceat semper meditatus venit.

Quis miserum sciret, verba nisi haberet dolor?
Quam miserum est cum se renovat consumptum malum!

A sorry thing to complain of a good deed you've done!

How happy the life which has passed without strife!

600 Whatever is to be top springs from the bottom.

A pity when chance beats design!

Whatever fortune bedizens is soon despised.

Any possession beyond the needful overburdens you.

He who can hurt is dreaded even when not upon the scene.

605 Him you have failed to control by fair means, you must restrain by foul.

What a senior says all take for advice.

Pity it is when your supposed defenders take you prisoner!

Everyone commends his hobby to himself by praising it.

It's ill complaining even about the very friend you love.

610 Who comes to injure always comes with mind made up.

Who would know the wretched, if pain had no words?

What a pity when an outworn evil is renewed!

Quanto serius peccatur tanto incipitur turpius.

Quam miser est qui excusare sibi se non potest!

Quo caveas, cum animus aliud verba aliud petunt?

Qui invitus servit, fit miser, servit tamen.

Quod est timendum decipit si neglegas.
Quid tibi pecunia opus est, si uti non potes?
Quod fugere credas saepe solet occurrere.

Quamvis acerbus qui monet nulli nocet.
Z Qui numerosis studet amicis is etiam inimicos ferat.

† Qui semet accusat ab alio non potest criminari.

Qui dormientem necat absentem ulciscitur.

Quod est venturum sapiens ut praesens cavet.

[615] cavetis F: caveas *Bothe, Woelfflin, Spengel, Meyer*: cavet is *Orelli.*

[621] *sic Haupt.*: qui numerosis s. a. et inimicos necesse est ferat T: q. studet multis a. multos i. f. *Meyer.*

[622] qui se ipse accusat, accusari non potest *Ribbeck*: *alii alia.*

The later the sin in coming, the more disgraceful its start.

How wretched the man who cannot make his excuses to himself!

615 How take precautions when heart seeks one thing and words another?

The unwilling slave grows wretched, but is still a slave.

The object of your fear tricks you, if you overlook it.

Why do you need money, if you can't use it?

What you suppose to be in flight is often wont to face you.

620 The warning voice, however sharp, hurts none.

He who is devoted to numerous friends should likewise put up with foes.

He who accuses himself cannot be accused by another.[a]

The slayer of a sleeping man is taking vengeance on the absent.

The wise man guards against what is to come, as if it were present.

[a] *criminari* is deponent in classical Latin.

O Quem diligas, ni recte moneas, oderis.

626 (Quod vult habet qui velle quod satis est potest.)
Ψ Ratione non vi vincenda adulescentia est.
Rei nulli prodest mora nisi iracundiae.
Reus innocens fortunam non testem timet.

Rarum esse oportet quod diu carum velis.
Rapere est accipere quod non possis reddere.
Regnat non regitur qui nihil nisi quod vult facit.

Rivalitatem non amat victoria.
Ruborem amico excutere amicum est perdere.
Rex esse nolim ut esse crudelis velim.

Res quanto est maior tanto est insidiosior.
Roganti melius quam imperanti pareas.
Respicere nihil consuevit iracundia.
Rapere est, non petere, quicquid invito auferas.

Remedium frustra est contra fulmen quaerere.

640 remedium fraus F: remigium frustra *Gruter in notis postumis.* flumen F: fulmen *Bentley.*

325 You will hate the man you love, unless you admonish him aright.

He who can wish for what is enough has his wish.[a]

Youth must be mastered not by force but by reason.

Anger is the one thing benefited by delay.

The innocent man on trial fears fortune, but not a witness.

330 Rare must be that which you would long hold dear.

It is robbery to take what you could never return.

He is a king and no subject who does only what he likes.

Victory loves not rivalry.

Wring a blush from a friend and you lose him.

335 I'd fain have no kingly power with its promptings to cruelty.

The bigger the affair, the greater the snare.

A request is better to comply with than an order.

Anger's way is to regard nothing.

It's no request, it's robbery, to take from the unwilling.

340 It's no good to seek an antidote for a thunderbolt.

[a] The Latin is from Sen. *Ep.* cviii. 11.

Rogare officium servitus quodammodo est.

Z Reddit non perdit cui quod alienum est perit.

Ψ † Semper iratus plus se posse putat quam possit.

Spes est salutis ubi hominem obiurgat pudor.

Suadere primum dein corrigere benivoli est.

Sapiens contra omnes arma fert cum cogitat.

Sanctissimum est meminisse cui te debeas.

Stulti timent fortunam, sapientes ferunt.

Sensus, non aetas, invenit sapientiam.

Semper beatam se putat benignitas.

Sapiens locum dat requiescendi iniuriae.

Solet esse in dubiis pro consilio temeritas.

Semper consilium tunc deest cum opus est maxime.

Sapiens quod petitur, ubi tacet, breviter negat.

Semper plus metuit animus ignotum malum.

642 *sic Haupt*: qui quod alienum erat persolvit T.

643 se posse plus iratus quam possit putat *Pithoeus*: *fortasse trochaicus* semper iratus plus sese posse quam possit putat *A. M. Duff.*

To ask a favour is slavery of a sort.

To lose what is not your own is not to lose but to give back.

Anger always thinks it has power beyond its power.

When shame rebukes a man, there's hope for his soul's health.

It's the well-wisher's way to advise before he corrects.

The sage bears arms against the world when he thinks.

'Tis most just to remember to whom you owe yourself.

Fools fear fortune, wise men bear it.

Wisdom is found by sense, not years.

Bounty holds herself ever rich.

The wise man gives an injury room to settle down.

In a hazard venturesomeness replaces deliberation.

Counsel is ever lacking when most needed.

It's a curt refusal when the wise man meets a request with silence.

The mind always fears the unknown evil more.

---

[651] *sic Spengel*: † sapiens semper quiescendi dat locum iniuriae F, *Meyer*: saepe ignoscendo das iniuriae locum *Gruter*: semper quiescens des iniuriae locum *Meyer in not.*

[654] *sic* F: cum . . . si . . . graviter O, *Meyer*.

Secunda in paupertate fortuna est fides.
Si nihil velis timere, metuas omnia.
Summissum imperium non tenet vires suas.
Secundus est a matre nutricis dolor.
Sibi supplicium ipse dat quem admissi paenitet.

Suum sequitur lumen semper innocentia.
Stultum est ulcisci velle alium poena sua.

Sibi primum auxilium eripere est leges tollere.

Suis qui nescit parcere inimicis favet.

Sine dolore est vulnus quod ferendum est cum victoria.
Semper metuendo sapiens evitat malum.
Stultum est queri de adversis, ubi culpa est tua.

Solet hora quod multi anni abstulerunt reddere.

Spina etiam grata est ex qua spectatur rosa.

In poverty faith is fortune renewed.[a]

If you want to fear nothing, you should dread all.

Diminished power keeps not its strength.

The nurse's pangs are second to the mother's.

He who repents his deed inflicts punishment on himself.

Innocence ever follows her own light.

It's folly to want vengeance on another by punishing oneself.

To destroy the laws is to rob oneself of one's first support.

He who cannot spare his own folk befriends his foes.

It's a painless wound that the victor must bear.

By constant fear the wise man escapes harm.

Silly to grumble about misfortune when the fault's your own.

An hour often restores what many years have taken away.

Pleasant even the thorn which yields a rose to view.

[a] *i.e.* if a man reduced to poverty retains a faith in better times to come, that is in some degree a restoration of fortune.

670 Stultum est vicinum velle ulcisci incendio.

Stultum facit Fortuna quem vult perdere.
Spes inopem, res avarum, mors miserum levat.

Se damnat iudex innocentem qui opprimit.
Sibi ipsa improbitas cogit fieri iniuriam.
675 Satis est beatus qui potest cum vult mori.
Solet sequi laus, cum viam fecit labor.
Socius fit culpae qui nocentem sublevat.
Suspicio sibi ipsa rivales parit.
Semper metuendum quicquid irasci potest.
680 Seditio civium hostium est occasio.
Salutis causa bene fit homini iniuria.
Stultitia est insectari quem di diligunt.
Sat magna usura est pro beneficio memoria.
Sero in periclis est consilium quaerere.
Z Sua servat qui salva esse vult communia.

686 Satis est superare inimicum, nimium est perdere.
Suspiciosus omnium damnat fidem.

It's silly to want vengeance on a neighbour by firing the house.

Fortune makes a fool of him whom she would ruin.[a]

Hope eases the beggar, wealth the miser, death the wretched.

A judge who crushes the guiltless is self-condemned.

Villainy compels injury to be done to itself.

Happy enough he who can die when he wills!

Praise ever follows when toil has made the way.

To help the guilty is to share his crime.

Suspicion doth breed rivals for herself.

What can show anger must ever be dreaded.

Discord mid citizens is the foeman's chance.

Injury may well be done a man for safety's sake.

'Tis folly to upbraid the favourite of heaven.

'Tis high enough interest for a benefit to remember it.

'Tis too late in perils to search for advice.

He who wishes safety for the common property is the guardian of his own.

It is enough to beat a foe, too much to ruin him.

The suspicious man condemns the good faith of all.

[a] A more familiar form of this idea is *quem Iuppiter vult perdere dementat prius.*

Suspicio probatis tacita iniuria est.

Superari a superiore pars est gloriae.

690 Supplicem hominem opprimere virtus non est sed crudelitas.

Sat est disertus e quo loquitur veritas.

Ψ Thesaurum in sepulcro ponit qui senem heredem facit.

Taciturnitas stulto homini pro sapientia est.

Tam deest avaro quod habet quam quod non habet.

Z Tarde sed graviter sapiens ⟨mens⟩ irascitur.

696 Tuti sunt omnes unus ubi defenditur.

O Temptando cuncta caeci quoque tuto ambulant.

Tam de se iudex iudicat quam de reo.

Ψ Ubi fata peccant, hominum consilia excidunt.

700 Voluptas e difficili data dulcissima est.

Ubi omnis vitae metus est, mors est optima.

Unus deus poenam affert, multi cogitant.

691 de quo T: pro quo O: e quo *Casp. Orelli in not.*
695 *alii alia*: mens *Bickford-Smith.*
702 u. deus poenam affert quam m. cogitant F: dies (*delevit* quam) *Gruter*: citant *Buecheler*: irrogant *Meyer*: coquunt *Friedrich.*

Suspicion is an unspoken wrong to tested worth.

To be bested by a better means a share in the glory.

To crush the suppliant is not valour but barbarity.

Eloquent enough is he who has the accent of truth.

He stows treasure in the tomb who makes an old man his heir.

For a fool it is wisdom to hold his tongue.

The miser lacks what he has as much as what he hasn't.[a]

A wise mind grows angry slowly but seriously.[b]

All are safe when one is defended.

By testing everything even the blind walk safely.

A judge passes judgement on himself as much as on the accused.

When fate goes awry, human counsels fail.

Out of difficulty comes the sweetest pleasure.

When life is all one terror, death is best.

God alone brings punishment, though many intend it.

[a] One of the best known lines of Publilius: it is quoted by Seneca, *Controv.* vii. 3 (18) 8; Quintilian, viii. 5, 6 and ix. 3, 64; Hieronymus, *Epist.* liii, 10 *sub fin.* Jerome's order is *avaro tam deest* . . .

[b] *Cf.* 550.

Ubi peccat aetas maior, male discit minor.
Ubi nihil timetur, quod timeatur nascitur.
Ubi sis cum tuis et absis, patriam non desideres.

Verum est quod pro salute fit mendacium.
Ubicumque pudor est, semper ibi sancta est fides.
Utilius ferrum est in sulco quam orichalcum est in proelio.
Ubi innocens formidat damnat iudicem.
Voluntas impudicum non corpus facit.
Virtuti melius quam fortunae creditur.
Verbum omne refert in quam partem intellegas.
Virum bonum natura non ordo facit.
Ubi coepit ditem pauper imitari, perit.
Veterem ferendo iniuriam invites novam.
Virtutis spolia cum videt, gaudet labor.
Virtutis vultus partem habet victoriae.
Virtute quod non possis blanditia auferas.
Utrumque casum adspicere debet qui imperat.

[705] absis patria *Meyer*: patriam desideres F: non *add. Orelli.*

[708] *om. Meyer*: Utilius est vero in sulco quam gravis galea in proelio *Par.* 8027 *servat solus*: veru est *Woelfflin*: ferrum est *alii*: quam orichalcum *Friedrich.*

When seniors blunder, juniors learn but ill.

When nothing is feared, something arises to fear.

When far away with your own folk, you would not miss your fatherland.

Falsehood for safety's sake is true.

Where scruples are, there faith is ever revered.

Steel in the furrow is more useful than yellow copper in battle.

Innocence in terror condemns the judge.

The will, not the body, makes impurity.

It's better trusting to valour than to luck.

For any word it matters how you understand it.

Nature, not rank, makes the gentleman.

When the poor man starts to ape the rich, he's lost.

Tolerate an old wrong and you may invite a new one.

The sight of valour's spoil makes the delight of toil.[a]

Bravery's countenance has a share in the victory.

Coaxing may win what the stout heart could not.

A ruler should look at both the sides of chance.

[a] *Labor* is personified: hard-wrought soldiers, after the fight, look with joy on the spoil which proves their victorious bravery.

Voluptas tacita metus est mage quam gaudium.
Viri boni est nescire facere iniuriam.
Vultu an natura sapiens sis, multum interest.

Virtuti amorem nemo honeste denegat.
Z Ubi libertas cecidit, audet libere nemo loqui.
Vita otiosa regnum est et curae minus.
Ubi omnes peccant, spes querelae tollitur.

Ut plures corrigantur, † rite pauci eliduntur.
Virtutis omnis impedimentum est timor.
Ubi iudicat qui accusat, vis non lex valet.
Ubi emas aliena, caveas ne vendas tua.

O Ubi peccatum cito corrigitur, fama solet ignoscere.

Ubi innocens damnatur, pars patriae exsulat.

Vincere est honestum, opprimere acerbum, pulchrum ignoscere.

φ (Velox consilium sequitur paenitentia.)

720 magis F, *Spengel*, *Meyer* : mage metus *Gruter*.
727 *sic* T : rite unus perit *Casp. Orelli in not.* : ut plures sanes recte paucos amputes *Friedrich*.

720 Dumb pleasure is rather fear than joy.

Goodness means inability to do a wrong.

It makes a wide difference whether you were born wise or only look it.

From virtue no man honourably withholds his love.

Where freedom has fallen, none dare freely speak.

725 The life of ease is a kingdom without the worry.

Where all go wrong, the hope of remonstrance is removed.

A few are justly destroyed that more may be reformed.

All virtue finds an obstacle in fear.

When the accuser is judge, force, not law, has power.

730 In buying others' goods, see you don't have to sell your own.

When an offence is soon corrected, scandal commonly overlooks it.

When the innocent is found guilty, part of his native land is exiled.

It is honourable to conquer, bitter to crush, handsome to forgive.

Repentance follows on a hasty plan.

---

730 *sic Meyer in apparatu* : invenies necesse est tua T.

ELEGIAE IN MAECENATEM

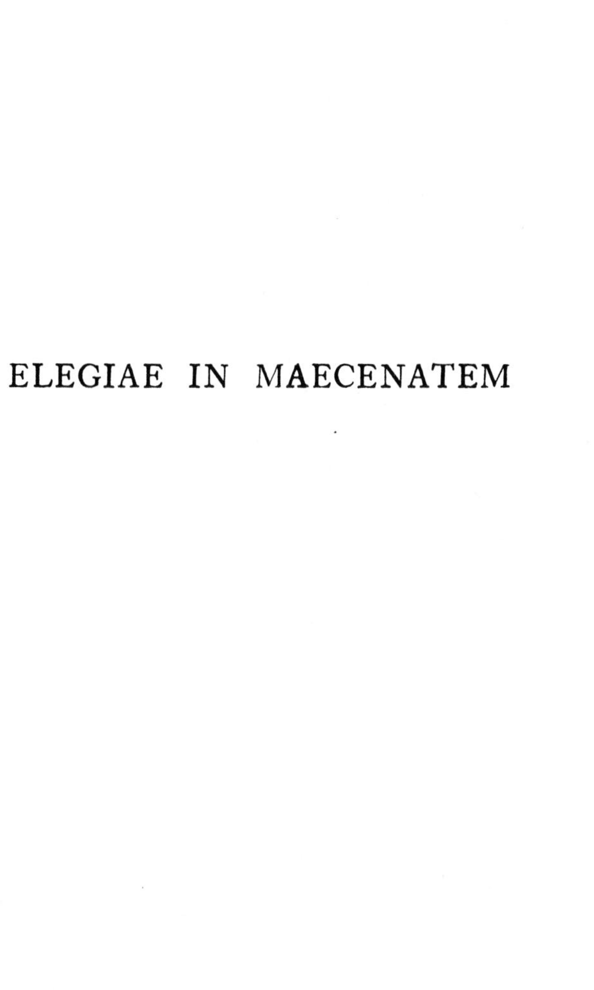

INTRODUCTION

TO THE ELEGIES

These two elegies are transmitted as a single continuous poem in manuscripts of the minor "Virgilian" works (*Culex*, *Dirae*, *Copa*, *Moretum*). The ascription to Virgil is chronologically impossible; for Maecenas died in 8 B.C., eleven years after Virgil. Scaliger first separated the longer poem from the thirty-four lines which give the "Dying Words of Maecenas," and he propounded the guess (once considered attractive) that both elegies, as well as the *Consolatio ad Liviam*, might be the work of Albinovanus Pedo. To some extent modern opinion inclines to accept as genuine the claim of the author (*Eleg*. I. 1–2 : *cf*. II. 3–4) to have already written the consolatory lament addressed to Livia on the death of Drusus.[a] The repetition of the phrases *Caesaris illud opus* and *illa rapit iuvenes*[b] as well as the noteworthy parallelism between two other passages[c] strengthens the case, though it is conceded that the *Elegiae* are artistically inferior to the *Consolatio*. They have, however, a similar rhetorical ring; and the metrical technique of the elegies, while it shows fewer elisions than does the *Consolatio*, is in keeping with that of the Augustan

[a] The *Consolatio* is translated in the Loeb Library: Ovid, *Art of Love and other Poems*, pp. 325 sqq.

[b] *Cons*. 39, *Eleg*. II. 6; *Cons*. 372, *Eleg*. I. 7.

[c] *Cons*. 47–48, *Eleg*. I. 15–16.

period. Haupt's endeavour to regard the first elegy as a defence of Maecenas against a charge of *tunicae solutae* in Seneca's 114th letter has been successfully rebutted by Skutsch:[a] Seneca's letter contains other censures which the poet could not have left unanswered, if he had ever seen them. In this elaborate letter on decadence, and in particular on speech as a mirror of morals, emphasis is laid upon Maecenas' undisciplined style as a parallel to the dishabille which he notoriously affected. There are no convincing allusions to prove that the poem followed the letter, and we should not expect a reply to it to ignore the instances adduced.[b]

The contents and tone of the poems give the impression that the author stood close to the facts introduced.[c] This direct contact with reality, which appears to underlie the allusions to Maecenas' war-service, to his *cura urbis* and intellectual interests,

[a] P. W. *Realencyclopädie*, IV. 1901 : art. on 'Consolatio ad Liviam.'

[b] Th. Birt, like Haupt, considers the *Elegiae* post-Senecan, and holds that the passage about the beryl (I. 19–20) refers to the wide difference between Maecenas' style and the common level of expression (*Ad hist. hexam. latini symb.*, Bonn, 1876, p. 66).

[c] Prof. R. S. Radford in *The Culex and Ovid, Philologus*, 1930, 86, 1, defends the Ovidian authorship of both *Consolatio* and the *Elegiae*. Dealing with *The Order of Ovid's Works* (*Trans. Amer. Philol. Assoc.*, 1923) he assigns the former to 9 B.C., the latter to 8 B.C. In E. Wagner's *De Martiale Poetarum Augusteae aetatis imitatore*, Regimonti (=Königsberg), 1880, similarities of phraseology between Elegy I and Martial were unduly stressed as suggestive of a difference in style between Elegy I and Elegy II. A few years earlier M. Hertz in *Analecta ad carm. Horat. historiam*, Breslau, 1876, had discovered echoes of Horace in I, but none in II. This sort of internal "evidence" amounts to very little.

makes a pleasant contrast to the occasional declamatory or mythological passages. There is something agreeably personal in the tenderness of the farewell to Terentia (II. 7–10) and in the poet's confession that, though he had not himself belonged to Maecenas' intimate circle, Lollius had put him in a position to compose this memorial poem (I. 10). The Lollius here meant had been consul in 20 B.C., and died in 1 B.C.

EDITIONS

Th. Gorallus (Clericus). *C. Pedonis Albinovani Elegiae III.* Amsterdam, 1703 (assigning both elegies and the *Consolatio ad Liviam* to Albinovanus).

P. Burman. *Anthologia Veterum Latinorum Epigrammatum et Poematum* (ascribing the Elegiae to an "incertus auctor"), I. pp. 251–287. Amsterdam, 1759.

C. Wernsdorf. *Poetae Latini Minores,* III. p. 155 sqq. Altenburg, 1782.

J. Plumtre. *The Elegies of C. Pedo Albinovanus with an English version* (heroic couplets). Kidderminster, 1807.

J. H. F. Meineke. *Drei dem C. Pedo Albinovanus zugeschriebene Elegien . . . mit einer metrischen Uebersetzung.* Quedlinburg, 1819.

H. Meyer. *Anthologia vet. Lat. epigram. et poematum* (based on Burman), Nos. 109 and 110. Leipzig, 1835.

O. Ribbeck. *Appendix Vergiliana,* pp. 193–204. Leipzig, 1868.

E. Baehrens. *Poetae Latini Minores,* I. pp. 122–136. Leipzig, 1879.

F. Bücheler, and A. Riese. *Anthologia Latina*, I. 2, ed. 2. Leipzig, 1906.
R. Ellis. *Appendix Vergiliana*. Oxford, 1907.
J. Middendorf. *Elegiae in Maecenatem* (text and notes). Marburg, 1912.
F. Vollmer. *Poetae Latini Minores*, I. pp. 143–155. Leipzig, 1927.

Relevant Works

E. Hübner. In *Hermes*. 13 (1878), p. 239.
E. Wagner. *De Martiale poetarum Augusteae aetatis imitatore* (pp. 42–46 on points of style in *Elegiae* and *Consolatio*).
F. Skutsch. P. W. *Realencyclopädie*, IV. col. 944 sqq. 1901.
F. Lillge. *De Elegiis in Maecen. quaestiones*, diss. Breslau, 1901.
B. Axelson. In *Eranos*, xxviii. (1930), 1 sqq. (Contention that the *Elegiae* and the *Consolatio ad Liviam* belong to a date not earlier than that of Statius and Martial.)
R. B. Steele. *The Nux, Maecenas, and Consolatio ad Liviam*. Nashville, Tennessee, U.S.A., 1933. (One of the contentions here is that similarities of diction in the works of Seneca to the *Consolatio* and to the Maecenas poems fix their publication within or later than the reign of Nero.)

SIGLA

Ω = archetype of all the codices.
S = Scaliger's lost manuscript whose readings are preserved in his "Virgilii Appendix. . . ." pp. 528–541. Leyden, 1573.

F = codex Fiechtianus, now Mellicensis, 11th cent. (contains lines 1–25).
B = codex Bruxellensis 10676, 12th cent.
P = codex Parisinus lat. 16236, 10th cent. (contains lines 1–43).
Z = a lost codex represented by three 15th century MSS.:
 H = Helmstadiensis 332.
 A = Arundelianus, Brit. Mus. 133.
 R = Rehdigeranus, Breslau Public Library.
M = Monacenses (manuscripts in Munich), including:
 m = Mon. lat. 305, 11th–12th cent.
 n = Mon. lat. 18059, 11th cent.
V = Vossianus lat. oct. 81 (Leyden), 15th cent.
ς = any correction by Italian scholars in the later MSS. or early editions.

Considerable departures have been made from Vollmer's text in readings and in punctuation.

Bibliographical addendum (1982)

Elegiae in Maecenatem, ed. E. J. Kenney in *Appendix Vergiliana* (*OCT*) pp. 83–95, Oxford 1966.

ELEGIAE IN MAECENATEM

I

Defleram iuvenis tristi modo carmine fata,
  sunt etiam merito carmina danda seni.
ut iuvenis deflendus enim tam candidus et tam
  longius annoso vivere dignus avo.
irreligata ratis, numquam defessa carina,
  it, redit in vastos semper onusta lacus:
illa rapit iuvenes prima florente iuventa,
  non oblita tamen sed † repetitque senes.
nec mihi, Maecenas, tecum fuit usus amici,
  Lollius hoc ergo conciliavit opus;
foedus erat vobis nam propter Caesaris arma
  Caesaris et similem propter in arma fidem.
regis eras, Etrusce, genus; tu Caesaris almi
  dextera, Romanae tu vigil urbis eras.
omnia cum posses tanto tam carus amico,
  te sensit nemo posse nocere tamen.

6 et Ω (= *codd.*), *Vollmer*: it *ed. Ascens.* 1507.
11 fidus Ω: foedus *Heinsius.*
13 almi Ω: alti *Heinsius.*

TWO ELEGIES ON MAECENAS

I

My saddened muse of late had mourned a young man's[a] death: now to one ripe in years also let songs be duly offered. As youth is mourned, so must we mourn for one so white-souled, so worthy to live beyond the span of an age-laden grandsire. The barque that knows no fastening, the never-wearied keel, goes and returns for ever with its load across the vasty pools: it carries off the young in the first bloom of their youth, yet unforgetful claims the old as well. At one time, my Maecenas, I lacked converse with thee as a friend: my present task, then, 'twas Lollius[b] won for me. For between you two was a bond because of your war-service for Caesar and your equal loyalty to Caesar's service. Thou wert of royal race, O Tuscan-born, thou wert the right hand of bounteous Caesar, thou wert the guardian of the Roman city. All-powerful though thou wert in such favour with so exalted a friend, yet no man ever felt thou hadst the power to hurt.

[a] *i.e.* Drusus, who died in 9 B.C., the year before Maecenas' death.

[b] M. Lollius, consul 20 B.C., died 1 B.C. Gorallus and Meineke take *opus* of gaining Maecenas' friendship for the author. *Opus*, however, seems odd in this connexion, and here Wernsdorf's view is followed that the *opus* is the present elegy.

Pallade cum docta Phoebus donaverat artes:
tu decus et laudes huius et huius eras,
vincit vulgares veluti beryllus harenas,
litore in extremo quas simul unda movet.
quod discinctus eras, animo quoque, carpitur unum:
diluitur nimia simplicitate tua.
sic illi vixere, quibus fuit aurea Virgo,
quae bene praecinctos postmodo pulsa fugit.
livide, quid tandem tunicae nocuere solutae
aut tibi ventosi quid nocuere sinus?
num minus urbis erat custos et Caesaris opses?
num tibi non tutas fecit in urbe vias?
nocte sub obscura quis te spoliavit amantem,
quis tetigit ferro, durior ipse, latus?
maius erat potuisse tamen nec velle triumphos,
maior res magnis abstinuisse fuit.

[19] *sic Birt*: vincit vulgares vincit FBPHMV, *Vollmer*: vicit vulgares vicit AR: sicut volgares vincit *Riese, Middendorf.* beritus FBPH *m*: berithus AR: peritus *n* V: berillus *Ald.* 1517: Berytus *Ellis.*

[22] diluvii hoc Ω (ac V): diluis hoc *Oudendorp, Baehrens, Vollmer*: diluitur *Ald.* 1517, *Riese.*

[27] obses (op- B) Ω: hospes A[1].

Apollo with learned Minerva had conferred their arts on thee: thou wert the ornament and glory of both—even as the beryl[a] surpasses the common sands which the wave tosses about along with it on the shore's edge. That thou wert luxurious in mind as in dress is the one slander urged against thee: it is dispelled by thine exceeding plainness of life. So did they live among whom dwelt the golden Maid[b] who soon fled into exile from the bustle of mankind. Backbiter, say what harm his loosened tunic did you, or dress through which the air could play? Was he a whit less guardian of the city, and less a hostage for our absent emperor? Did he make the streets of Rome unsafe for you? 'Neath the murk of night who could rob you in an amour. or who in excess of heartlessness drive steel into your side? Greater it was to have had the power, yet not to wish for triumphs: a greater thing it was to refrain from mighty deeds.

[a] With an allusion to Maecenas' fondness for jewels. Among terms applied to Maecenas in a jocular letter from Augustus were *Cibriorum smaragde . . . berylle Porsennae* (Macrob. *Saturn.* II. iv. 12). The beryl (βήρυλλος) is a transparent gem, usually sea-green, and, though now found in many parts of the Old World and the New, was mainly known to the ancients as coming from India (Plin. *N.H.* XXXVII. 5, 20, *India eos gignit raro alibi repertos*, a passage which tempts one to take *extremo in litore* as " on a distant shore " : cf. *extremos equos*, 56). Pliny rightly associates it with the emerald. Since one species was the aquamarine, some knowledge of this may have prompted the reference to the sea-shore in 20. It is difficult, however, to imagine that this product of granitic rocks can have been often washed up among the sands of the sea, though Gorallus quotes Greek hexameters from Dionysius Periegetes, of which one interpretation supports the view.

[b] Astraea, or Justice, sojourned among men in the Golden Age, but was driven from earth by the growth of depravity.

maluit umbrosam quercum lymphasque cadentes
paucaque pomosi iugera certa soli:
Pieridas Phoebumque colens in mollibus hortis
sederat argutas garrulus inter avis.
marmorea Aonii vincent monumenta libelli:
vivitur ingenio, cetera mortis erunt.
quid faceret? defunctus erat comes integer, idem
miles et Augusti fortis et usque pius:
illum piscosi viderunt saxa Pelori
ignibus hostilis reddere ligna ratis;
pulvere in Emathio fortem videre Philippi;
quam nunc ille tener, tam gravis hostis erat.
cum freta Niliacae texerunt lata carinae,
fortis erat circa, fortis et ante ducem,
militis Eoi fugientis terga secutus,
territus ad Nili dum fugit ille caput.
pax erat: haec illos laxarunt otia cultus:
omnia victores Marte sedente decent.
Actius ipse lyram plectro percussit eburno,
postquam victrices conticuere tubae.

[33] nymphas Ω: lymphas *Wernsdorf.* cadentes BP: canentes ZMV.

[37] marmora m(a)eonii ARMV: marmora minei SPH: marmorea Aonii *vel* marmora Smyrnaei *Scaliger.*

[44] tam . . . tam B, *Vollmer.*

[45] l(a)eta BZ, *Vollmer*: lata MV, *Ellis.*

He chose rather the shady oak, the falling waters, the few sure acres of fruit-bearing soil. Honouring the Muses and Apollo in luxurious gardens, he reclined babbling verse among the tuneful birds. Aonian writings[a] will eclipse marble monuments: genius means life, all else will belong to death. What was he to do? He had filled his part as blameless comrade, yea, as Augustus' warrior, gallant and devoted throughout. The rocks of Pelorus abounding in fish saw him give the enemy's craft for fuel to the flames:[b] Philippi[c] saw his bravery amid Emathian dust: as tender of heart as he is to-day, so dread a foe was he then. When (Antony's) Egyptian ships covered the waters wide, Maecenas showed bravery around and bravery in front of his leader,[d] following in the wake of the fugitive Oriental warrior, while he flees panic-stricken to the mouth of the Nile. Peace came: its leisure brought a slackening of those ways: when the War-god sits idle, everything beseems the conquerors.

The very god of Actium[e] smote the lyre with ivory quill after the bugles of victory were hushed. He

[a] *i.e.* poetic: "Aonian" is an epithet of the Muses.

[b] The reference is to the fighting against Sextus Pompeius in Sicilian waters, 38–35 B.C.

[c] Philippi, on the borders of Thrace, is here called "Emathian" (*i.e.* Macedonian). The allusion is to the defeat of Brutus and Cassius by Octavian Caesar and Antony, 42 B.C.

[d] *i.e.* at Actium in 31 B.C. Most authorities accept the testimony of Dio, li. 3. 5, that Maecenas was in Rome when Actium was fought. See E. Groag, art. "Maecenas," P. W. *Realencl.* XIV. i. col. 210, and Gardthausen, *Augustus und seine Zeit,* I. i. p. 365. This *Elegia* is the one ancient source which suggests the contrary view.

[e] Apollo. In the games instituted at Actium by Augustus in honour of his victory, musical performances were included.

hic modo miles erat, ne posset femina Romam
  dotalem stupri turpis habere sui;
hic tela in profugos—tantum curvaverat arcum—
  misit ad extremos exorientis equos:
Bacche, coloratos postquam devicimus Indos,
  potasti galea dulce iuvante merum,
et tibi securo tunicae fluxere solutae,
  te puto purpureas tunc habuisse duas.
sum memor et certe memini sic ducere thyrsos
  bracchia purpurea candidiora nive,
et tibi thyrsus erat gemmis ornatus et auro,
  serpentes hederae vix habuere locum;
argentata tuos etiam sandalia talos
  vinxerunt certe nec, puto, Bacche negas.
mollius es solito mecum tum multa locutus
  et tibi consulto verba fuere nova.
impiger Alcide, multo defuncte labore,
  sic memorant curas te posuisse tuas,
sic te cum tenera laetum lusisse puella
  oblitum Nemeae, iamque, Erymanthe, tui.

61 thyrsos Ω: tigres *Burman, Vollmer.*
62 Bacchea RMV: bracchia *Ald.* 1517. purpurea Ω: hyperborea *Vollmer.*
65 talaria Ω, *Vollmer*: sandalia V.
71 multum BHM, *Vollmer*: laetum *Ascens.* 1507.

was of late a warrior to prevent a woman[a] from having Rome as a marriage-gift for her foul lewdness : he sped his arrows after the runaways—so mighty the bow he had bent—far as the furthest steeds of the rising sun.

O Bacchus,[b] after we subdued the dark-skinned Orientals, thou didst drink sweet wine with thy helmet's aid, and in thy care-free hour loose flowed thy tunics—'twas the time, I fancy, when thou didst wear two[c] of brilliant colour. My memory works, and certes I remember that thus arms whiter than the gleaming snow led the Bacchic wands, and thy wand was adorned with gems and gold—the trailing ivy scarce had room thereon; silvern surely were the slippers which bound thy feet: this I trow, Bacchus, thou dost not deny. Softer e'en than thy wont was much that thou saidst then in converse with me : 'twas of set design that thy words were new to the ear.

O Hercules unwearied, after mighty toil performed, 'twas even so, they relate, thou didst lay aside thy cares, and even so didst hold joyous sport with tender damsel, forgetful of Nemea, forgetful now of Erymanthus.[d]

[a] Apollo is fancied to have fought for Octavian against Cleopatra of Egypt and her lover Antony.

[b] Vollmer takes ll. 57–68 as a "dithyramb" addressed by Apollo to Bacchus. Antony's historic posing as Bacchus gives point to the passage.

[c] To wear two was a sign of luxury.

[d] Hercules' twelve labours included the slaying of the Nemean lion and of the Erymanthian boar. An oracle having ordered Hercules to undergo for penance a period of menial service, he placed himself under the charge of Omphale, princess of Lydia, and found favour with her by spinning and dressing like a woman, while she donned his lion's skin. The tale of the strong hero relaxing into effeminacy is adduced here as an apology for Maecenas' luxury after he had accomplished great tasks.

ultra numquid erat? torsisti pollice fusos,
  lenisti morsu levia fila parum.
percussit crebros te propter Lydia nodos,
  te propter dura stamina rupta manu.
Lydia te tunicas iussit lasciva fluentis
  inter lanificas ducere saepe suas.
clava torosa tua pariter cum pelle iacebat,
  quam pede suspenso percutiebat Amor.
quis fore credebat, premeret cum iam impiger infans
  hydros ingentes vix capiente manu,
cumve renascentem meteret velociter Hydram,
  frangeret immanes vel Diomedis equos,
vel tribus adversis communem fratribus alvom
  et sex adversas solus in arma manus?
fudit Aloidas postquam dominator Olympi,
  dicitur in nitidum percubuisse diem,
atque aquilam misisse suam, quae quaereret, ecqui
  posset amaturo digna referre Iovi,
valle sub Idaea dum te, formose sacerdos,
  invenit et presso molliter ungue rapit.
sic est: victor amet, victor potiatur in umbra,
  victor odorata dormiat inque rosa;
victus aret victusque metat; metus imperet illi,
  membra nec in strata sternere discat humo.
tempora dispensant usus et tempora cultus,
  haec homines, pecudes, haec moderantur avis.
lux est; taurus arat: nox est; requiescit arator,
  liberat et merito fervida colla bovi.

83 terret Ω: tereret *Ald.* 1517: meteret *Struchtmeyer*, *Vollmer*.
89 ecquid BAR, *Vollmer*: et quid HM: et qui V: ecquis ς: ecqui *Baehrens*, *Ellis*.
90 signa Ω: digna *Heinsius*: vina *edd. var.*
91 sacerdos Ω: iacentem *Heinsius*: *fortasse* satelles *Ellis*.

Could aught exceed this?—twirling spindles with the thumb, and biting the rough threads smooth with the mouth! Lydian Omphale beat thee for leaving too many knots or for breaking the threads with that hard hand. The sportive Lydian bade thee often wear loose-flowing robes among her spinning-maids. The knotty club was thrown down along with thy lion-skin, and on it the Love-god danced with light-poised toe. That this would come who was like to believe in the hour when the active babe strangled monstrous serpents which his hand could hardly grasp? or when he nimbly lopped each Hydra-head as it grew again? or conquered the savage steeds of Diomede or the body common to three confronting brothers, and the six confronting hands,[a] which he fought unaided? After the Ruler of Olympus routed the sons of Aloeus,[b] they say he lay asleep till the bright dawn, and sent his eagle in quest of one who could render fitting service to Jove bent on love, until in Ida's vale he found thee, fair priest,[c] and carried thee off in talons softly closed.

Such is the world's way: the victor must love, the victor have the mastery in the shade, the victor must sleep on scented rose-leaves: the vanquished must plough, the vanquished must reap: fear must be his lord: never must he learn to rest his limbs on the cushioned ground. The seasons regulate different habits and ways in life: the seasons rule mankind and cattle and birds. 'Tis dawn—the bull ploughs: 'tis night—the ploughman rests; he frees the steaming neck of the ox which has

[a] *i.e.* of the three-headed monster Geryon.

[b] Giants who had warred against the Gods.

[c] Ganymede is thereafter to minister to Jove.

conglaciantur aquae; scopulis se condit hirundo:
  verberat egelidos garrula vere lacus.
Caesar amicus erat: poterat vixisse solute,
  cum iam Caesar idem quod cupiebat erat.
indulsit merito: non est temerarius ille:
  vicimus: Augusto iudice dignus erat.
Argo saxa pavens postquam Scylleia legit
  Cyaneosque metus, iam religanda ratis,
viscera dissecti mutaverat arietis agno
  Aeetis sucis omniperita suis:
his te, Maecenas, iuvenescere posse decebat,
  haec utinam nobis Colchidos herba foret!
redditur arboribus florens revirentibus aetas:
  ergo non homini quod fuit ante redit?
vivacesque magis cervos decet esse paventis
  si quorum in torva cornua fronte rigent?
vivere cornices multos dicuntur in annos:
  cur nos angusta condicione sumus?
pascitur Aurorae Tithonus nectare coniunx
  atque ita iam tremulo nulla senecta nocet:

107 Scilleia BHA: Scylleia R. legit Ω: Scyllaea relegit *Salmasius.*

109 disiecti BARV: directi SH^1: dissecti *Vat.* 3269. agni Ω: agno *Ald.* 1517.

done its work. The streams are frozen—then the swallow shelters 'mid the crags: in spring loud-twittering she skims the genial meres.

The Emperor was Maecenas' friend: so he was free to live a life of ease when the Emperor was now all he longed to be. He granted indulgence to Maecenas' merits: nor is Maecenas reckless: we have won our victory [a]: 'twas the judgement of Augustus that counted him deserving.[b] After the Argo had skirted in affright the reefs of Scylla [c] and the peril of the Clashing Rocks, when the barque had now to be moored, the daughter [d] of Aeetes, all-skilled in her magic juices, had changed into a lamb the body of the ram she had cut up. 'Twas right, Maecenas, that by such means thou shouldst have power to grow young again: would that we had the herb of the Colchian (sorceress)!

Trees reclothed in green have the bloom of their life restored: and to man then does not that which was his before come again? Is it meet that the timid deer with stiff horns on their wild foreheads should have longer life? Crows, 'tis said, live for many a year: why do we men exist on narrow terms? Tithonus, as Aurora's consort, feeds on nectar, and so, though he be palsied now, no length of age can work him harm. That thy life, Maecenas, might

[a] As Antony has been overthrown, easy-going relaxation is no longer a danger.

[b] *i.e.* to indulge in a more luxurious life after Antony's defeat.

[c] The Argo would not naturally pass by Scylla and Charybdis on the outward voyage to Colchis.

[d] Medea, princess of Colchis, famous for her powers in sorcery.

ut tibi vita foret semper medicamine sacro,
te vellem Aurorae complacuisse virum.
illius aptus eras croceo recubare cubili
et, modo puniceum rore lavante torum,
illius aptus eras roseas adiungere bigas,
tu dare purpurea lora regenda manu,
tu mulcere iubam, cum iam torsisset habenas
procedente die, respicientis equi.
quaesivere chori iuvenum sic Hesperon illum,
quem nexum medio solvit in igne Venus,
quem nunc in fuscis placida sub nocte nitentem
Luciferum contra currere cernis equis.
hic tibi Corycium, casias hic donat olentis,
hic et palmiferis balsama missa iugis.
nunc pretium candoris habes, nunc redditus umbris:
te sumus obliti decubuisse senem.
ter Pylium flevere sui, ter Nestora canum,
dicebantque tamen non satis esse senem:

129 chori SBHAM: thori V. iuvenem Ω: iuvenum *Scaliger*. 131 infusci BM: infusi Z: in fluscis *corr. in* fuscis V: infusa *Vollmer*. placida Ω: placide *Baehrens*: placidus *Vollmer*.

---

[a] *i.e.* caused Hesperos to set; in myth, Hesperos was a fair youth elevated by Venus into the "Evening-star," which was by the ancients correctly identified with Phosphoros (Lucifer),

last for ever in virtue of a holy drug, I could wish thou hadst found favour with Aurora as husband. Worthy wert thou to recline on her saffron bed, and, as the morning-dew was just moistening the purple couch, worthy wert thou to yoke the two steeds to her rosy car, worthy to give the reins for guidance by the bright-hued hand, worthy to stroke the mane of the horse as it looked back (on its nightly course), now that Aurora had turned the reins at the advance of day.

In such a way did the bands of his youthful comrades feel the loss of Hesperos, whom Venus attached to herself and released in the midst of his fiery course:[a] thou canst see him now as Lucifer gleaming in the dark 'neath the stilly night and charioting his steeds on an opposite course.[b] He it is that presents to thee the Corycian saffron-flower, he presents the aromatic cinnamon, he too the balsams sent from palm-growing hills.

Now hast thou, Maecenas, the guerdon of sincerity, now that thou art given to the shades: we have forgotten that thou didst die an old man.[c] His people mourned the King of Pylos, Nestor, hoary after three generations of life; and yet they said he had not fully reached old age. Thou wouldst

the "Morning-star." Actually it is the planet Venus. The allusion is to the fact that, after a cycle of brilliancy, the planet's apparent height above the horizon at sunset gradually diminishes and it sinks into invisibility.

[b] Lucifer, particularly associated with the East, appropriately offers, in honour of Maecenas, fragrant Oriental plants, *crocus* from Corycus in Cilicia (Plin. *N.H.* XXI. 6. 17), *casia* from Arabia Felix (*ib.* XII. 18, 41), and balsam from Judaea (Joseph. *Ant. Jud.* XIV. 4 (7)).

[c] *i.e.* we do not realise that you were old when you died, because in life you always seemed young, and in our thoughts you still retain the charm of perpetual youth.

Nestoris annosi vicisses saecula, si me
  dispensata tibi stamina nente forent.
nunc ego, quod possum: "Tellus, levis ossa teneto,
  pendula librato pondus et ipsa tuom.
semper serta tibi dabimus, tibi semper odores,
  non umquam sitiens, florida semper eris."

II

Sic est Maecenas fato veniente locutus,
  frigidus et iam iam cum moriturus erat:
"mene," inquit, "iuvenis primaevi, Iuppiter, ante
  angustam Drusi non cecidisse diem!
pectore maturo fuerat puer, integer aevo
  et magnum magni Caesaris illud opus.
discidio vellemque prius"—non omnia dixit
  inciditque pudor quae prope dixit amor,

[140] nempe Ω: nente *Ald.* 1517.
[4] augustam AR, *Vollmer*: angustam BHMV, *Heinsius.* bruti Ω: Drusi *Francius et I.F. Gronovius.* fidem Ω, *Vollmer*: diem *Heinsius.*

have surpassed the generations of long-lived Nestor, if I had been spinner to assign thee the threads of destiny. But as things are, all that I can, I pray: "O Goddess Earth, light be thy touch on his bones; o'erhanging keep thine own weight as in a balance suspended: so shall we ever give thee wreaths, and ever fragrances: never shalt thou feel thirst, but ever be decked with flowers."

II

[Scaliger was the first to distinguish this as a separate poem: in the MSS. it runs on after Elegia I without break.]

Thus spoke Maecenas at the coming of fate, chill on the very brink of death. "Why," said he, "did I not sink in death, O Jupiter, before young Drusus' narrow day of life? He had shown himself a youth of ripe judgement, a stalwart for his years—the mighty achievement of mighty Caesar's training.[a] Would that before our civil strife . . ."[b] The rest he never spoke: scruples cut short what affection nearly said—yet was he clearly understood:[c] dying,

[a] *Caesaris illud opus* is used similarly, *Consol. ad Liviam*, 39.

[b] Maecenas recalls the hostilities between Octavian Caesar and Mark Antony.

[c] *Manifestus erat moriens* might be taken, with Scaliger, as a Graecism, δῆλος ἦν ἀποθνήσκων, "it was clear he was dying."

sed manifestus erat: moriens quaerebat amatae
  coniugis amplexus oscula verba manus.
"sed tamen hoc satis est: vixi te, Caesar, amico
  et morior" dixit, "dum moriorque, satis.
mollibus ex oculis aliquis tibi procidet umor,
  cum dicar subita voce fuisse tibi.
hoc mihi contingat: iaceam tellure sub aequa.
  nec tamen hoc ultra te doluisse velim.
sed meminisse velim: vivam sermonibus illic;
  semper ero, semper si meminisse voles.
et decet et certe vivam tibi semper amore
  nec tibi qui moritur desinit esse tuus.
ipse ego quicquid ero cineres interque favillas,
  tunc quoque non potero non memor esse tui.
exemplum vixi te propter molle beati,
  unus Maecenas teque ego propter eram.
arbiter ipse fui; volui, quod contigit esse;
  pectus eram vere pectoris ipse tui.
vive diu, mi care senex, pete sidera sero:
  est opus hoc terris, te quoque velle decet.
et tibi succrescant iuvenes bis Caesare digni
  et tradant porro Caesaris usque genus.

[16] potuisse Ω: doluisse *Heinsius*.
[23] beate Ω: beati *Salmasius*.
[24] unus Ω: unctus *Maehly*.
[25] voluit, q.c. esse, pectus eram *Vollmer*: voluit Ω: volui *Ald.* 1517.

he sought for his beloved wife's embraces, her kisses, words and hands:

"Yet after all this is enough," he said, "I have lived and I die in thy friendship, Caesar; and, as I die, it is enough. From thy kindly eyes some drop will fall, when thou art told the sudden news that I am gone. This be my lot, to lie 'neath the impartial earth: nor yet would I have thee longer grieve for this. But I would wish for remembrance: there in thy talk would I live; for I shall always exist, if thou wilt always remember me. 'Tis fitting so, and I shall surely live for thee in affection ever; thy dying friend ceases not to be thine own. Myself, whatever I shall be among the ashes and the embers, e'en then I shall not be able to forget Caesar. 'Tis thanks to thee I have lived the luxurious pattern of bliss, thanks to thee that I was the one Maecenas of the day. I was my own controller: I willed to be what fell to my lot:[a] I was truly the heart of thine own heart.

Long mayest thou live, old friend I love so well; late mayest thou pass to heaven: the earth hath need of this: this should be thy will too. May the youths doubly worthy of Caesar[b] grow up to thy support and thenceforward hand on to the future the house

[a] As captain of his fate, Maecenas did not aim at rising above his equestrian rank.

[b] Gaius and Lucius, the sons of Agrippa by Julia, were adopted by Augustus in 17 B.C. as "Caesares." "Doubly" is variously explained: it may refer to their paternity by blood and by adoption; or to their personal qualities added to adoption; or, as Gorallus thought, simply to the fact that they were two. Lucius died A.D. 2, and Gaius A.D. 4.

sit secura tibi quam primum Livia coniunx,
  expleat amissi munera rupta gener.
cum deus intereris divis insignis avitis,
  te Venus in patrio collocet ipsa sinu."

31 sit secura tibi Ω : set tibi securo V : sed tibi sit curae *Ellis*.

33 cum Ω : tum *Wernsdorf* : tu *Baehrens*. in terris Ω : intersis *Ribbeck* : intereris *Vollmer* : cur deus in terris ? *Ellis*.

34 patrio Ω : proprio *Ribbeck, Riese, Baehrens*. ipsa BHM : alma AR.

of Caesar. Right soon may thine Empress Livia be free from anxiety: let a son-in-law fulfil the broken duties of him who is lost.[a] When thou hast taken thy place, a god distinguished among a line of deities, let Venus' own hand set thee in the paternal bosom."[b]

[a] Tiberius is the *gener*: Agrippa, the *gener amissus*. In 11 B.C. Augustus had forced Tiberius to divorce Vipsania Agrippina and marry his daughter Julia, the widow of Agrippa. This marriage, it is hoped in the couplet 31–32, will both assure Livia of descendants through her own son Tiberius and, at the same time, strengthen dynastic prospects by adding to the number of Augustus' grandchildren, now that Agrippa is dead.

[b] *i.e.* the bosom of Julius Caesar, Augustus' adoptive father. The reference to Venus is appropriate, as the Julian *gens* claimed descent from her (Suet. *Jul.* 6).

GRATTIUS

INTRODUCTION

TO GRATTIUS

The period of Grattius is fixed as Augustan by one of Ovid's pentameters, *Ep. ex Ponto*, IV. 16. 34, "aptaque *venanti* Grattius arma daret." This is a specific reference to Grattius' twenty-third line, whether the reading there be *venanti* or *venandi*, and it places him in a list of Ovid's contemporaries before A.D. 8. It is possible, though not certain, that his work was known to Manilius : otherwise, antiquity is silent about him. If it were as certain that he borrowed from the *Aeneid* as it is that he borrowed from the *Georgics*, then his work could be placed between the limits 19 B.C. and A.D. 8. His title to the epithet *Faliscus*, reported to have been in a manuscript now vanished, is not admitted by all. *Nostris Faliscis* of l. 40 does not necessarily imply that he was a native of Falerii :[a] any Italian or even Sicilian might have used the phrase; and indeed there is a possibility that he was connected with Sicily; for he mentions (435–36) that he had frequently seen ailing dogs dipped in the bituminous pools of Sicily. *Silvis nostris* of 137, though taken by Curcio to mean "our Roman woods," may not imply more than "our western woods" in contrast

[a] Among recent writers Vollmer and P. J. Enk are convinced that he was Faliscan.

with the East which Grattius had just mentioned. There is more of the Roman note in the allusion to the simple board of ancient heroes of Rome (321); but it must always be remembered how, from Ennius onwards, Latin authors born far from the capital itself tended to speak and write as Romans. If, then, we cannot add the descriptive *Faliscus* to his name, it is left " Grattius "[a] without cognomen or praenomen.

If Grattius ever wrote lyric poetry,[b] it is long since lost. His sole surviving work is his *Cynegetica*, of which we have one book of about 540 hexameters mutilated towards its end. Here, like several other writers of antiquity, he treats of the chase and especially of the rearing and training of dogs for hunting purposes. The sources of his material are not easy to trace.[c] Some authorities affirm, while others deny, his debt to the *Cynegeticus* of Xenophon (or pseudo-Xenophon) and to Plutarch. It seems at least likely that some Greek author of the Alexandrian period lay behind his list of dogs, in which the Asiatic breeds come before the European, with the " Celtae "[d] sandwiched between " Medi " and " Geloni " (155–57). The Latin influence which is most noticeable upon Grattius is that of Virgil, especially his *Georgics*.

The debt of subsequent writers to Grattius was of the slightest; largely for the reason that a

[a] The spelling *Gratius* in Ovid is less correct. Buecheler, *Rh. Mus.* 35 (1880), p. 407: *cf. C.I.L.* vi. 19–117 *sqq.*

[b] This hypothesis is briefly discussed by Enk, *proleg.* pp. 2–3.

[c] Enk, *op. cit.* pp. 31–32.

[d] Can his Greek original have meant " Galatian " instead of " Gaulish " ? Radermacher, *Rh. Mus.* 60 (1905), p. 249.

didactic poem on so restricted a subject had little chance of a great vogue. Even upon Nemesianus, who handled the same theme in the third century, his influence has been doubted. But while Schanz, Curcio and others hold that Grattius was unknown to Nemesianus, Enk has made out a good case to support the belief that the earlier author was consulted by the later.[a]

Grattius' method of treatment is, after his proem (1–23), to treat first (24–149) of the huntsman's equipment in the means of catching and killing game, and secondly (150–541) of his companions in the chase, dogs and horses, with a brief sub-section on the dress to be worn by hunters. The longest portion is that devoted to dogs (150–496) and it thus justifies the title of the poem; but, besides handling their breeds and breeding, their points and diseases, it is, on the whole fortunately, broken by episodes. These episodes, although in them rhetoric contends with poetry, are enlivening additions or insertions. They are four, and concern a renowned hunter Hagnon (213–62); the miserable effects of luxury on human beings (310–25), somewhat quaintly appended to the prescription of plain fare for dogs; a grotto in Sicily (430–66); and a sacrifice to Diana (480–96). The earlier part on nets, devices for frightening game, on snares, springes, spears and arrows, is also diversified with episodes, namely, a eulogy of the chase (61–74) and of the ingenious hunter Dercylus (95–110). Many readers will welcome these digressions as pleasant side-paths; for it is not everyone to whom the methods of the ancient hunter can make appeal. At the same time

[a] *Mnemos.* 1917, pp. 53–68.

the subject has decidedly antiquarian interest, and it is only fair to remember that great scholars of the past, including Julius Caesar Scaliger and Nicolaus Heinsius, awarded high praise to Grattius' elegance.

His well-turned hexameters show that he was an apt student of Virgil; and his alliteration may indicate admiration for still older poets of Rome. There is also an independent turn in him which shows itself in his employment of words in unusual senses, e.g. *nodus*, 32, of a mesh; *vellera*, 77, of feathers; *verutus*, 110, of a weapon's teeth; *caesaries*, 273, of a dog's hair; *populari*, 376, of spoiling; *dulcedo*, 408, of scratching. There are several ἅπαξ εἰρημένα in his poem: *plagium*, 24; *cannabius*, 47 (? *cannabinus*, Vollmer); *praedexter*, 68; *apprensat*, 239; *perpensare*, 299; *delecta* from *delicio*, 303 (if that be the reading and not *dilecta* or even *de lacte*); *nardifer*, 314; *offectus*, 406; *termiteus*, 447.

EDITIONS

G. Logus (de Logau): Editio princeps (with Ovid's *Halieutica*, Nemesianus and Calpurnius). Venice, 1534.

J. Ulitius (van Vliet): In *Venatio Novantiqua.* Leyden, 1645, 1655.

Thos. Johnson: *Gratii Falisci Cynegeticon* (cum poematio Nemesiani). London, 1699.

R. Bruce and S. Havercamp: In *Poetae latini rei venaticae scriptores et bucolici antiqui* (cum notis Barthii, Ulitii, Johnsonii). [Elaborate commentary at end.] Leyden, 1728.

P. Burman: In *Poetae latini minores* I. Leyden, 1731.

TO GRATTIUS

C. A. Küttner: *Gratii Cynegeticon et Nemesiani Cyneg.* (cum notis selectis Titii, Barthii, Ulitii, Johnsonii et Burmanni integris). Mitaviae (= Mitau), 1775.

J. C. Wernsdorf: In *Poetae latini minores* I. Altenburg, 1780.

R. Stern: *Gratii et Nemesiani carmina venatica* . . . Halle, 1832.

M. Haupt: *Ovidii Halieutica, Gratii et Nemesiani Cynegetica.* [Important as a critical edition.] Leipzig, 1838.

E. Baehrens: In *Poetae latini minores* I. Leipzig, 1879.

G. Curcio: In *Poeti latini minori* I. Acireale, 1902.

J. P. Postgate: In *Corpus poetarum latinorum* II. London, 1905.

F. Vollmer: In *Poetae latini minores* II. 1. Leipzig, 1911.

P. J. Enk: *Gratti Cynegeticon quae supersunt* (cum proleg., not. crit., comm. exeget.). [A learned edition showing genuine appreciation of Grattius.] Zutphen, 1918.

TRANSLATION

Grati Falisci Cynegeticon, or a poem on hunting by Gratius the Faliscian, Englished and illustrated by Chris. Wase, w. commendatory poem by Edmund Waller. London, 1654.

RELEVANT WORKS

Th. Birt: *Ad historiam hexametri latini symbola*, diss. Bonn, 1876.

Fr. Buecheler: *Coniectanea* in *Rhein. Mus.* 35 (1880), p. 407 [defends spelling " Grattius "].

Robinson Ellis: *Ad Grattii Cyneg.* in *Philolog.* 52 (1894).

H. Schenkl: *Zur Kritik und Ueberlief. des Grattius u. anderen lateinischen Dichtern*, Teubner (= Fleck. Jahrb. Suppl. xxiv. 1898 pp. 387–480).

L. Radermacher: *Interpretationes latinae* in *Rhein. Mus.* 60 (1905), pp. 246–49.

G. Pierleoni: *Fu poeta Grattius?* in *Riv. fil.* 1906, pp. 580–97. [A depreciatory criticism on Grattius' style, answered by P. J. Enk in the *Prolegomena* to his edition.]

F. Vollmer: art. *Grattius* in Pauly-Wissowa, *Real-encycl.*

J. Herter: *Grattianum* in *Rhein. Mus.* (N. F. 78), 1929, pp. 361–70.

A. J. Butler: *Sport in Classic Times.* London, 1930. [A fuller list is given in P. J. Enk's edn., 1918.]

SIGLA

A = codex Vindobonensis lat. 277 : saec. ix.

B = ex A descriptus:[a] Parisinus lat. 8071 : saec. ix.

Sann.= emendationes factae a Giacomo Sannazaro in apographis quae extant in codice Vindob. lat. 277 fol. 74-83 et in codice Vindob. lat. 3261 fol. 43-72.

Ald.= editio princeps, anno 1534 a Georgio de Logau curata.

[a] L. Traube, in *Berlin. philol. Wochenschrift*, 1896, p. 1050. As a copy of A, B does not give independent evidence. It contains lines 1–159.

TO GRATTIUS

Bibliographical addendum (1982)

Il Cinegetico (introduction, text, Italian translation, notes), ed. M. Cacciaglia, Rome 1970.

GRATTI CYNEGETICON

Dona cano divom, laetas venantibus artes,
auspicio, Diana, tuo. prius omnis in armis
spes fuit et nuda silvas virtute movebant
inconsulti homines vitaque erat error in omni.
post alia propiore via meliusque profecti
te sociam, Ratio, rebus sumpsere gerendis.
hinc omne auxilium vitae rectusque reluxit
ordo et contiguas didicere ex artibus artes
proserere, hinc demens cecidit violentia retro.
sed primum auspicium deus artibus altaque circa
firmamenta dedit; tum partes quisque secutus
exegere suas tetigitque industria finem.

[2] inermis *Barth* (*in not.* "forte legend."): in armis A.

GRATTIUS

THE CHASE

Under thine auspices, Diana, do I chant the gifts of the gods [a]—the skill that has made the hunters glad. Erstwhile their sole hope lay in their weapons: [b] men untrained stirred the woods with prowess unaided by skill: [c] mistakes beset life everywhere. Afterwards, by another and a more fitting way, [d] with better schooling they took thee, Reason, to aid their enterprises. From Reason came all their help in life: the true order of things shone forth: men learned out of arts to produce kindred arts: from Reason came the undoing of mad violence. But 'twas a divinity who gave the first favouring impulse to the arts, putting around them their deep-set props: then did every man work out the portions of his choice, and industry

[a] Like Xenophon or the pseudo-Xenophon, *Cyn.* ad init. τὸ μὲν εὕρημα θεῶν κ.τ.λ., Grattius claims a divine origin for hunting.

[b] Good sense is got without taking *armis* from *armi*, "members," as Vollmer does with Barth, Burman and others. A. E. Housman, *Cl. Rev.* 14 (1900), 465–66, and P. J. Enk, in his edn. 1918, take *armis* from *arma*.

[c] *Nuda virtute*: *cf.* 153 *nudo marte* contrasted with *ex arte*.

[d] *i.e.* by training they attained to a more convenient and suitable method (*via*) than the old haphazard hunting. For sense of *propior cf.* Cic. *ad Att.* XIV. xix., *nos alium portum propiorem huic aetati videbamus*.

tu trepidam bello vitam, Diana, ferino,
qua primam quaerebat opem, dignata repertis
protegere auxiliis orbemque hac solvere noxa.
adscivere tuo comites sub nomine divae
centum: omnes nemorum, umentes de fontibus omnes
Naides, et Latii ⟨satyri⟩ Faunus⟨que subibant⟩
Maenaliusque puer domitrixque Idaea leonum
mater et inculto Silvanus termite gaudens.
his ego praesidibus nostram defendere sortem
contra mille feras et non sine carmine iussus,
carmine et arma dabo et venandi persequar artes.
  armorum casses plagiique exordia restes.
prima iubent tenui nascentem iungere filo
limbum et quadruplices tormento adstringere limbos:

[17] gentem *Radermacher, Schenkl, Vollmer*: centem A: mentem *Haupt*: centum B *ex. corr., Postgate, Enk.*

[18] *sic Enk*: Faunusque subibat *Vollmer in not.*: iuvabant *vel* favebant *Herter*: Latii cultor qui Faunus amoeni *Ald.*

[22] lusus A: nisus *Ulitius*: iussus *Graevius*. *post v.* 23 *videntur Vollmero restituendi vv.* 61–74.

[23] et venandi A: venanti et *Ulitius*. *cf. Ov. ex Ponto* IV. xvi. 34 cum . . . aptaque venanti Grattius arma daret.

[24] plagii *sic* A (*vocabulum a* plaga *formatum*). exordia restes *Vollmer*: exordiar estis A: exordiar astus *Ald. et vulgo.*

attained its goal. The life that was imperilled by warfare against wild beasts, where most it needed help, thou, Diana, didst deign to shield with aids of thy discovery, and to free the world from harm so great. Under thy name the goddesses joined to them a hundred comrades:[a] all the nymphs of the groves, all the Naiads dripping from the springs, and Latium's satyrs and the Faun-god came in support; Pan, too, the youth of the Arcadian mount, and the Idaean Mother, Cybele, who tames the lions, and Silvanus rejoicing in the wilding bough. I by these guardians ordained—and not without song—to defend our human lot against a thousand beasts, with song too will furnish weapons and pursue the arts of the chase.

The beginning of hunting equipment consists in nets and the ropes of the snare.[b] First of all, experts prescribe that the rope along the edge of the net be twined, at the start, of thin thread and then fourfold strands be drawn tight to form the twist;[c]

[a] Herter, *Rhein. Mus.*, 78 (1929), p. 366, takes *centum* with *divae*.

[b] With lines 24–60, 75–94, on hunting-nets, *cf.* Xen. *Cyn.* ii. 3–8; Arrian, *Cyn.* 1; Pollux, *Onomast.* V. 26–32; Oppian, *Cyn.* I. 150–51; Nemes. *Cyn.* 299 *sqq.* The Latin *rete* (δίκτυον) means net in general, or specifically a large "hay"; *plaga* (ἐνόδιον) means a net placed in the known run or track of the game; *cassis* (ἄρκυς) means a funnel-shaped net resembling, according to Pollux, a κεκρύφαλος (*reticulum*)—which may be applied either to a network cap for the hair or to the bag-shaped reticule, pouch or belly of a hunting-net.

[c] *Limbus*, the rope along the edge of the net, corresponds to the τόνος in Xen. *Cyn.* x. 2, Pollux V. 27. Grattius uses *limbi*, the plural, for the *fila linea* out of which the *limbus* is made (*Limbus grandis et capitalis linea illa est cui minores limbi quadrangulo sinuamine circumstringuntur*, Barth).

illa operum patiens, illa usus linea longi.
tunc ipsum e medio cassem quo nascitur ore
per senos circum usque sinus laqueabis, ut omni
concipiat tergo, si quisquam est plurimus, hostem.
at bis vicenos spatium praetendere passus
rete velim plenisque decem consurgere nodis;
ingrati maiora sinus impendia sument.

optima Cinyphiae, ne quid cunctere, paludes
lina dabunt; bonus Aeolia de valle Sibyllae
fetus et aprico Tuscorum stuppea campo
messis contiguum sorbens de flumine rorem,
qua cultor Latii per opaca silentia Thybris
labitur inque sinus magno venit ore marinos.
at contra nostris imbellia lina Faliscis
Hispanique alio spectantur Saetabes usu.
vix operata suo sacra ad Bubastia lino
velatur sonipes aestivi turba Canopi:
ipse in materia damnosus candor inerti
ostendit longe fraudem atque exterruit hostes.
at pauper rigui custos Alabandius horti
cannabi⟨n⟩as nutrit silvas, quam commoda nostro
armamenta operi. gravis ⟨est⟩ tutela, sed illis
tu licet Haemonios includas retibus ursos.
tantum ne subeat vitiorum pessimus umor

[a] *Ingrati* is predicative: "Thankless (*i.e.* profitless) will be the nets that demand greater expense."

that makes a length to stand its work; that will serve many a day. The snare itself, at the central mouth which it has when being made, you must entangle all round with six pouches so that in the whole cavity it may catch the savage quarry, however big he is. But I should have the whole net extend forty paces in length and rise ten full meshes in height from the ground. Nets likely to cost more outlay are unremunerative.[a]

The Cinyphian marshes,[b] doubt it not, will yield excellent thread-material; there is fine produce from the Aeolian valley[c] of the Sibyl, and there is the flax harvest on the sunny Tuscan meadow drinking in the neighbouring moisture from the river, where Tiber that fertilises Latium glides through the shady silences and meets with mighty mouth the gulfs of the sea. But on the other hand our Falerians have flax-crops unfit for conflict, and (those of) the Spanish Saetabes are tested by a different use.[d] The dancing crowds of sultry Canopus[e] are scarcely veiled by their transparent native linen when sacrificing in the ritual at Bubastis: its very whiteness, ruinous in a material useless for nets, reveals the deceit afar off and frightens away the beasts. Yet the poor guardian of a well-watered estate at Alabanda[f] can rear a growth of hemp, right fitting equipment for this task of ours. Burdensome is the care needed, but you may entrap within such toils the bears of Thessaly. Only, first take pains that no moisture, worst of plagues, steal thereon:

[b] In North Africa between the two Syrtes.

[c] At Cumae on the Bay of Naples.

[d] *i.e.* are unsuitable for nets.

[e] In Egypt. [f] In Caria, Asia Minor.

ante cave: non est umentibus usus in armis,
nulla fides. ergo seu pressa flumina valle
inter opus crassaeque malum fecere paludes
sive improvisus caelo perfuderit imber,
illa vel ad flatus Helices oppande serenae
vel caligineo laxanda reponite fumo.
idcirco et primas linorum tangere messes
ante vetant quam maturis accenderit annum
ignibus et claro Plias se prompserit ortu.
imbiberint: tanto respondet longior usus.

magnum opus et tangi, nisi cura vincitur, impar.
nonne vides veterum quos prodit fabula rerum
semideos—illi aggeribus temptare superbis
caeli iter et matres ausi ⟨a⟩ttrectare deorum—
quam magna mercede meo sine munere silvas
impulerint? flet adhuc et porro flebit Adonin
victa Venus ceciditque suis Ancaeus in armis
(et praedexter erat geminisque securibus ingens).
ipse deus cultorque feri Tirynthius orbis,

[53] clausaeque *Barth*: causaeque A: crassaeque *Sann.*[2], *Ald.*
[59] prompserit *Sann.*: promiserit A.
[60] imbiberit A: -int *Burman.*
[64] Jr& fr&a (*sic* = iret freta *contra metrum*) A: ire freta et *Ulitius, Johnson, Stern et alii*: aethera tum *Heinsius*: aethera et ad *Haupt*: sidera et ad (ad *cum* trectare *per tmesin*) *Vollmer*: caeli iter et *Enk.*: ausi *Heinsius*: ausit A. trectare A: tractare *Sann.*: ⟨a⟩ttrectare *Heinsius.*

in damp equipment there is no use, no dependence. Therefore, whether streams in a narrow valley and sluggish swamps have wrought harm amid the hunter's task, or unforeseen rain from heaven shall have drenched the nets, either unfold them to face the northern breezes of serene Helice [a] or set them in murky smoke to slacken. For such reasons too it is forbidden to touch the first crops of flax before the Pleiad [b] has kindled the year with ripening fires and appeared in its brilliant rising. If nets drink in breeze or smoke,[c] their longer service answers accordingly.

The chase is a mighty task, unfit to be handled, save it is mastered by pains.[d] Do you not see the demigods whom old mythic lore records (they dared on proud-piled mountains to essay the way to heaven [e] and assault the mothers of the gods)—at what mighty cost they hunted the woodlands without the boon of my teaching? Venus, baffled, still weeps and long will weep Adonis: Ancaeus [f] fell, arms in hand (yet was he right skilful and imposing with the double axe). The god himself, he of Tiryns, who civilised a barbarous world,

[a] Ursa Major.

[b] Summer began with the rising of the constellation of the Seven Pleiades (Lat. *Vergiliae*), and winter with their setting.

[c] *i.e. si lina imbiberint flatus vel fumum* : *cf.* 55–56.

[d] Lines 61–74 are by some editors transposed to follow either 23 or 24.

[e] Unsatisfying attempts have been made to read *ire freta* and explain it as applicable either to the giants traversing the ocean of the sky in their attack on heaven or even to the Argonauts crossing the sea, which is Curcio's strange suggestion.

[f] A son of Neptune and an Argonaut, who, like Adonis, was killed by a boar.

quem mare, quem tellus, quem praeceps ianua Ditis
omnia temptantem, qua laus erat obvia, passa est,
hinc decus et famae primum impetravit honorem.
exige, si qua meis respondet ab artibus, ergo,
gratia quae vires fallat collata ferinas.
  sunt quibus immundo decerptae vulture plumae
instrumentum operis fuit et non parva facultas.
tantum inter nivei iungantur vellera cygni,
et satis armorum est. haec clara luce coruscant
terribiles species, at vulture dirus ab atro
turbat odor silvas meliusque alterna valet res.
sed quam clara tuis et pinguis pluma sub armis,
tam mollis tactu et non sit creberrima nexu,
ne reprensa suis properantem linea pennis
implicet atque ipso mendosa coarguat usu.
hic magis in cervos valuit metus; ast ubi lentae
interdum Libyco fucantur sandyce pennae
linteaque expositis lucent anconibus arma,
rarum si qua metus eludet belua falsos.
nam fuit et laqueis aliquis curracibus usus:

71 obvia *Sann.*: obula A. passi A, *Vollmer*: passa est *Haupt*.

to whom sea and earth and the sheer gateway of Pluto yielded as he essayed all things where glory's path lay open, even he (Hercules) won from the chase the chiefest ornament and honour of his fame. Consider, then, what benefit, derived from the arts I treat, can trick the strong beasts when matched against them.

Some hunters have found in plumes plucked from the filthy vulture a handy means of working and no slight help. Only, at intervals along the line there must be added the down of the snow-white swan, and that is implement enough: the white feathers glitter in clear sunlight, formidable appearances for game,[a] whereas the dread stench from the black vulture disturbs the forest-creatures; and the contrast of colour works the better effect. But, while the plumage hanging from your device has its bright gleam or heavy scent, let it be at the same time soft to handle and not very closely entwined, so that the cord when pulled in will not entangle you with its feathers in your hurry and by its faultiness convict you in the very using. This device of terror has more use against stags; but when the pliant feathers are sometimes dyed with African vermilion and the flaxen cord gleams from its projecting forks,[b] it is rare for any beast to escape the counterfeit terrors. Yes, and there is also some use in "running"

[a] The *linea pinnis distincta* intended to drive game into snares was called a "formido" (*cf. metus,* 85); Sen. *Dial.* iv. 11. 5; *Phaedra* 46–48; Virg. *G.* III. 372; Lucan IV. 437–38.

[b] The *ancon* (ἀγκών) was a forked pole on which to spread nets. A pure Latin term for a similar trestle was the *ames* of Hor. *Epod.* ii. 33: *cf. varae,* Lucan, *Phars.* IV. 439; and in Greek στάλικες, σταλίδες, or σχαλίδες; Xen. *Cyn.* ii. 7, Oppian, *Cyn.* I. 151.

cervino iussere magis contexere nervo;
fraus teget insidias habitu mentita ferino.
quid qui dentatas iligno robore clausit
venator pedicas? quam dissimulantibus armis
saepe habet imprudens alieni lucra laboris!
o felix, tantis quem primum industria rebus
prodidit auctorem! deus ille an proxima divos
mens fuit, in caecas aciem quae magna tenebras
egit et ignarum perfudit lumine vulgus?
dic age Pierio, fas est, Diana, ministro.
Arcadium stat fama senem, quem Maenalus auctor
et Lacedaemoniae primum vidistis Amyclae
per non adsuetas metantem retia valles
Dercylon. haut illo quisquam se iustior egit,
haut fuit in terris divom observantior alter:
ergo illum primis nemorum dea finxit in arvis
auctoremque operi digna⟨ta⟩ inscribere magno
iussit adire suas et pandere gentibus artes.
ille etiam valido primus venabula dente
induit et proni moderatus vulneris iram
omne moris excepit onus; tum stricta verutis

100 auctor A: altor *Turnebus, Postgate.*
103 haud *Sann.*: aut A.
104 hau fuit *Baehrens*: au fuit A: auṭ (t *deleta*) fuit *Paris.* 8071.

nooses:[a] it is recommended to compose these of deer's leather preferably: the deceit will cloak the snare through falsely suggesting a creature of the wild.[b] What of the hunter who to his toothed springe adds an oaken stake? How often, thanks to these tricksome devices, does one unexpectedly reap the fruit of another's toil![c]

Fortunate the man whose industry made him first inventor of arts so great! Was he a god or was that mind close kin to the gods which mightily sped its clear gaze into blind darkness and flooded the uninstructed crowd with light? Come speak, Diana, for 'tis heaven's will, unto a servant of the Muses. The story stands secure that it was an old Arcadian whom you, Maenalus, his witness, and you, Lacedaemonian Amyclae, first saw laying out hunting-nets in unaccustomed vales—Dercylos his name. Never did man bear himself more justly than he: on earth there was no other more regardful of the gods. He then it was whom the goddess fashioned in primeval fields,[d] and deigning to inscribe him as author of a mighty work, she enjoined him to go and unfold her own arts to the nations. He was the first also to dress hunting-spears with a strong tooth, and, controlling the angry onslaught of a forward thrust, to receive all the (boar's) weight on projecting spear-guards.[e]

[a] Enk, pp. 36–38, has a full note on different interpretations of *laquei curraces*.

[b] *i.e.* the *cervinus nervus* will have the smell of the *cervus*.

[c] An animal partly lamed or dragging with it the *robur* would be easily caught.

[d] Arcadia.

[e] The term *morae* is applied to projecting metal *alae* or *orbes* fixed behind the spear-head so as to hinder the spear from going too deeply into the beast.

dentibus et gemina subiere hastilia furca
et quidam totis clauserunt ensibus ⟨hastas⟩,
ne cessaret iners in vulnere massa ferino.
blandimenta vagae fugies novitatis: ibidem
exiguo nimiove nocent. sed lubricus errat
mos et ab expertis festinant usibus omnes.
quid, Macetum immensos libeat si dicere contos?
quam longa exigui spicant hastilia dentes!
aut contra ut tenero destrictas cortice virgas
praegravat ingenti pernix Lucania cultro!
omnia tela modi melius finxere salubres.
quocirca et iaculis habilem perpendimus usum,
ne leve vulnus eat neu sit brevis impetus illi.
ipsa arcu Lyciaque suos Diana pharetra
armavit comites: ne tela relinquite divae:
magnum opus et volucres quondam fecere sagittae.
  disce agedum et validis dilectum hastilibus omnem.
plurima Threiciis nutritur vallibus Hebri
cornus et umbrosae Veneris per litora myrtus
taxique pinusque Altinatesque genestae

112 *post* ensibus *nihil in* A: orbes *male add. Ald.*: tortis . . hastas *H. Schenkl.*
117 dicere A: ducere *Baehrens.*
120 praegravat *Ald.*: -av& A.
123 neu leve A: ne leve *Sann.*

Later, there succeeded to them weapons furnished with spit-like teeth and twofold fork, and some gave their spear-ends a ring of sharp points to prevent the thick steel remaining inactive in the wounded quarry.[a] You are to shun the allurements of fleeting novelty: in this same field of hunting they do harm by a small or excessive size of spear. But slippery fashion goes its wandering round, and all men are in haste to discard usages which have been tried. What if I choose to speak of the enormous Macedonian pikes? How long are the shafts and how small the teeth which furnish their spikes! Or, on the other hand, how does nimble Lucania overload with a huge point thin rods stripped of their tender bark! All weapons have been the better fashioned by healthy moderation. Wherefore for javelins too we weigh thoroughly their manageable handling, lest their wounding power speed lightly or the weapon's force fall short.[b] Diana herself armed her own comrades with bow and Lycian quiver: abandon ye not the weapons of the goddess: once on a day great work was wrought by swift arrows.

Now, moreover, learn the whole range of choice for strong spears. The cornel tree grows abundantly in the Thracian valleys of the Hebrus; there are shady myrtles along the shores of Venus;[c] there are yew trees and pines and the broom-plants of Altinum,[d] and the lopped bough more likely to help

[a] The sharp points would make the wound worse.

[b] *Vulnus* is used of the weapon which wounds in Virg. *Aen.* IX. 745, X. 140; Sil. Ital. I. 397; Val. Flacc. III. 197. *Illi* sc. *vulneri* i.e. *iaculo*.

[c] *i.e.* in Cyprus.

[d] On the Adriatic shore, not far from Venice.

et magis incomptos opera iuturus agrestes
termes. ab Eois descendit virga Sabaeis
mater odorati multum pulcherrima turis:
illa suos usus intractatumque decorem
(sic nemorum iussere deae) natalibus hausit
arbitriis; at enim multo sunt ficta labore
cetera quae silvis errant hastilia nostris:
numquam sponte sua procerus ad aera termes
exiit inque ipsa curvantur stirpe genestae.
ergo age luxuriam primo fetusque nocentes
detrahe: frondosas gravat indulgentia silvas.
post ubi proceris generosa⟨m⟩ stirpibus arbor
se dederit teretesque ferent ad sidera virgae,
stringe notas circum et gemmantes exige versus.
his, si quis vitium nociturus sufficit umor,
ulceribus fluet et venas durabit inertes.
in quinos sublata pedes hastilia plena
caede manu, dum pomiferis advertitur annus
frondibus et tepidos autumnus continet imbres.
  sed cur exiguis tantos in partibus orbes
lustramus? prima illa canum, non ulla per artes
cura prior, sive indomitos vehementior hostes
nudo marte premas seu bellum ex arte ministres.

131 in comptos A: in contos *Johnson.* opera A: superat *Stern.* lutores A: lotaster *Johnson*: iuturus *Sudhaus.* agstis (-st- *ex* -rt- *corr.*) A: agrestis *Sann.*

148 avertitur *Vollmer*: advertitur A.

with its service the uncouth country-folk. From the Arabians in the East comes the branch that is far the fairest mother of fragrant frankincense: it draws from the laws of its birth (so have the goddesses of the groves ordained) its own uses and its natural shapeliness; but it is only with much toil that the other stems widely grown in our western woods are fashioned into spear-shafts. Never did bough of its own accord rise tall into the air; and the broom curves even in its lower stem. Come, then, strip off at once the excessive growth and harmful branches: indulgence overloads trees with leaves. Later, when the tree proves its goodliness in its tall stems and the shapely branches tend starwards, cut round the places where suckers start and remove the rows of sprouting branches. If any sap of an injurious sort causes harm, it will flow out of these wounds and so harden the weak veins. When the shafts have risen to a height of five feet, cut them with full grasp, while the year approaches the season of fruit-laden leafage and autumn holds back the warm showers.

But why do we traverse these wide rounds amidst small details? The foremost care is that of dogs;[a] no other care comes before that throughout the whole system of hunting, whether you energetically pursue the untamed quarry with bare force or use skill to manage the conflict. Dogs belong to a

[a] On dogs generally see Xen. *Cyn.* iii–iv, vii; Aristotle, *Hist. An.* 574a 16 *sqq.* and *passim*; Arr. *Cyn.* 2 *sqq.*; Poll. *Onom.* V. 37 *sqq.*; *Geoponica* (10th cent.) xix. 1 *sqq.*; Virg. *G.* III. 404 *sqq.*; Varro, *R.R.* II. 9; Plin. *N.H.* VIII. 142 *sqq.*; Colum. *R.R.* VII. 12–13; Nemes. *Cyn.* 103 *sqq.*; Oppian, *Cyn.* I. 368–588; Claud. *Stil.* III. 298–301.

mille canum patriae ductique ab origine mores
quoique sua. magna indocilis dat proelia Medus
magnaque diversos extollit gloria Celtas.
arma negant contra martemque odere Geloni,
sed natura sagax: Perses in utroque paratus.
sunt qui Seras alant, genus intractabilis irae;
at contra faciles magnique Lycaones armis.
sed non Hyrcano satis est vehementia gentis
tanta suae: petiere ultro fera semina silvis;
dat Venus accessus et blando foedere iungit.
tunc et mansuetis tuto ferus errat adulter
in stabulis ultroque gravem succedere tigrin
ausa canis maiore tulit de sanguine fetum.
sed praeceps virtus: ipsa venabitur aula
ille tibi et pecudum multo cum sanguine crescet.
pasce tamen: quaecumque domi sibi crimina fecit,
excutiet silva magnus pugnator adepta.
at fugit adversos idem quos repperit hostes
Umber: quanta fides utinam et sollertia naris,
tanta foret virtus et tantum vellet in armis!
quid, freta si Morinum dubio refluentia pont⟨o⟩
veneris atque ipsos libeat penetrare Britanno⟨s⟩?

---

[a] *i.e.* the breeds are innumerable: *cf.* Oppian, *Cyn.* I. 400, τὰ δὲ μυρία φῦλα πέλονται.

[b] A Sarmatian tribe in the region of the modern Ukraine.

[c] In pugnacity and sagacity.

[d] Or, possibly, Tibetan.

[e] British dogs were, Strabo tells us, IV. v. 2 (C 199), exported as εὐφυεῖς πρὸς τὰς κυνηγεσίας. *Cf.* Nemes. 225, *divisa*

thousand lands[a] and they each have characteristics derived from their origin. The Median dog, though undisciplined, is a great fighter, and great glory exalts the far-distant Celtic dogs. Those of the Geloni,[b] on the other hand, shirk a combat and dislike fighting, but they have wise instincts: the Persian is quick in both respects.[c] Some rear Chinese[d] dogs, a breed of unmanageable ferocity; but the Lycaonians, on the other hand, are easy-tempered and big in limb. The Hyrcanian dog, however, is not content with all the energy belonging to his stock: the females of their own will seek unions with wild beasts in the woods: Venus grants them meetings and joins them in the alliance of love. Then the savage paramour wanders safely amid the pens of tame cattle, and the bitch, freely daring to approach the formidable tiger, produces offspring of nobler blood. The whelp, however, has headlong courage: you will find him a-hunting in the very yard and growing at the expense of much of the cattle's blood. Still you should rear him: whatever enormities he has placed to his charge at home, he will obliterate them as a mighty combatant on gaining the forest. But that same Umbrian dog which has tracked wild beasts flees from facing them. Would that with his fidelity and shrewdness in scent he could have corresponding courage and corresponding will-power in the conflict! What if you visit the straits of the Morini, tide-swept by a wayward sea, and choose to penetrate even among the Britons?[e]

Britannia mittit Veloces nostrique orbis venatibus aptos: Claud. *Stil.* III. 301, *magnaque taurorum fracturae colla Britannae.* The Morini were northern Gauls whose chief town Gesoriacum became Bononia (Boulogne).

o quanta est merces et quantum impendia supra!
si non ad speciem mentiturosque decores
pronus es (haec una est catulis iactura Britannis),
at magnum cum venit opus promendaque virtus
et vocat extremo praeceps discrimine Mavors:
non tunc egregios tantum admirere Mol⟨os⟩s⟨os⟩.
comparat his versuta suas Athamania ⟨gentes⟩
Azorusque Pheraeque et clandestinus Acar⟨nan⟩:
sicut Acarnanes subierunt proelia furto,
sic canis illa suos taciturna supervenit hostes.
at clangore citat quos nondum conspicit apros
Aetola quaecumque canis de stirpe: malignum
officium, sive illa metus convicia rupit
seu frustra nimius properat favor. et tamen ill⟨ud⟩
ne vanum totas genus aspernere per artes:
mirum quam celeres et quantum nare merentur,
tum non est victi quoi concessere labori.
idcirco variis miscebo gentibus usum:
quondam inconsultis mater dabit Umbrica Gallis

178 pronis (*ut sit principium parenthesi*) *Vollmer*: pronuis A, *Postgate*, ἅπαξ εἰρημένον: pronus es *H. Schenkl*: protinus *Sann. et vulgo, extra parenthesin.*

182 *finis versus periit in* A: fraudes *add. Ald.*: gentes *Vollmer.*

183 Azorusque *Wernsdorf*: Acirusque A.

189 furor A, *Burm.*, *Wernsdorf*, *Stern*: favor *Gronov*, *Johnson*: cf. 230 favore, 240 faventem.

O how great your reward, how great your gain beyond any outlays! If you are not bent on looks and deceptive graces (this is the one defect of the British whelps), at any rate when serious work has come, when bravery must be shown, and the impetuous War-god calls in the utmost hazard, then you could not admire the renowned Molossians [a] so much. With these last [b] cunning Athamania compares her breeds; as also do Azorus, Pherae and the furtive Acarnanian: just as the men of Acarnania steal secretly into battle, so does the bitch surprise her foes without a sound. But any bitch of Aetolian pedigree rouses with her yelps the boars which she does not yet see—a mischievous service, whether it is that fear makes these savage sounds break out or excessive eagerness speeds on uselessly. And yet you must not despise that breed as useless in all the accomplishments of the chase; they are marvellously quick, marvellously efficient in scent; besides, there is no toil to which they yield defeated. Consequently, I shall cross the advantages of different breeds:—one day an Umbrian mother will give to the unskilled Gallic pups [c] a smart disposition;

[a] Molossian dogs are frequently mentioned in ancient literature: *e.g.* Aristoph. *Thesm.* 416; Poll. V. 37; Opp. *Cyn.* I. 375; Plaut. *Capt.* 86; Lucr. V. 1063; Virg. *G.* III. 405; Hor. *Epod.* vi. 5; *Sat.* II. vi. 114; Lucan IV. 440; Sen. *Phaedra*, 33; Stat. *Theb.* III. 203, *Silv.* II. vi. 19; *Ach.* I. 747; Mart. XII. i. 1; Claud. *Stil.* II. 215, III. 293; Nem. *Cyn.* 107.

[b] It seems appropriate to take *his* of Molossian dogs rather than of British, as the proper names refer to neighbouring districts of Epirus, Thessaly, Aetolia and Acarnania. Athamania is a district in Epirus near the Pindus range.

[c] *Cf.* the qualities suggested in 171–73, and 156. "Gallic" in 194 may mean "Galatian": see Introduction.

sensum agilem, traxere animos de patre Gelonae
Hyrcano et vanae tantum Calydonia linguae
exibit vitium patre emendata Molosso.
scilicet ex omni florem virtute capessunt
et sequitur natura favens. at te leve si qua
ta⟨n⟩git opus pavidosque iuvat compellere dorcas
aut versuta sequi leporis vestigia parvi,
Petronios (haec fama) canes volucresque Sycambros
et pictam macula Vertraham delige flava:
ocior affectu mentis pennaque cucurrit,
sed premit inventas, non inventura latentes
illa feras, quae Petroniis bene gloria constat.
quod si maturo pressantes gaudia lusu
dissimulare feras tacitique accedere possent,
illis omne decus, quod nunc, metagontes, habetis,
constaret: silva sed virtus irrita damno est.
at vestrum non vile genus, non patria. vulgo

196 tantum A: natum *Stern.*
202 cani *Haupt*: cana A: Petroniost haec fama cani *Vollmer.*
203 vertraham *sic* A: *cf. Mart.* XIV. cc. falsa A: flava *vel* fulva *Johnson.*
210 *ante* silva *primus distinxit Baehrens.*

puppies of a Gelonian mother have drawn spirit from a Hyrcanian sire;[a] and Calydonia,[b] good only at pointless barking, will lose the defect when improved by a sire from Molossis. In truth, the offspring cull the best from all the excellence of the parents, and kindly nature attends them. But if in any wise a light sort of hunting captivates you, if your taste is to hunt the timid antelope or to follow the intricate tracks of the smaller hare, then you should choose Petronian[c] dogs (such is their reputation) and swift Sycambrians[d] and the Vertraha[e] coloured with yellow spots—swifter than thought or a winged bird it runs, pressing hard on the beasts it has found, though less likely to find them when they lie hidden; this last is the well-assured glory of the Petronians. If only the latter could restrain their transports until the completion of their sport, if they could affect not to be aware of their prey and approach without barking, they would be assured all the honour which you dogs of the *metagon*[f] breed now hold: as it is, in the forest ineffectual spirit means loss. But you *metagontes* have no ignoble pedigree or home.

[a] *Cf.* 157–58 and 161–63.

[b] *i.e.* Aetolia: *cf.* 186–92.

[c] *Petroni*: possibly dogs workable on stony ground (*petra*).

[d] *Sycambri*, a tribe of Western Germany near the Rhine.

[e] Perhaps *Vertagra*: *cf.* Italian *veltro*, a greyhound. MSS. of Martial, XIV. cc. 1 give the forms *vertrăcus*, *vertăgus*, *vetrăgus*. The word seems to be Celtic: Arrian, *Cyneg.* 3. 6, αἱ δὲ ποδώκεις κύνες αἱ Κελτικαὶ καλοῦνται μὲν οὐέρτραγοι φωνῇ τῇ Κελτῶν . . . It has sometimes been explained as a "tumbler" dog that inveigled game by rolling himself into a heap to disguise his appearance.

[f] The μετάγων is mentioned only by Grattius. Burman suggested the word implied the tracking of game: Ulitius and Curcio take it of the cross-breeding of the dog.

Sparta suos et Creta suos promittit alumnos:
sed primum celsa lorum cervice ferentem,
Glympice, te silvis egit Boeotius Hagnon,
Hagnon Astylides, Hagnon, quem plurima semper
gratia per nostros unum testabitur usus.
hic trepidas artes et vix novitate sedentes
vidit qua propior peteret via nec sibi turbam
contraxit comitem nec vasa tenentia longe:
unus praesidium atque operi spes magna petito
adsumptus metagon lustrat per nota ferarum
pascua, per fontes, per quas trivere latebras.
primae lucis opus: tum signa vapore ferino
intemerata legens si qua est qua fallitur eius
turba loci, maiore secat spatia extera gyro;
atque hic egressu iam tum sine fraude reperto
incubuit, spatiis qualis permissa Lechaeis
Thessalium quadriga decus, quam gloria patrum
excitat et primae spes ambitiosa coronae.
sed ne qua ex nimio redeat iactura favore,

212 Sparta suos A: Sparte vos *Baehrens*: Sparte quos *H. Schenkl.*
218 peteret viam A: patuit via *Ald.*: ferret via *Baehrens.*

Sparta,[a] by common report, and Crete[b] alike claim you as their own nurslings. But, Glympic[c] hound, you were the first to wear leash on high-poised neck and he that followed you in the forest was the Boeotian Hagnon, Hagnon son of Astylos, Hagnon, to whom our abundant gratitude shall bear witness as pre-eminent in our practice of the chase. He saw where the easier road lay to a calling as yet nervously timorous and owing to its newness scarce established: he brought together no band of followers or implements in long array: his single *metagon* was taken as his guard, as the high promise of the longed-for spoil; it roams across the fields which are the haunts of beasts, over the wells and through the lurking-places frequented by them. 'Tis the work of early dawn: then, while the dog is picking out the trail as yet unspoiled by another animal's scent, if there is any confusion of tracks in that place whereby he is thrown off, he runs an outside course in a wider circle and, at last discovering beyond mistake the footprints coming out, pounces on the track like the fourfold team, the pride of Thessaly, which is launched forth on the Corinthian race-course, stirred by ancestral glory and by hopes covetous of the first prize. But lest loss be the outcome of excessive zeal, the dog's

[a] For Spartan or Lacedaemonian dogs *cf.* Soph. *Aj.* 8; Xen. *Cyn.* iii. 1; Opp. *Cyn.* I. 372; Pollux, V. 37; Virg. *G.* III. 405; Hor. *Epod.* vi. 5; Ov. *Met.* III. 208, 223; Sen. *Phaedra,* 35; Lucan, IV. 441; Claud. *Stil.* III. 300 (*tenuesque Lacaenae*); Nemes. *Cyn.* 107, etc.

[b] For Cretan dogs *cf.* Xen. *Cyn.* x. 1; Poll. V. 37; Opp. *Cyn.* I. 373; Ov. *Met.* III. 208, 223; Sen. *Phaedra,* 34; Claud. *Stil.* III. 300 (*hirsutae Cressae*), etc.

[c] The reference is to a locality on the Argive and Laconian border.

lex dicta officiis: neu voce lacesseret hostem
neve levem praedam aut propioris pignora lucri
amplexus primos nequiquam effunderet actus;
iam vero impensum melior fortuna laborem
cum sequitur iuxtaque domus quaesita ferarum,
et sciat occultos et signis arguat hostes:
aut effecta levi testatur gaudia cauda
aut ipsa infodiens uncis vestigia plantis
mandit humum celsisve apprensat naribus auras.
et tamen, ut ne prima faventem pignora fallant,
circum omnem aspretis medius qua clauditur orbi⟨s⟩
ferre pedem accessusque abitusque notare ferarum
admonet et, si forte loco spes prima fefellit,
rusum opus incubuit spatiis; at, prospera si res,
intacto repetet prima ad vestigia gyro.
ergo ubi plena suo rediit victoria fine,
in partem praedae veniat comes et sua norit
praemia: sic operi iuvet inservisse benigne.
  hoc ingens meritum, haec ultima palma tropae⟨i⟩,
Hagnon magne, tibi divom concessa favore:

233 offenderet A, *Vollmer*: effunderet *Johnson, vulgo.*
236 & sciat A: ut sciat *Sann.*
240 faventem (= *studiosum, cf. v.* 230).
241 orbis *Sann.*: orbi A: orbem *Baehrens.*

duties are regulated: he must not assail his foe with barking;[a] he must not seize on some trivial prey or on signs of a nearer catch and so blindly lose the fruit of his first activities. When, however, better fortune already attends the outlay of toil, and the sought-for lair of the wild beasts is near, he must both know his enemies are hidden and prove this by signs: either he shows his new-won pleasure by lightly wagging the tail, or, digging in his own footprints with the nails of his paws, he gnaws the soil and sniffs the air with nostrils raised high. And yet to prevent the first signs from misleading the dog in his keenness, the hunter bids him run all about the inner space encircled by rough ground and nose the paths by which the beasts come and go; then, if it happens that the first expectation has failed him in the place,[b] he turns again to his task in wide coursings; but, if the scent was right, he will make for the first trail again as the quarry has not crossed the circle. Therefore, when full success has arrived with its proper issue, the dog must come as comrade to share the prey and must recognise his own reward: thus let it be a delight to have given ungrudging service to the work.

Such was the mighty benefit, such the surpassing prize of triumph granted to thee, great Hagnon, by favour of the gods: so shalt thou live for ever, as long

[a] *Cf.* Lucan, *Phars.* IV. 441, *nec creditur ulli Silva cani nisi qui presso vestigia rostro Colligit et praeda nescit latrare reperta,* and Pliny's description of the silent tracking of game, *N.H.* VIII. 147, *quam silens et occulta sed quam significans demonstratio est cauda primum deinde rostro.*

[b] *i.e.* if the animal has already escaped and is no longer lying hidden there.

ergo semper eris, dum carmina dumque manebunt
silvarum dotes atque arma Diania terris.
hic et semiferam thoum de sanguine prolem
finxit. non alio maior sub pectore virtus,
sive in lora voces seu nudi ad pignora martis.
thoes commissos (clarissima fama) leones
et subiere astu et parvis domuere lacertis;
nam genus exiguum et pudeat, quam informe, fateri;
vulpina species: tamen huic exacta voluntas.
at non est alius quem tanta ad munia fetus
exercere velis, aut te tua culpa refellet
inter opus, quo sera cadit prudentia damno.
iunge pares ergo et maiorum pignore signa
feturam prodantque tibi metagonta parentes,
qui genuere sua pecus hoc immane iuventa.
et primum expertos animi, quae gratia prima est,
in venerem iungam. tum sortis cura secunda,
ne renuat species aut quem detractet honorem.
sint celsi vultus, sint hirtae frontibus aures,
os magnum et patulis agitatos naribus ignes
spirent, adstricti succingant ilia ventres,
cauda brevis longumque latus discretaque collo

255 lora *Ellis*: ora A.
262 quom *Gronov*: quo A.
265 tenuere A: genuere *Gesner*.
268 aut quem *Baehrens*: atque A: aut quae *Ald.*: aut qua *Barth.*

as my songs shall last, as long as the woods keep their treasures and Diana's weapons abide on earth.

'Twas he too who developed a species with a wild strain from the blood of the *thoes*.[a] Beneath no other breast is there higher courage, whether you call them to the leash or to the test of open conflict. The *thoes* (their reputation is famous) can steal craftily on lions pitted against them[b] and overcome them with their short legs; for it is a small-sized breed, and one may scruple to own how ugly: it has a fox-like look: still its resolution is perfect. But there is no other breed which you could wish to train for tasks so important; or else your own mistake will find you out in the hunt when loss of game makes late-learned wisdom vain.

Now then couple well-matched mates[c] and mark the offspring with the pledge of their pedigree, letting the parents who produce this wonderful progeny in the vigour of their youth yield you a fine *metagon*. First I shall mate dogs tried in courage, the foremost quality: the next care in the apportionment is that outward appearance shall not belie descent or lower any of its merits. They should have the face high, they should have shaggy ears by their foreheads, the mouth big, and they should breathe fiery blasts from wide nostrils; a neat belly should gird their flanks below; tail should be short and sides long, hair parted on the neck, and that

[a] The θῶες of Oppian, *Cyneg.* III. 336–38, are jackals sprung from a union of wolves with leopards. The θώς of Aristotle is perhaps rather a civet than a jackal. Pliny, *N.H.* VIII. 123, mentions *thoes* as a kind of wolf.

[b] *e.g.* in the public games at Rome.

[c] For the mating of dogs, with 263 *sqq.* *cf.* Nemesianus, *Cyn.* 103 *sqq.*; Oppian, *Cyn.* I. 376 *sqq.*

caesaries neu pexa nimis neu frigoris illa
impatiens; validis tum surgat pectus ab armis,
quod magnos capiat motus magnisque supersit.
effuge qui lata pandit vestigia planta:
mollis in officio. siccis ego dura lacertis
crura velim et solidos haec in certamina calces.
sed frustra longus properat labor, abdita si non
altas in latebras unique inclusa marito ⟨est⟩
femina: nec patres veneris sub tempore magnos
illa neque emeritae servat fastigia laudis.
primi complexus, dulcissima prima voluptas:
hunc veneri dedit impatiens natura furorem.
si tenuit custos et mater adultera non est,
da requiem gravidae solitosque remitte labores:
vix oneri super illa suo. tum deinde monebo,
ne matrem indocilis natorum turba fatiget,
percensere notis iamque inde excernere pravos.
signa dabunt ipsi. teneris vix artubus haeret
ille tuos olim non defecturus honores,
iamque illum impatiens aequae vehementia sortis
extulit: affectat materna regna sub alvo,
ubera tota tenet, a tergo liber aperto,

280 in latebras *Sann.*: illecebras A. est *add. Lachmann.*
281 patres *Sann.*: patre A.
285 custos A: castus *Ellis*: fastus *Lachmann*: renuit cunctos *Pith., Burm.*
289 pravos *Burman*: parvos A.
294 tenet, a tergo ς: ten& eatergo A: tenetque a tergo *Baehrens.*

neither too shaggy nor yet unable to stand cold; and then from strong limbs [a] must rise a breast capable of drawing deep breaths, and with strength left for more. Avoid the dog that spreads his steps with a broad foot: he is weak in hunting-duty. I should want hardy legs with firm muscles and I should want solid feet for such struggles.

But zealous and prolonged trouble is all in vain unless the bitch is shut up in some deep retreat and secluded for a single male: otherwise she cannot at the time of coupling maintain unspoilt the pedigree of a fine sire or the pitch of past distinction won. The first unions, the first pleasure is sweetest: such frenzy has uncontrolled nature given to love. If the attendant has kept her shut up and the pregnant bitch has no unions with other dogs, [b] give her rest and remit her usual tasks: she is barely sufficient for her own burden. Then later I shall suggest, to prevent an unruly litter of whelps from wearing their mother out, that you examine them by their points and thereupon pick out the inferior ones. They will themselves give indications. The puppy that one day will not fail [c] your pride in him [d] is scarcely yet firm in his tender limbs, and already his vigour, impatient of equality with the rest, has raised him above them: he aims at sovereignty beneath his mother's belly, keeps her teats wholly to himself, his back unen-

[a] The shoulder-blades should be broad, as in Oppian, *Cyn.* I. 409, εὐρέες ὠμοπλάται: *cf.* Xen. *Cyn.* iv. 1; Pollux, V. 58; Arr. *Cyn.* 5. 9; Colum. *R.R.* VII. xii. 4.

[b] Vollmer's inclusion of the *si tenuit* clause in the preceding sentence, with *hunc . . . furorem* as a parenthesis, is unsatisfactory.

[c] *Cf.* note on *illum . . . mergentem*, 424–5.

[d] Or " high tasks to which you may call him."

dum tepida indulget terris clementia mundi;
verum ubi Caurino perstrinxit frigore vesper,
ira iacet turbaque potens operitur inerti.
illius et manibus vires sit cura futuras
perpensare: leves deducet pondere fratres:
nec me pignoribus, nec te mea carmina fallent.
  protinus et cultus alios et debita fetae
blandimenta feres curaque sequere merentem:
illa perinde suos, ut erit † dilecta, minores
ad longam praestabit opem. tum denique, fetu
cum desunt, operis fregitque industria matres,
transeat in catulos omnis tutela relictos.
lacte novam pubem facilique tuebere maza,
nec luxus alios avidaeque impendia vitae
noscant: haec magno redit indulgentia damno.
nec mirum: humanos non est magis altera sensus,
tollit ni ratio et vitiis adeuntibus obstat.
haec illa est Pharios quae fregit noxia reges,
dum servata cavis potant Mareotica gemmis

297 ire plac& A: ira iacet *Ulitius*: irreptat *Radermacher*.
298 et *Heinsius*: e A.
299 leuis A.
303 de lacte *Sann.*, *Vollmer*: delacta A: dilecta *Stern*: suo saturat de lacte *Johnson* 1699 *ed.*: delecta (*particip. a delicere*) *Heinsius*.
304–5 fetu A: fetus cum desunt operi *Ellis*. operis *Ulitius*: operi A.
311 ni *Graevius*: se A.

cumbered and unpressed by the others so long as the genial warmth of the heavens is kind to earth;[a] but when evening has shrivelled him with north-western chilliness, his bad temper flags and this strong pup lets himself be snugly covered by the sluggish crowd (of the rest). It must be your care thoroughly to weigh his promised strength in your hands: he will humble his light brothers with his weight.[b] In these signs my poems will mislead neither myself nor you.

As soon as she has produced young, you are to offer the mother different treatment and the comforts due to her, and to attend her carefully as she deserves. Exactly as she is kindly treated, she will maintain her little ones until a long service of nurture has been rendered.[c] Then finally, when the mothers fail their offspring and their assiduity in the task of suckling has shattered them, let all your concern pass over to the deserted whelps. You must sustain the young brood with milk and a simple pap: they must not know other luxuries and the outlays of a gluttonous life: such indulgence comes home at mighty cost. Nor is this surprising: no other life eats more into the senses of mankind, unless reason banishes it and bars the way against the approach of vices. Such was the fault that ruined Egyptian kings, as they drank old Mareotic wines in goblets of precious stone, reaping the perfumes

[a] *i.e.* during the sunny day.

[b] *Cf.* Livy IX. 34 . . . *ad servorum ministerium deduxisti* (= brought down, degraded). The reference is not to exact weighing in a *trutina* or balance.

[c] The text is uncertain; but the sense required is that the greater the care lavished on the mother, the longer she will be able to give milk to her pups.

nardiferumque metunt Gangen vitiisque ministrant.
sic et Achaemenio cecidisti, Lydia, Cyro:
atqui dives eras ⟨ac⟩ fluminis aurea venis.
scilicet ad summam ne quid restaret habendi,
tu quoque luxuriae fictas dum colligis artes
et sequeris demens alienam, Graecia, culpam,
o quantum et quotiens decoris frustrata paterni!
at qualis nostris, quam simplex mensa Camillis!
qui tibi cultus erat post tot, Serrane, triumphos!
ergo illi ex habitu virtutisque indole priscae
imposuere orbi Romam caput, actaque ab illis
ad caelum virtus summosque tetendit honores.

scilicet exiguis magna sub imagine rebus
prospicies, quae sit ratio, et quo fine regendae.
idcirco imperium catulis unusque magister
additur: ille dapes poenamque operamque ⟨moramque⟩
temperet, hunc spectet silvas domitura iuventus.
nec vile arbitrium est: quoicumque haec regna dicantur,
ille tibi egregia iuvenis de pube legendus,

329 *in fine nullum lacunae signum in* A: ministrans *add. Ald.*: peraeque *Baehrens*: moramque *H. Schenkl.*

of nard-bearing Ganges and ministering to vice. By this sin fell you too, Lydia, beneath Persian Cyrus; and yet you were rich and golden in the veins of your river.[a] In good truth, so that nothing might be left to crown the possession of wealth, how much and how often, O Greece, did you too fall short of ancestral honour by gathering together the arts which luxury fashioned and by madly following the faults of other nations! But of what sort, how simple, was the table of our Camilli![b] What was your dress, Serranus, after all your triumphs![c] These were the men who, in accord with the bearing and character of ancient virtue, set o'er the world Rome as its head; and by them was virtue exalted to heaven, and so she reached highest honours.

In truth, taught by great precedent you will be able to provide for small details, finding the right system and the limits which should govern them. Therefore rule is imposed on the whelps in the shape of a single keeper: he must control their food and punishments, their service and rest: the young pack that is to master the woods must look to him. It is no trumpery charge: whosoever has such power dedicated to him should be a youth picked by you from young folk of merit, at once prudent

[a] The river Pactolus was famous for its golden sands. Postgate's *Pactolique aurea venis* suggests that *fluminis* was a gloss on the original reading.

[b] The plural alludes rhetorically to M. Furius Camillus, the conqueror of Veii, who saved Rome after the Allian disaster: for his poverty *cf.* Hor. *Od.* I. xii. 42 *sqq.*

[c] C. Atilius Regulus Serranus was consul in 257 and in 250 B.C. He was summoned from farm-work to undertake a military command, Val. Max. IV. iv. 5; Virg. *Aen.* VI. 845.

utrumque et prudens et sumptis impiger armis.
quod nisi et accessus et agendi tempora belli
noverit et socios tutabitur hoste minores,
aut cedent aut illa tamen victoria damno est.
  ergo in opus vigila † factusque ades omnibus armis:
arma acuere viam; tegat imas fascia suras:
⟨sit pell⟩is vitulina, suis et tergore fulvo
i⟨re decet, niteant⟩ canaque e maele galeri,
ima Toletano praecingant ilia cultro
terribilemque manu vibrata falarica dextra
det sonitum et curvae rumpant non pervia falces.
  haec tua militia est. quin et Mavortia bello
vulnera et errantes per tot divertia morbos
causasque affectusque canum tua ⟨cura⟩ tueri est.
stat Fatum supra totumque avidissimus Orcus
pascitur et nigris orbem circumsonat alis.
scilicet ad magnum maior ducenda laborem
cura, nec expertos fallet deus: huic quoque nostrae

337 vigil affectusque *Vollmer.*

338 arma hacuere uitã A: arma acuere viam (virum *Johnson*) *Ald. versuum* 339 *et* 340 *initia perierunt in* A *praeter primam v.* 340 *litteram, quae tamen utrum* j *an* p *fuerit dubitandum* (p *legit Sann.*).

339 *ante* inulina *potest fuisse* us *vel* is: inulina A: sit famulis vitulina tuis *Ulitius, Burm., Wernsd.* suĭs (*genit.,* = suīs) A.

345 divertia A: divortia *vulgo.*

350 huic *Baehrens*: hinc A.

and, when he grasps his weapons, unflagging. But unless he knows the right ways of approach and the right moments for attack and can protect his allies when unequal to their enemy, then either the dogs will run away or the victory so won is after all too dear.

So then be wakeful for your work and attend equipped[a] with weapons fully. Weapons make the way of the chase more keen[b]: let bandaging protect the lower parts of the leg: the leather should be calf's leather, and tawny pig-skin is fit for the march: the caps should gleam with the grey of the badger:[c] close under the hunter's flanks should be girt a knife of Toledo steel: a missile weapon brandished in the right hand should give a terrifying sound, while curved reaping-hooks must break through thickets which block the way.

Such is your active service in the chase. But especially is it your concern to care for the martial wounds suffered in fight, the maladies which stray along so many different paths, their causes and the symptoms shown by your dogs. Above stands Fate: the insatiable Death-god devours everything and echoes round the world on sable wings. Clearly for a great task still greater care must be employed, nor will the deity[d] play the experienced false: for this our care too there is another divinity[e] easy to

[a] *factus*, if sound, must have the force of *instructus*.

[b] *Via* is the method of the hunt, *cf*. 5. Johnson's *virum* is attractive, "make the hunter keen."

[c] The nose, chin, lower sides of the cheeks and the mid forehead of the badger (*maeles*) are white: the ends of the hairs on the body are at bottom yellowish-white, in the middle black, and at the ends ash-coloured or grey: hence the proverb "as grey as a badger." The skin dressed without removing the hair can be used for caps or pouches.

[d] Diana. [e] Paean.

est aliud, quod praestet opus, placabile numen.
nec longe auxilium, licet alti vulneris orae
abstiterint atroque cadant cum sanguine fibrae:
inde rape ex ipso qui vulnus fecerit hoste
virosam eluviem lacerique per ulceris ora
sparge manu, venas dum sucus comprimat acer:
mortis enim patuere viae. tum pura monebo
circum labra sequi tenuique includere filo.
at si pernicies angusto pascitur ore,
contra pande viam fallentesque argue causas
morborum: in vitio facilis med⟨icina recenti⟩;
sed tacta impositis mulcent p⟨ecuaria palmis⟩
(id satis) aut nigrae circum picis unguine signant;
quodsi destricto levis est in vulnere noxa,
ipse habet auxilium validae natale salivae.
illa gravis labes et curis altior illis,
cum vitium causae totis egere latentes
corporibus seraque aperitur noxia summa.
inde emissa lues et per contagia mortes
venere in vulgum iuxtaque exercitus ingens
aequali sub labe ruit, nec viribus ullis
aut merito venia est aut spes exire precanti.
quod sive a Stygia letum Proserpina nocte
extulit et Furiis commissam ulciscitur iram,
seu vitium ex alto spiratque vaporibus aether

352 orae *Barth*: ora A.
353 atroque *Sann.*: utroque A.
355 ulceris *Ald.*: viceris A.
357 pura monebo *Sann.*: purmo bebo A.
360 pande *Ald.*: prande A.
361 med⟨icina recenti⟩ *Ald.*: med⟨icina reperto⟩ *Baehrens*.
362 sed A: seu *Heinsius*. tacta A: tactu *Sann.* p⟨ecuaria palmis⟩ *Ald.*
369 morbi *Sann.*, *Vollmer*: morbis A: mortes *Stern.*
370 fusaque *Vollmer*: Iusaque A: iuxtaque *Sann.*

be entreated who can guarantee the work of healing. Nor is aid far distant, though the lips of a deep wound have parted and the fibres are dripping with dark blood: thereupon seize from the very enemy that has dealt the wound some of his fetid urine, sprinkling it with the hand over the mouth of the torn wound, till the acid juice compresses the veins: for the avenues of death lie open. Then my advice will be to go round the lips till they are clean and sew them fast with a slender thread. But if deadly danger battens in a narrow wound, contrariwise, widen the outlet and expose the treacherous causes of corruption: the remedy is easy in a newly-found mischief; but the beasts which are infected they soothe with strokes of the hands (that is enough), or seal the sore around with an ointment of black pitch: if, however, there is merely a trivial hurt in a slight wound, the dog has the natural remedy of efficacious saliva.[a] It is a serious plague, too deep for the treatments mentioned, when hidden causes have sped the malady through all the bodies of the pack and the damage is only discovered in its final consummation. Then has pestilence been let loose, and by contagion deaths have come upon the pack at large, and the great host alike perishes beneath an infection that falls on all: neither is there indulgence granted for any strength or service, nor is there hope of escape in answer to prayer. But whether it be that Proserpina has brought death forth from Stygian darkness, satisfying her wrath for some offence entrusted to the Furies to avenge, whether the infection is from on high and ether breathes with contagious vapours, or whether earth

[a] *i.e.* he licks the wound.

pestiferis, seu terra suos populatur honores,
fontem averte mali. trans altas ducere calles
admoneo latumque fuga superabitis amnem.
hoc primum effugium leti: tunc ficta valebunt
auxilia et nostra quidam redit usus ab arte.
sed varii motus nec in omnibus una potestas:
disce vices et quae tutela est proxima tempta.
plurima per catulos rabies invictaque tardis
praecipitat letale malum: sit tutius ergo
antire auxiliis et primas vincere causas.
namque subit, nodis qua lingua tenacibus haeret,
(vermiculum dixere) mala atque incondita pestis.
ille ubi salsa siti praecepit viscera longa,
aestivos vibrans accensis febribus ignes,
moliturque fugas et sedem spernit amaram.
scilicet hoc motu stimulisque potentibus acti
in furias vertere canes. ergo insita ferro
iam teneris elementa mali causasque recidunt.
nec longa in facto medicina est ulcere: purum
sparge salem et tenui permulce vulnus olivo:
ante relata suas quam nox bene compleat umbras,
ecce aderit factique oblitus vulneris ultro
blanditur mensis cereremque efflagitat ore.

376 seu terra suos *Sann.*: si litaeras vos A.
384 praecipitat *Pithou*: prȩcipiat A. sit tutius *Sann.*, *qui et* securius *coniecit*: sicutius A: sic tutius *Ald.*
388 longae A: longa *Sann.*: longe *Vollmer, Curcio.*
390 amarã A: amatam *Ulitius.*

is devastating her own fair products,[a] remove the source of the evil. I warn you to lead the dogs over the high mountain-paths: you are to cross the broad river in your flight. This is your first escape from destruction: thereafter the aids we have devised will avail and some service is secured from our lore. But varied are the onsets of disease, nor is there the same force in all of them: learn their phases and make trial of the medicine which is most available. Rabies, prevalent among young dogs and uncontrollable for those who delay treatment, launches a deadly evil: it must be safer then to forestall it with remedies and overcome its first causes. For the mischievous and barbarous plague—it has been described as a tiny worm—steals in where the tongue is rooted to its firm ligaments. When the worm has seized on the inwards briny with prolonged thirst, darting its sweltering fires with fevers aflame, it works its escape and spurns its bitter[b] quarters. Impelled, it is plain, by its activity and potent goads, dogs turn frantic. So, when they are quite young, it is usual to cut out with the knife the deep-seated elements and causes of disease. Prolonged treatment is not needed for the wound so made: sprinkle clean salt and soothe the affected part with a little olive-oil: before returning night can well complete her shadows, look, the dog will be on the scene, and, forgetting the wound made, is actually fawning at table and pleading for bread[c] with his mouth.

[a] *i.e.* with the result that they rot and cause disease.

[b] With the meaning of *amaram* compare *salsa* in 388.

[c] The goddess' name is put by metonymy for bread: *cf.* Nemes. *Cyn.* 154, *cererem cum lacte ministra*: so for corn, Virg. *G.* I. 297; Cic. *N.D.* II. 23. 60; *Aetna*, 10.

quid, priscas artes inventaque simplicis aevi
si referam? non illa metus solacia falsi,
tam longam traxere fidem. collaribus ergo
sunt qui lucifugae cristas inducere maelis
iussere aut sacris conserta monilia conchis
et vivum lapidem et circa Melite⟨n⟩sia nectunt
curalia et magicis adiutas cantibus herbas.
ac sic offectus oculique venena maligni
vicit tutela pax impetrata deorum.

at si deformi lacerum dulcedine corpus
persequitur scabies, longi via pessima leti:
in primo accessu tristis medicina, sed una
pernicies redimenda anima, quae prima sequaci
sparsa malo est, ne dira trahant contagia vulgus.
quodsi dat spatium clemens et promonet ortu
morbus, disce vias et qua sinit artibus exi.
tunc et odorato medicata bitumina vino

408 deformis *Ios. Wassius, Vollmer*: deformi A, *Postgate*.
413 promonet A: praemonet *Titius*.
415 vino *Johnson*: viro A. *cf. v.* 476 *et Veget. mulom.* 2. 135. 5.

---

[a] The omission of a punctuation mark after *falsi* would imply in Grattius an Epicurean disdain for primitive superstition: "those consolations of a groundless fear did not continue to command such a lasting belief." According to

What need to record primitive devices and the inventions of an unsophisticated age? Of no groundless fear were those the consolations: so lasting a confidence have they prolonged.[a] Thus there are some whose prescription has been to fasten cock's combs upon the dog-collars made from the light-shunning badger,[b] or they twine necklets around, strung of sacred shells,[c] and the stone of living fire[d] and red coral from Malta and herbs aided by magic incantations. And so the peace of the gods won by the protective amulet is found to vanquish baleful influences and the venom of the evil eye.

But if the mange pursues a body torn with the ugly itch for scratching, it is the cruellest road of slow death: at the first onset, the remedy is a melancholy one, but destruction must be bought off by the one life (of the dog) which has first been contaminated with the infectious disease, to prevent the whole pack from contracting the dread contagion. If, however, the ailment is slight, giving time and forewarnings at the start, learn the methods of cure and by skilled devices escape wherever feasible. Then fire is found to blend and into one whole unite

the text here accepted, Grattius seems to admit that superstitious cures soothed reasonable fears, and remained long in vogue.

[b] The badger burrows underground, confining itself to its hole during the day and feeding at night.

[c] Among prophylactic amulets the *conchae* were sacred to Venus. Pliny, *N.H.* XXXII, 2–6, mentions the shell *echeneis* or *remora*, believed to have power to stop ships by adhering to the hull. The marvellous properties of such shells, he considers, became the more credible because they were preserved and consecrated in the temple of Venus at Cnidos.

[d] *Pyrites*: *cf.* Pliny, *N.H.* XXXVI. 137, *molarem quidam pyriten vocant*: *cf. Aetna*, 454.

Hipponiasque pices neclectaeque unguen amurcae
miscuit et summam complectitur ignis in unam.
inde lavant aegros: ast ira coercita morbi
laxatusque rigor. quae te ne cura timentem
differat, et pluvias et Cauri frigora vitent;
duc magis, ut nudis incumbunt vallibus aestus,
a vento clarique faces ad solis, ut omne
exsudent vitium subeatque latentibus ultro
quae facta est medicina vadis. nec non tamen illum
spumosi catulos mergentem litoris aestu
respicit et facilis Paean adiuvit in artes.
o rerum prudens quantam Experientia vulgo
materiem largita boni, si vincere curent
desidiam et gratos agitando prendere fines!
  est in Trinacria specus ingens rupe cavique
introsum reditus, circum atrae moenia silvae
alta premunt ruptique ambustis faucibus amnes;

416 Hippŏniasque *primus agnovit Haupt*: iponiasque A: impone atque pices, *vel* impositasque pices *vel denique* fraces *Heinsius.* neclectaeque *Haupt*: nec liceat quę A: immundaeque *Ald.*

418 ast A: est *Ald.*: atque *Barth.*

419 ne cura timentem *Sann.*: nec urat in mentem A.

421 duc *H. Schenkl*: sic A: stent *Postgate.*

426 paean adiuvit *Sann.*: paeana divint A.

doses of bitumen, mixed with fragrant wine, and portions of Bruttian[a] pitch and ointment from the unregarded dregs of olive-oil. Therewith they bathe the ailing dogs: then the anger of the malady is curbed and its severity relaxed. Let not this treatment, for all your anxiety, distract you (from further precautions): the dogs must avoid both rains and the chills of the north-west wind: rather, when sultry heats hang over the bare valleys, take them (to heights) away from the wind to meet the rays of the bright sun, so that they may sweat out all the infection and moreover that the healing which has been effected may steal into their hidden veins.[b] Besides the Healing-God, kindly disposed to our skill, fails not to regard favourably and to aid him who dips[c] his whelps in the tide of the foaming beach. O Experience, foreseeing in affairs, how much material benefit hast thou lavished on the mass of men, if they make it their care to overcome sloth and by vigorous action to get a grip of fair ideals!

There is in Sicily a grotto enormous in its rocky mass—with hollow windings which return upon themselves; high ramparts of black woodland enclose it around and streams bursting from volcanic jaws—

[a] Ἱππώνιον is Vibo Valentia on the Via Popilia in the territory of the Bruttii. Curcio thinks that Hippo in Numidia is meant.

[b] *Vadis* is also explained as (1) pores (Enk), (2) intestines (Radermacher). Vollmer imagines a contrast between *latentibus vadis,* meaning *ex aquis reconditis,* and the open sea of the next sentence.

[c] The Latin of *illum mergentem* in the sense of *illum qui mergit* is questionable; but *cf. ille . . . defecturus,* 291. Vollmer proposes tentatively *illic* or *ullum.*

Vulcano condicta domus. quam supter eunti
stagna sedent venis oleoque madentia vivo.
huc defecta mala vidi pecuaria tabe
saepe trahi victosque malo graviore magistros.
" te primum, Vulcane, loci, pacemque precamur,
incola sancte, tuam: da fessis ultima rebus
auxilia et, meriti si nulla est noxia tanti,
tot miserare animas liceatque attingere fontes,
sancte, tuos " ter quisque vocant, ter pinguia libant
tura foco, struitur ramis felicibus ara.
hic (dictu mirum atque alias ignobile monstrum)
adversis specibus ruptoque e pectore montis
venit ovans Austris et multo flumine flammae
emicat ipse: manu ramum pallente sacerdos
termiteum quatiens " procul hinc extorribus ire
edico praesente deo, praesentibus aris,
quis scelus aut manibus sumptum aut in pectore motum est "
inclamat: cecidere animi et trepidantia membra.
o quisquis misero fas umquam in supplice fregit,
quis pretio fratrum meliorisque ausus amici
sollicitare caput patriosve lacessere divos,
illum agat infandae comes huc audacia culpae:
discet commissa quantum deus ultor in ira
pone sequens valeat. sed cui bona pectore mens est

433 supter *Sann.*: super A.
438 fessis *Sann.*: fissis A.
439 meriti *Sann.*: meritis A.
440 miserare A: -rere *Ald.*
441 vocant ter *Sann.*: vocanter A.

---

[a] *ira commissa* (a curious condensation recalling *commissa piacula*, Virg. *Aen.* VI. 569) is here taken with Wernsdorf to

Vulcan's acknowledged haunt. As one passes beneath, the pools lie motionless oozing in veins of natural bituminous oil. I have often seen dogs dragged hither fordone from mischievous wasting, and their custodians overcome by still heavier suffering. "Thee first, O Vulcan, and thy peace, holy dweller in this place, do we entreat: grant final aid to our wearied fortunes, and, if no guilt is here deserving penalty so great, pity these many lives and suffer them, holy one, to attain to thy fountains"—thrice does each one call, thrice they offer rich incense on the fire, and the altar is piled with fruitful branches. Hereat (wondrous to tell and a portent elsewhere unknown) from the confronting caves and the mountain's riven breast there has come, exultant in southern gales and darting forth 'mid a full flood of flame, the God himself: his priest, waving in pallid hand the olive branch, proclaims aloud: "In the presence of the God, in the presence of the altars, I ordain that all go out of the land far from here, who have put their hands to crime or contemplated it in their heart": forthwith droop their spirits and their nervous limbs. Oh! whoso has ever impaired heaven's law in the case of a wretched suppliant, whoso for a price has dared to aim at the life of brothers or of faithful friend or to outrage ancestral gods—if such a man be impelled hither by audacity, the comrade of unutterable sin, he will learn how mighty is the power of the God who followeth after as the avenger in wrath for crime committed.[a] But he whose mind

mean *ira quae commissis sceleribus provocata est.* The sense is different in 374, *Furiis commissam . . . iram,* unless 455 can imply "in wrath assigned to him to vent."

obsequitur⟨que⟩ deo, deus illam molliter aram
lambit et ipse, suos ubi contigit ignis ⟨hon⟩ores,
defugit a sacris rursumque reconditur antro:
huic fas auxilium et Vulcania tangere dona.
nec mora, si medias exedit noxia fibras,
his lave praesidiis affectaque corpora mulce:
regnantem excuties morbum. deus auctor, et ipsa
artem aluit natura suam. quae robore pestis
acrior aut leto propior via? sed tamen illi
hic venit auxilium valida vementius ira.
  quod primam si fallet opem dimissa facultas,
at tu praecipitem qua spes est proxima labem
aggredere: in subito subita et medicina tumultu.
stringendae nares et ⟨bi⟩na ligamina ferro
armorum, geminaque cruor ducendus ab aure:
hinc vitium, hinc illa est avidae vehementia pesti.
ilicet auxiliis fessum solabere corpus
subsiduasque fraces defusaque Massica prisco
sparge cado: Liber tenues e pectore curas
exigit, et morbo Liber medicina furenti.
  quid dicam tusses, quid inertis damna veterni

463 excuties *Barth*: -iens A.
466 hic A: hinc *Ald.*
468 at tu *Sann.*: ad tu A: actu *Baehrens.*
470 &na A: et bina *Haupt*: scindenda *Burm. et alii.*
477 inertis *Sann.*: maestis A: moesti *Ald.* veterni *Sann.*: -nis A.

is good at heart and is reverent to the God, has his altar-gift gently caressed by the Fire-god, who himself, when the flame has reached the sacrifices offered in his honour, retreats from the holy ritual and again conceals himself in his cave. For such a one 'tis right to attain relief and Vulcan's kindliness. Let there be no delay: if the malady has gnawed right into the fibres, bathe with the remedies specified[a] and soothe the suffering bodies: so will you expel the tyrannous disease. The God lends support, and nature herself nourishes her own skilful remedy.[b] What plague is sharper than "robur"[c] or what path nearer to death? But still for it there comes here assistance more active than the powerful anger of the ailment.

Yet if a lost opportunity baffles first aid, then you must attack the furious pestilence where prospects are likeliest: sudden disturbance calls for sudden relief. The nostrils must be cut slightly with the steel, as well as the two muscles of the shoulders, and blood is to be drawn off from both ears: from the blood comes the corruption, from the blood the violence of the insatiate plague. Forthwith you will comfort the wearied body with palliatives, and you must sprinkle on the wounds the sediment of oil-dregs and Massic wine outpoured from its ancient cask—Bacchus expels light cares from the heart: Bacchus also is healing for the fury of disease.

Why mention coughs, why the afflictions of a

[a] *e.g.* the oil from the bituminous lake of 434.

[b] In the form of fire and bitumen.

[c] The disease has the symptoms of tetanus according to veterinary writers: Vegetius, *Mulomedicina* 2, 88; Chiron, 315; Pelagonius, ed. Ihm, 294.

aut incurvatae si qua est tutela podagrae?
mille tenent pestes curaque potentia maior.
mitte age (non opibus tanta est fiducia nostris),
mitte, anime: ex alto ducendum numen Olympo,
supplicibus⟨que⟩ vocanda sacris tutela deorum.
idcirco aeriis molimur compita lucis
spicatasque faces sacrum ad nemorale Dianae
sistimus et solito catuli velantur honore,
ipsaque per flores medio in discrimine luci
stravere arma sacris et pace vacantia festa.
tum cadus et viridi fumantia liba feretro
praeveniunt teneraque extrudens cornua fronte
haedus et ad ramos etiamnum haerentia poma,
lustralis de more sacri, quo tota iuventus
lustraturque deae proque anno reddit honorem.
ergo impetrato respondet multa favore
ad partes, qua poscis opem; seu vincere silvas
seu tibi fatorum labes exire minasque
cura prior, tua magna fides tutelaque Virgo.
  restat equos finire notis, quos arma Dianae
admittant: non omne meas genus audet in artes.

478 incurvatae *ed. Gryph.* 1537 : incuratae A.
484 nemorale *Turnebus, Postgate*: nemora alta A, *Burm., Wernsd., Stern, Curcio, Enk.*

---

[a] 483–96, description of an Ambarval sacrifice to Diana, with allusion to her worship near Aricia.

[b] *Multa*, nom. sing. fem., agreeing with *dea* understood: *i.e.* "in full force" (like πολὺς ῥεῖ in Greek). Enk thinks *multa* neut. plur.; Vollmer takes it for *mulcta* in the sense of "mollified."

sluggish lethargy or any prophylactic there is for gout that twists the limbs? A thousand plagues hold their victims, and their power transcends our care. Come, dismiss such cares (our confidence is not so great in our own resources)—dismiss them, my mind: the deity must be summoned from high Olympus and the protection of the gods invoked by suppliant ritual. For that reason we construct cross-road shrines in groves of soaring trees [a] and set our sharp-pointed torches hard by the woodland precinct of Diana, and the whelps are decked with the wonted wreath, and at the centre of the cross-roads in the grove the hunters fling down among the flowers the very weapons which now keep holiday in the festal peace of the sacred rites. Then the wine-cask and cakes steaming on a green-wood tray lead the procession, with a young goat thrusting horns forth from tender brow, and fruit even now clinging to the branches, after the fashion of a lustral ritual at which all the youth both purify themselves in honour of the Goddess and render sacrifice for the bounty of the year. Therefore, when her grace is won, the Goddess answers generously [b] in those directions where you sue for help: whether your greater anxiety is to master the forest or to elude the plagues and threats of destiny, the Maiden is your mighty affiance and protection.

It remains to define by their characteristics the horses which Diana's equipment can accept as useful.[c] Not every breed has the courage needed for my

[c] *Dianae arma* = the chase. For horses in general see Xen. *Cyn.* 1; Pollux, *Onom.* I. 188 *sqq.*; Virg. *G.* III. 72 *sqq.*; Varro *R. R.* II. 7; Columella, VI. 26–29; Plin. *N.H.* VIII. 154; Nemes. *Cyn.* 240 *sqq.*; Oppian, *Cyn.* I. 158–367.

est vitium ex animo, sunt quos imbellia fallant
corpora, praeveniens quondam est incommoda virtus.
consule, Penei qualis perfunditur amne
Thessalus aut patriae quem conspexere Mycenae
glaucum? nempe ingens, nempe ardua fundet in auras
crura. quis Eleas potior lustravit harenas?
ne tamen hoc attingat opus: iactantior illi
virtus quam silvas durumque lacessere martem.
nec saevos miratur equos terrena Syene
scilicet, et Parthis inter sua mollia rura
mansit honor; veniat Caudini saxa Taburni
Garganumve trucem aut Ligurinas desuper Alpes:
ante opus excussis cadet unguibus. et tamen illi
est animus fingetque meas se iussus in artes:
sed iuxta vitium posuit deus. at tibi contra
Callaecis lustratur ⟨e⟩quis scruposa Pyr⟨ene⟩,
non tamen Hispano martem temptare m⟨inistro⟩
ausim: ⟨in⟩ muricibus vix ora tenacia ferr⟨o⟩
concedunt. at tota levi Nasam⟨onia virga⟩
fingit equos: ipsis Numidae solver⟨e capistris⟩

507 syenae A: Sidene *Burm.*: Cyrene *Wesseling.*
515 m⟨inacem⟩ *Ald.*: m⟨inistro⟩ *H. Schenkl*: m⟨aligno⟩ *Birt.*
516 ferr⟨o⟩ *Sann.*
517 at *Ulitius*: aut A: ast *H. Schenkl.* virga *Ulitius, cf. Lucan* IV. 683.

profession. Some show deficiency on the score of spirit; some have feeble bodies to play them false; at times excessive mettle is unsuitable. Bethink you—what sort of Thessalian horse bathes in Peneus' stream, or what is the grey sort on which its native Mycenae fixes its gaze? Assuredly it is huge, assuredly it will throw its legs high in air. What better steed ever traversed the race-course in Elis?[a] Yet let it not touch our hunting-work: its vigour is too impetuous for an attack on the hard fighting of the forests. Doubtless Syene[b] on the level plain has horses to admire which are not wild, and those of Parthia have kept their reputation in their own flat country: if such a horse comes to the crags of Taburnus near the Caudine Forks or to rugged Garganus[c] or over the Ligurian Alps, he will collapse before his task with hoofs battered.[d] And yet he has spirit and will mould himself to my methods if ordered: but heaven alongside of merit imposes defects. On the other hand, you find the horses of the Callaeci[e] can traverse the jagged Pyrenees. I should not, however, venture to try the conflict with a Spanish steed to serve me: amid sharp stones they scarce yield their stubborn mouths to the steel; but all Nasamonia[f] controls her horses with light switches. The bold and hard-toiling Numidian folk free theirs even

[a] *i.e.* at the Olympic games.

[b] Syene (Assouan) in Upper Egypt below the First Cataract.

[c] Taburnus was in Samnium: Garganus in Apulia.

[d] *i.e.* owing to the stony nature of the ground.

[e] The Callaeci were a people of Hispania Tarraconensis.

[f] The Nasamonian tribe dwelt in the eastern part of the Syrtis Major in N. Africa.

audax et patiens operum g⟨enus. ille vigebit⟩
centum actus spatiis atque eluctabitur iram.
nec magni cultus: sterilis quodcumque remisit
terra sui tenuesque satis producere rivi.
sic et Strymonio facilis tutela Bisaltae:
possent Aetnaeas utinam se ferre per arces,
qui ludus Siculis. quid tum, si turpia colla
aut tenuis dorso curvatur spina? per illos
cantatus Graiis Acragas victaeque fragosum
Nebroden liquere ferae: o quantus in armis
ille meis quoius dociles pecuaria fetus
sufficient! quis Chaonios contendere contra
ausit, vix merita quos signat Achaia palma?
spadices vix Pellaei valuere Cerauni;
at tibi devotae magnum pecuaria Cyrrhae,
Phoebe, decus meruere, leves seu iungere currus
usus, seu nostras agere in sacraria tensas.

519 g⟨enus. ille vigebit⟩ *Ald.*
529 illa . . . coetus *Vollmer*: ille . . . coetus A: foetus *Ald.*
533 & A: at *Vollmer.*

[a] In Thrace. Grattius proceeds to express a wish that these Thracian horses could have the chance of showing their powers on the mountains of Sicily. The Sicilian horses are mentioned for their swiftness, Oppian, *Cyn.* I. 272. Their victories in horse-racing and chariot-racing are the themes of many of Pindar's odes: *e.g. Pyth.* i. celebrates a victory won by Hieron of Aetna (*cf.* Gratt. 524). The qualities of speed and sure-footedness requisite in Sicilian sport (*cf. qui ludus Siculis,* 525, and *fragosum Nebroden,* 527–528) explained to Grattius' mind how, though not of prepossessing appearance, these

from halters: the horse will show his vigour careering in a hundred race-courses and will work off his temper in the contest. Nor does his keep cost much: whatsoever of its own the barren earth or the small rivulet doth yield, is enough to support him. So too maintenance is easy for horses of the Bisaltae[a] near the Strymon: oh, that they could career along the highlands of Aetna, the sport which Sicilians make their own! What then, though their necks are ugly or though they have a thin spine curving along their back? Thanks to such steeds Acragas was praised in song by the Greeks,[b] thanks to such, the vanquished creatures of the wild quitted craggy Nebrodes.[c] Oh, how stalwart will he be in hunting whose herds shall yield colts that can be trained! Who could dare pit against them the horses of Epirus, which are distinguished by Greece with honour scarce deserved? The chestnut-brown horses of Macedonian[d] Ceraunus have scanty worth as hunters: but the herds of Cyrrha,[e] sacred to thee, O Apollo, have won high honour, whether the need be to yoke light vehicles or pull our (image-laden) cars in procession to

horses could be trained to win glory in the games of Greece (*cantatus Graiis Acragas*, 527).

[b] Pindar, *Olymp.* iii. 2, κλεινὰν Ἀκράγαντα (= Agrigentum in Sicily, now Girgenti). *Olympian Odes* ii. and iii. celebrate victories won by Theron of Acragas in chariot-racing; *Pyth.* vi. and *Isthm.* ii. similar victories by Xenocrates of Acragas.

[c] A Sicilian mountain. *Fragosum* indicates the serviceability of Sicilian horses as hunters on rocky ground.

[d] The fact that Pella was in Macedonia and the Ceraunian range in Epirus does not justify the epithet *Pellaei*; but, as Enk says, "poeta parum curat geographiam."

[e] Cyrrha or Cirrha, a seaport in Phocis, near Parnassus on which was the Delphic oracle of Apollo.

venanti melius pugnat color: optima nigr⟨a⟩
⟨cru⟩ra illi badiosque leg⟨a⟩nt et . . .
⟨et quo⟩rum fessas imitantur terga favillas.
⟨o quan⟩tum Italiae (sic di voluere) parentes
⟨praestant⟩ et terras omni praecepimus usu
⟨nostraque quam pernix⟩ collustrat prata ⟨iuventus⟩!

. . . .

536 melius A: mellis *Graevius*: vineus *Burman*: maelis *Birt*: medius *H. Schenkl.* nigr . . . A: nigri *Ald.*: nigra *Enk.*

537 ⟨cru⟩ra *Ulitius*: ⟨o⟩ra *Birt*: ⟨cu⟩ra *Vollmer.* leg⟨u⟩nt *Ald.*: leg⟨a⟩nt *Vollmer.* & avedon *videtur legi in* A: in pectore crines *edd.*: glaucosque periti *Birt.*

538 ⟨et quo⟩rum *Ald.* terda A: terga *Ald.*

539 ⟨o quan⟩tum *Ulitius.*

540 ⟨praestant⟩ et *Ulitius.*

541 ⟨nostraque quam pernix⟩ *Ulitius et post* prata *add.* ⟨iuventus⟩.

the shrines. For the hunter the horse's colour is a better ally (than its origin). His legs had best be black: let brown steeds be chosen . . . and those whose backs resemble spent embers. Oh, how much do the mares of Italy (such is heaven's will) excel in their foals; how much have we outstripped the world in every practice of life; and how active the young breed which brightens our meadows! . . .[a]

[a] A portion of the poem is lost—presumably of no great extent, as *restat* of 497 suggests that the author was drawing to a conclusion.

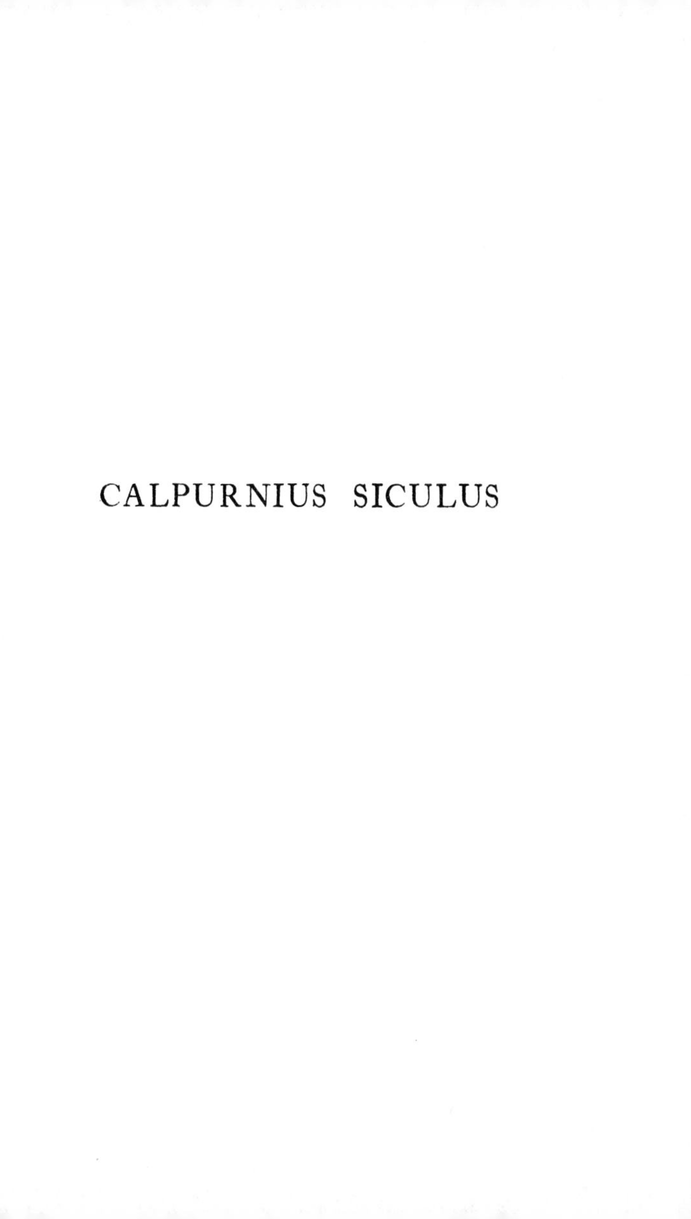

CALPURNIUS SICULUS

INTRODUCTION

TO CALPURNIUS SICULUS

The group of poems consisting of the pastorals by T. Calpurnius Siculus and by Nemesianus, the *Laus Pisonis* and two short Einsiedeln eclogues[a] present a bundle of interconnected and, though baffling, still not uninteresting problems. Certain questions arise at once. On separating the eclogues of Calpurnius from those of Nemesianus, to what dates should one assign their authors? Why did "Calpurnius Siculus" bear these two names? Had he a relationship with C. Calpurnius Piso, the conspirator of A.D. 65, to whom, according to most authorities, the *Laus Pisonis* was addressed?[b] If so, did Calpurnius Siculus write that panegyric in praise of Piso as his patron, and can "Meliboeus," the patron in two Calpurnian eclogues, have been the same Calpurnius Piso? If he was not, was he Seneca, or someone else? Again, can the Einsiedeln eclogues have emanated from the same hand as the Calpurnian eclogues or the *Laus Pisonis*, or are they products of a school of Neronian poets influenced by a transient passion for pastoral themes,

[a] For these other poems see pp. 289–315, pp. 319–335, and pp. 451–485 in this volume.

[b] See Introduction to the *Panegyric on Piso*, p. 289.

to which school M. Hubaux [a] has ascribed *Catalepton* IX bequeathed to us in the *Appendix Vergiliana*?

To most of these and to several related questions, the most contradictory answers have been given,[b] which cannot here be more than lightly touched upon. Since Haupt in his classic essay of 1854, *De carminibus bucolicis Calpurnii et Nemesiani*, divided,[c] on principles of style, the eleven eclogues which had often passed together under the name of Calpurnius Siculus into seven by him and the remaining four by Nemesianus, there has been no serious doubt about the gap in date between the two sets. Indeed, attention to certain *subscriptiones* and headings in the manuscripts (including a tell-tale blunder in *Riccardianus* 363, *Titi Calphurnii bucolicum carmen ad Nemesianum Karthaginiensem* [d]) ought to have led to an earlier separation of the poems by all editors. In any case, it is now generally agreed that Calpurnius Siculus belongs to the Neronian age and the

[a] In *Les thèmes bucoliques dans la poésie latine*, Brussels, 1930.

[b] For a résumé of the different hypotheses, see Groag, "C. Calpurnius Piso," P. W. *Realencycl.* III. (1899); Skutsch, "T. Calpurnius Siculus," *ibid.*; Schanz, *Gesch. der röm. Literatur*, II. 2; Clementina Chiavola, *Della vita . . . di Tito Calpurnio Siculo*, 1921.

[c] Haupt was the first to make clear the Neronian date of Calpurnius' seven eclogues; but the Aldine edition of 1534 prints the two sets separately—in fact *Nemesiani Bucolica* precede *Calpurnii Siculi Bucolica.*

[d] This confusion, which quite impossibly makes Nemesianus contemporary with Calpurnius, may be due either to a misreading of a double manuscript title, giving the names of both poets at the beginning of the eclogues, or to a corruption of words separating the two collections *finis bucolicorum Calphurnii Aurelii Nemesiani poetae Carthaginiensis egloga prima.*

eclogues of Nemesianus to the author of the *Cynegetica* in the third century A.D. Features of style and of metre, like the preservation of length in final -*o* and a paucity of elision, clearly distinguish the verse of Calpurnius from that of Nemesianus,[a] imitator of Calpurnius Siculus though he was. Some of the decisive points in favour of the Neronian date for Calpurnius consist in such allusions as those to the comet of 54 A.D. (i. 77–83), to the wooden amphitheatre of 57 A.D. (vii. 23–24) and to the young prince of golden promise, handsome, eloquent, divine,[b] who can be identified with no one so aptly as with Nero at the outset of his reign.

About the poet's name there is no means of determining whether it argues a relationship with the C. Calpurnius Piso to whom it is usually thought that the *Laus Pisonis* was addressed. One hypothesis suggests that he might have been a son of one of Piso's freedmen. Certainty is equally unattainable as to the meaning of the epithet "Siculus": it may indicate Sicilian origin in the geographical sense, but it may just as well record the literary debt of the eclogues to Theocritus. "Meliboeus," the patron in Calpurnius Siculus' first and fourth eclogues, is drawn as an actual personage in a position enabling him to recommend the author's verses to the emperor, and skilled in poetry and weather-lore. Sarpe's contention that this fits Seneca as the writer of tragedies and of the *Naturales Quaestiones* remains, on the whole, more plausible than the theory once maintained by Haupt and Schenkl, that the patron is the versatile Calpurnius Piso him-

[a] Birt, *Ad historiam hexametri latini symbola,* Bonn, 1877, 63.
[b] See i. 42–45, 84–88; iv. 84–87, 137; vii. 6, 83–84.

self. On the foundation of this latter theory was built the guess that the *Laus Pisonis* was the work of Calpurnius Siculus. But there is no consensus of opinion about the identification of "Meliboeus." While some have supposed him to represent Seneca or Calpurnius Piso, others have seen in him Columella[a] or M. Valerius Messala Corvinus,[b] consul with Nero in 58 A.D.: others still have dismissed all such identifications as sheer caprice. There is no more certainty about the two Einsiedeln eclogues. As the conjecture that they were composed by Piso[c] is countered with equal readiness to believe that Calpurnius wrote them,[d] discretion will acknowledge that there is not enough evidence to prove more than that they belong to the same literary environment as the Calpurnian poems.

The arrangement of the eclogues of Calpurnius does not follow the chronological order of composition. The four more strictly rural poems preceded in time the three which may be called "courtly" in virtue of their praises of the emperor (i, iv, vii): some, indeed, may have been written before Nero succeeded to the purple. There is much to be said for Haupt's suggested order of writing, namely, that the earliest and least finished is iii, the quarrel with Phyllis, which Scaliger considered an unamusing piece of clownishness; next, vi, a singing-match broken off by the umpire owing to the competitors' loss of temper—a weakish imitation of Theocritus iv and v and of Virgil's third eclogue; ii, somewhat

[a] Chytil, *Der Eklogendichter T. Calp. Siculus*, Znaim, 1894.
[b] Hubaux, *op. cit.*
[c] Groag, "Calp. Piso" in P. W. *Realencycl.*
[d] Hubaux, *op. cit.*

after the manner of Virgil's seventh eclogue, the amoebean praises of the pretty Crocale by two rivals, a herd and a gardener; and v, the aged Micon's expert advice to a young rustic on the management of flocks, based on *Georgics* III. 295–456. The three " courtly " poems, i, iv, vii, were written after these four and placed at the beginning, middle and end of the collection. In eclogue i, roughly modelled on Virgil's " Messianic " eclogue, the tuneful shepherds are imagined to discover a prophecy by Faunus heralding a renewal of the Golden Age under a new " Prince Charming," and they hope their poetry may reach the imperial ears through the good offices of their patron Meliboeus; in iv, the longest of the seven, hopes are expressed that the poetic eulogies on the emperor will be recommended to his majesty by Meliboeus, and it is indicated that some success had been already gained through his patronage; finally, in vii Corydon, newly back to the country from Rome, relates to Lycotas his impressions of the amphitheatre and of the handsome emperor.

Another feature of the arrangement may be noted. Eclogues ii, iv, vi are amoebean in form, and are sandwiched between eclogues which are not verse-dialogues in structure. In thought and manner, though there are, as we have seen, contemporary allusions, the pervasive influence is that of Virgil, and in a less degree that of Theocritus. The style also owes something to Ovid. Without being in the least deeply poetic, and in spite of the artificiality inherent in pastorals, the eclogues of Calpurnius breathe a rural atmosphere which makes them pleasant to read. Historically, they pass on the Virgilian tradition to Nemesianus.

EDITIONS

(The Eclogues of Calpurnius with those of Nemesianus.)

C. Schweynheim and A. Pannartz: (with Silius Italicus) eleven *Eclogae* under name of C. Calpurnius. Rome, 1471.

A. Ugoletus. *Calpurnii Siculi et Nemesiani bucolica.* Parma, *circ.* 1490. [For this edition Angelus Ugoletus used the codex of Thadeus Ugoletus: see *infra* under A in "Sigla."]

G. Logus. In edn. containing *Poetae tres egregii.* Aldus, Venice, 1534.

P. Burman. *Poet. Lat. Minores* I. Leyden, 1731.

J. C. Wernsdorf in *Poet. Lat. Minores,* Vol. II. Altenburg, 1780. [Wernsdorf gives an introductory essay and account of earlier editions.]

C. D. Beck. Recogn. annot. et gloss. instr. Leipzig, 1803.

C. E. Glaeser. *Calp. et Nemes. . . . recensuit.* Göttingen, 1842. [Glaeser's edn. made an advance in preferring the Codex Neapolitanus to the MSS. of the second group.]

E. Baehrens. In *Poet. Lat. Minores* III. Leipzig, 1881.

H. Schenkl. *Calp. et Nemes. bucol. rec.* Leipzig, 1885.

——. Re-edited in J. P. Postgate's *Corp. Poet. Lat.,* Vol. II. London, 1905.

C. H. Keene. *The Eclogues of Calpurnius Siculus and M. Aur. Olymp. Nemesianus* (introd., comment.). London, 1887.

CALPURNIUS SICULUS

C. Giarratano. *Calpurnii et Nemesiani Bucolica.* Naples, 1910.
——. *Calpurnii et Nemesiani Bucolica.* (Paravia ed.) Turin, 1924.

ENGLISH TRANSLATION

E. J. L. Scott. *The Eclogues of Calpurnius* (the seven in octosyll. verse). London, 1890.

RELEVANT WORKS

G. Sarpe. *Quaestiones philologicae.* Rostock, 1819. [Argues that " Meliboeus " = Seneca.]
M. Haupt. *De Carminibus bucolicis Calpurnii et Nemesiani.* Berlin, 1854. [Argues that " Meliboeus " = Calpurnius Piso.]
F. Chytil. *Der Eklogendichter T. Calpurnius Siculus und seine Vorbilder.* Znaim, 1894. [Identifies " Meliboeus " with Columella.]
F. Skutsch. Art. *Calpurnius Siculus.* P. W. *Realencycl.* col. 1401 *sqq.* 1899.
G. Ferrara. *Calpurnio Siculo e il Panegirico a Calpurnio Pisone.* Pavia, 1905.
Clementina Chiavola. *Della vita e dell' opera di Tito Calpurnio Siculo.* Ragusa, 1921.
J. Wight Duff. *A Literary History of Rome in the Silver Age*, pp. 330–338. London, 1927.
J. Hubaux. *Les thèmes bucoliques dans la poésie latine.* Brussels, 1930.
E. Cesareo. *La poesia di Calpurnio Siculo.* Palermo, 1931.

SIGLA

Used by H. Schenkl in Postgate's C. P. L.

The Best Group of MSS.

N = Neapolitanus 380, end of 14th cent. or beginning of 15th.
G = Gaddianus 90, 12 in Laurentian Library, Florence: 15th cent. [Akin to N, but somewhat inferior.][a]
A = Nicolaus Angelius' readings from the now lost MS. brought by Thadeus Ugoletus from Germany: they were entered in the year 1492 on the margin of codex Riccardianus 363 at Florence.
H = Readings in codex Harleianus 2578, 16th cent., apparently from a manuscript of Boccaccio's or the manuscript of Ugoletus.

Inferior MSS.

V = " vulgaris notae libri," of 15th or 16th cent. and interpolated. [Schenkl divides them into two classes :—

v = the slightly better;
w = the worst.
Giarratano dislikes Schenkl's subdivision into *v* and *w*.]

[a] Baehrens, the first collator of G, inclined to overvalue it: Schenkl, on the other hand, perhaps overvalued N. Giarratano pleads for a fair estimate of the merits of G, even if N is on the whole the better manuscript.

CALPURNIUS SICULUS

An Intervening Group

P = Parisinus 8049, 12th cent.; only reaches *Ecl.* IV. 12.

Exc. Par. = Extracts from Calpurnius and Nemesianus in two *florilegia*, liber Parisinus 7647, 12th cent., and liber Parisinus 17903, 13th cent.

[The texts of H. Schenkl and of Giarratano have been taken into account in determining the readings adopted.]

Bibliographical addendum (1982)

Hirtengedichte aus neronischer Zeit (with the Einsiedeln Eclogues), Latin with German translation, by D. Korzeniewski, Darmstadt 1971.

CALPURNIUS SICULUS

I

Corydon : Ornytus

C. Nondum solis equos declinis mitigat aestas,
quamvis et madidis incumbant prela racemis
et spument rauco ferventia musta susurro.
cernis ut ecce pater quas tradidit, Ornyte, vaccae
molle sub hirsuta latus explicuere genista?
nos quoque vicinis cur non succedimus umbris?
torrida cur solo defendimus ora galero?
O. hoc potius, frater Corydon, nemus, antra petamus
ista patris Fauni, graciles ubi pinea denset
silva comas rapidoque caput levat obvia soli,
bullantes ubi fagus aquas radice sub ipsa
protegit et ramis errantibus implicat umbras.
C. quo me cumque vocas, sequor, Ornyte; nam mea Leuce,
dum negat amplexus nocturnaque gaudia nobis,
pervia cornigeri fecit sacraria Fauni.
prome igitur calamos et si qua recondita servas.
nec tibi defuerit mea fistula, quam mihi nuper
matura docilis compegit harundine Ladon.

[1] declinis NA : declivis GV : declivus P.

CALPURNIUS SICULUS

ECLOGUE I

Corydon: Ornytus

C. Not yet doth the waning summer tame the sun's horses, although the wine-presses are squeezing the juicy clusters and a hoarse whisper comes from the foaming must as it ferments. Look, Ornytus, do you see how comfortably the cattle our father trusted us to watch have lain down to rest in the shaggy broom? Why do not we also make for the neighbouring shade? Why only a cap to protect our sunburnt faces?

O. Rather let us seek this grove, brother Corydon,—the grottoes over there, the haunt of Father Faunus, where the pine forest thickly spreads its delicate foliage and rears its head to meet the sun's fierce rays, where the beech shields the waters that bubble 'neath its very roots, and with its straying boughs casts a tangled shade.

C. Whithersoever you call me, Ornytus, I follow. For by refusing my embraces and denying me nightly pleasures, my Leuce has left it lawful for me to enter the shrine of horned Faunus. Produce your reed-pipes then and any song you keep stored for use. My pipe, you will find, will not fail you—the pipe that Ladon's skill fashioned for me lately out of a ripely seasoned reed.

O. et iam captatae pariter successimus umbrae.
sed quaenam sacra descripta est pagina fago,
quam modo nescio quis properanti falce notavit?
aspicis ut virides etiam nunc littera rimas
servet et arenti nondum se laxet hiatu?
C. Ornyte, fer propius tua lumina: tu potes alto
cortice descriptos citius percurrere versus;
nam tibi longa satis pater internodia largus
procerumque dedit mater non invida corpus.
O. non pastor, non haec triviali more viator,
sed deus ipse canit: nihil armentale resultat,
nec montana sacros distinguunt iubila versus.
C. mira refers; sed rumpe moras oculoque sequaci
quamprimum nobis divinum perlege carmen.
O. "qui iuga, qui silvas tueor, satus aethere Faunus,
haec populis ventura cano: iuvat arbore sacra
laeta patefactis incidere carmina fatis.
vos o praecipue nemorum gaudete coloni,
vos populi gaudete mei: licet omne vagetur
securo custode pecus nocturnaque pastor
claudere fraxinea nolit praesepia crate:
non tamen insidias praedator ovilibus ullas
afferet aut laxis abiget iumenta capistris.
aurea secura cum pace renascitur aetas
et redit ad terras tandem squalore situque
alma Themis posito iuvenemque beata sequuntur

25 codice GA.
35 fatis *Ulitius*: fagis *codd.*

[a] Themis, the Greek goddess of justice, was driven from earth by man's deterioration after the fabled Golden Age. Poets also called her "Astraea." *Squalore situque* conveys an image of the Goddess in her broken-hearted banishment, *squalore* suggesting mourning (as in Cicero often)

O. Now we have both come beneath the shade we sought. But what legend is this inscribed upon the hallowed beech, which someone of late has scored with hasty knife? Do you notice how the letters still preserve the fresh greenness of their cutting and do not as yet gape with sapless slit?

C. Ornytus, look closer. *You* can more quickly scan the lines inscribed on the bark high up. You have length enough of limb by the bounty of your father, and tall stature ungrudgingly transmitted by your mother.

O. These be no verses in wayside style by shepherd or by traveller: 'tis a very god who sings. No ring here of cattle-stall; nor do alpine yodellings make refrains for the sacred lay.

C. You tell of miracles! Away with dallying; and at once with eager eye read me through the inspired poem.

O. "I, Faunus of celestial birth, guardian of hill and forest, foretell to the nations that these things shall come. Upon the sacred tree I please to carve the joyous lay in which destiny is revealed. Rejoice above all, ye denizens of the woods; rejoice, ye peoples who are mine! All the herd may stray and yet no care trouble its guardian: the shepherd may neglect to close the pens at night with wattles of ash-wood—yet no robber shall bring his crafty plot upon the fold, or loosing the halters drive the bullocks off. Amid untroubled peace, the Golden Age springs to a second birth; at last kindly Themis,[a] throwing off the gathered dust of her mourning, returns to the earth; blissful ages attend the youthful prince who

and *situ* the dust that has gathered round her in her motionless grief. Now the poet pictures her springing to life again.

saecula, maternis causam qui vicit Iulis.
dum populos deus ipse reget, dabit impia victas
post tergum Bellona manus spoliataque telis
in sua vesanos torquebit viscera morsus
et, modo quae toto civilia distulit orbe,
secum bella geret: nullos iam Roma Philippos
deflebit, nullos ducet captiva triumphos;
omnia Tartareo subigentur carcere bella
immergentque caput tenebris lucemque timebunt.
candida pax aderit; nec solum candida vultu,
qualis saepe fuit quae libera Marte professo,
quae domito procul hoste tamen grassantibus armis
publica diffudit tacito discordia ferro:
omne procul vitium simulatae cedere pacis
iussit et insanos Clementia contudit enses.
nulla catenati feralis pompa senatus
carnificum lassabit opus, nec carcere pleno
infelix raros numerabit Curia patres.
plena quies aderit, quae stricti nescia ferri
altera Saturni referet Latialia regna,
altera regna Numae, qui primus ovantia caede
agmina, Romuleis et adhuc ardentia castris

45 vicit NP: vĭcit G: lusit V. iulis NGPV: in ulnis A.

55 quae *codd.*: ceu *Baehrens.*

57 iubila *Godofr. Hermann*: vulnera *Leo*: fulmina *H. Schenkl in not.*: publica *codd.* (*quo servato* confodit t. praecordia f. *Maehly*).

pleaded a successful case for the Iuli of the mother town (of Troy).[a] While he, a very God, shall rule the nations, the unholy War-Goddess shall yield and have her vanquished hands bound behind her back, and, stripped of weapons, turn her furious teeth into her own entrails; upon herself shall she wage the civil wars which of late she spread o'er all the world: no battles like Philippi shall Rome lament henceforth: no triumph o'er her captive self shall she celebrate. All wars shall be quelled in Tartarean durance: they shall plunge the head in darkness, and dread the light. Fair peace shall come, fair not in visage alone—such as she often was when, though free from open war, and with distant foe subdued,[b] she yet 'mid the riot of arms spread national strife[c] with secret steel. Clemency has commanded every vice that wears the disguise of peace to betake itself afar: she has broken every maddened sword-blade. No more shall the funereal procession of a fettered senate weary the headsman at his task; no more will crowded prison leave only a senator here and there for the unhappy Curia to count.[d] Peace in her fullness shall come; knowing not the drawn sword, she shall renew once more the reign of Saturn in Latium, once more the reign of Numa who first taught the tasks of peace to armies that rejoiced in slaughter and still drew from Romulus' camp their fiery spirit—Numa who first

[a] The reference is to an early oration by Nero on behalf of the inhabitants of Ilium (Suet. *Nero*, 7; Tac. *Ann.* xii. 58).

[b] This is best taken as a reference to the Roman invasion of Britain in Claudius' reign.

[c] If *publica* is right, *discordia* must be plural of *discordium*, a rare neuter form.

[d] There were many arbitrary executions ordered by Claudius.

pacis opus docuit iussitque silentibus armis
inter sacra tubas, non inter bella, sonare.
iam nec adumbrati faciem mercatus honoris
nec vacuos tacitus fasces et inane tribunal
accipiet consul; sed legibus omne reductis
ius aderit, moremque fori vultumque priorem
reddet et afflictum melior deus auferet aevum.
exultet quaecumque notum gens ima iacentem
erectumve colit boream, quaecumque vel ortu
vel patet occasu medione sub aethere fervit.
cernitis ut puro nox iam vicesima caelo
fulgeat et placida radiantem luce cometem
proferat? ut liquidum niteat sine vulnere plenus?
numquid utrumque polum, sicut solet, igne cruento
spargit et ardenti scintillat sanguine lampas?
at quondam non talis erat, cum Caesare rapto
indixit miseris fatalia civibus arma.
scilicet ipse deus Romanae pondera molis
fortibus excipiet sic inconcussa lacertis,
ut neque translati sonitu fragor intonet orbis
nec prius ex meritis defunctos Roma penates
censeat, occasus nisi cum respexerit ortus."

76 tepet *Postgate*: patet *codd.* fervit GP: servit NV.
79 niteat *Ulitius*: mutat NG: mittat P: nutet V *nonnulli*: nictet *Barth.*
87 prius a NG: pr̃ios = patrios *Diels apud Levy, Gnomon*, 1928, *pp.* 594 *sqq.*

[a] The comet of lines 77 *sqq.* is taken to be the comet of A.D. 54 which was believed to have heralded the death of

hushed the clash of arms and bade the trumpet sound 'mid holy rites instead of war. No more shall the consul purchase the form of a shadowy dignity or, silenced, receive worthless fasces and meaningless judgement-seat. Nay, laws shall be restored; right will come in fullest force; a kinder god will renew the former tradition and look of the Forum and displace the age of oppression. Let all the peoples rejoice, whether they dwell furthest down in the low south or in the uplifted north, whether they face the east or west or burn beneath the central zone. Do ye mark how already for a twentieth time the night is agleam in an unclouded sky, displaying a comet radiant in tranquil light? and how brightly, with no presage of bloodshed, twinkles its undiminished lustre? Is it with any trace of blood-hued flame that, as is a comet's way, it besprinkles either pole? does its torch flash with gory fire? But aforetime it was not such, when, at Caesar's taking off, it pronounced upon luckless citizens the destined wars.[a] Assuredly a very god shall take in his strong arms the burden of the massive Roman state so unshaken, that the world will pass to a new ruler without the crash of reverberating thunder, and that Rome will not regard the dead as deified in accord with merit ere the dawn of one reign can look back on the setting of the last."[b]

Claudius, Suet. *Claud.* 46. Similarly, Virgil, *Georg.* I. 487 *sqq.*, described the celestial portents accompanying the assassination of Julius Caesar.

[b] The words seem obscurely to imply a succession to imperial power without disturbance or interregnum. By one of his early acts, Nero proclaimed divine honours for his predecessor, Claudius.

C. Ornyte, iam dudum velut ipso numine plenum
me quatit et mixtus subit inter gaudia terror.
sed bona facundi veneremur numina Fauni.
O. carmina, quae nobis deus obtulit ipse canenda,
dicamus teretique sonum modulemur avena:
forsitan augustas feret haec Meliboeus ad aures.

II

Idas: Astacus: Thyrsis

Intactam Crocalen puer Astacus et puer Idas,
Idas lanigeri dominus gregis, Astacus horti,
dilexere diu, formosus uterque nec impar
voce sonans. hi cum terras gravis ureret aestas,
ad gelidos fontes et easdem forte sub umbras
conveniunt dulcique simul contendere cantu
pignoribusque parant: placet, hic ne vellera septem,
ille sui victus ne messem vindicet horti;
et magnum certamen erat sub iudice Thyrsi.
adfuit omne genus pecudum, genus omne ferarum
et quodcumque vagis altum ferit aera pennis.
convenit umbrosa quicumque sub ilice lentas
pascit oves, Faunusque pater Satyrique bicornes;
adfuerunt sicco Dryades pede, Naides udo,

[89] plenum NGP: plenus V.
II. [1] Crotalem N.
[5] ulmos PV: umbras NG.
[7] hic ne *Baehrens*: hic ut *codd.*
[11] quaecumque *codd.*: quodcumque *Ulitius.* altum *codd.*: avium *Barth.*

C. Ornytus, long has my very being, full of the god's own spirit, been thrilled with awe: mingling with my joy it steals upon me. Come, let us praise the kindly divinity of eloquent Faunus.

O. Let us rehearse the strains which the god himself has presented us to be sung; let us make music for it on our rounded reed-pipe. Haply these verses will be borne by Meliboeus [a] to our prince's ears.

ECLOGUE II

Idas: Astacus: Thyrsis

The virgin Crocale for long was loved by young Astacus and young Idas—Idas who owned a wool-bearing flock and Astacus a garden. Comely were both; and well-matched in tuneful song. These, upon a day when oppressive summer scorched the earth, met by a cooling spring—as it chanced, beneath the same shady tree; and made ready to contend together in sweet singing and for a stake. It was agreed that Idas, if beaten, should forfeit seven fleeces and Astacus the produce of his garden for the year. Great was the contest to which Thyrsis listened as their judge. Cattle of every kind were there, wild beasts of every kind, and every creature whose roving wing smites the air aloft. There met every shepherd who feeds his lazy flocks beneath the shady oak, and Father Faunus too and the twy-horned Satyrs. Dry-foot the wood-nymphs came; with watery feet the river-nymphs; and

[a] Meliboeus represents the poet's patron, an unidentified courtier, or Seneca according to some, or Calpurnius Piso according to others: see Introduction.

et tenuere suos properantia flumina cursus;
desistunt tremulis incurrere frondibus Euri
altaque per totos fecere silentia montes:
omnia cessabant, neglectaque pascua tauri
calcabant, illis etiam certantibus ausa est
daedala nectareos apis intermittere flores.
iamque sub annosa medius consederat umbra
Thyrsis et " o pueri me iudice pignora " dixit
" irrita sint moneo: satis hoc mercedis habeto,
si laudem victor, si fert opprobria victus.
et nunc alternos magis ut distinguere cantus
possitis, ter quisque manus iactate micantes."
nec mora: decernunt digitis, prior incipit Idas.
I. me Silvanus amat, dociles mihi donat avenas
et mea frondenti circumdat tempora taeda.
ille etiam parvo dixit mihi non leve carmen:
" iam levis obliqua crescit tibi fistula canna."
A. at mihi Flora comas pallenti gramine pingit
et matura mihi Pomona sub arbore ludit.
" accipe " dixerunt Nymphae " puer, accipe fontes:
iam potes irriguos nutrire canalibus hortos."
I. me docet ipsa Pales cultum gregis, ut niger albae
terga maritus ovis nascenti mutet in agna,

23 habete *Kempfer, Baehrens.*
31 crescat NGP: crescit V, *Keene*: crescet *Maehly.*
32 et APV: at NG. pallenti *De Rooy*: parienti *codd.* pingit NGP: cingit *Haupt.*
33 matura mihi *codd.* et mihi matura Pomona sub arbore plaudit *Haupt*: *alii alia.*

hastening torrents stayed their courses. East-winds ceased their rush upon the quivering leaves and so made deep silence over all the hills; everything stood idle; bulls trampled the pasture, which they heeded not; during that contest even the craftsman bee ventured to leave unvisited the nectar-yielding flowers. Now under the shade of an aged tree had Thyrsis taken his seat between them and said, "Lads, if I am to be judge, I urge that the stakes count for nothing. Let sufficient recompense be won herefrom, if the victor take the glory and the vanquished the reproach. Now, the better to mark off your alternate songs, raise in sudden movement each your hands three times."[a] They obey at once. The finger-trial decides, and Idas begins first.

I. I am loved of Silvanus—he gives me reeds to obey my will—he wreathes my temples with leaves of pine. To me while yet a boy he uttered this prophecy of no slender import: "Already upon the sloping reed there grows a slender pipe for thee."

A. But my locks doth Flora adorn with pale-green grasses, and for me Pomona in her ripeness sports beneath the tree. "Take, boy," said the nymphs, "take for yourself these fountains. Now with the channels you can feed your well-watered orchard."

I. Pales herself teaches me the breeding of a flock, how a black ram mated with a white ewe produces a changed colour in the fleece of the lamb born to

[a] In the Italian game of *mora*, the two players raise simultaneously any number of fingers they like, each calling out a number, which wins if it gives the correct sum of the fingers raised by both. Here the winner is the one who makes the best score out of three rounds.

quae neque diversi speciem servare parentis
possit et ambiguo testetur utrumque colore.
A. non minus arte mea mutabilis induit arbos
ignotas frondes et non gentilia poma:
ars mea nunc malo pira temperat et modo cogit
insita praecoquibus subrepere persica prunis.
I. me teneras salices iuvat aut oleastra putare
et gregibus portare novis, ut carpere frondes
condiscant primoque recidere gramina morsu,
ne depulsa vagas quaerat fetura parentes.
A. at mihi cum fulvis radicibus arida tellus
pangitur, irriguo perfunditur area fonte
et satiatur aqua, sucos ne forte priores
languida mutata quaerant plantaria terra.
I. o si quis Crocalen deus afferat! hunc ego terris,
hunc ego sideribus solum regnare fatebor;
secernamque nemus dicamque: "sub arbore numen
hac erit; ite procul—sacer est locus—ite profani."
A. urimur in Crocalen: si quis mea vota deorum
audiat, huic soli, virides qua gemmeus undas
fons agit et tremulo percurrit lilia rivo,
inter pampineas ponetur faginus ulmos.
I. ne contemne casas et pastoralia tecta:
rusticus est, fateor, sed non et barbarus Idas.
saepe vaporato mihi cespite palpitat agnus,
saepe cadit festis devota Parilibus agna.

41 genitalia *vulgo*: gentilia *w.*

47 vagos *codd.*: vagas *Scaliger.*

48 at NG: et PV. fulvis *codd.*: vulsis (*vel* furvis) *Burman.* arida NGA: altera PV.

49 panditur V.

54 decernamque NGPH: dicam namque V: discernamque *Glaeser*: secernamque *Gronov.*

55 hoc erit *codd.*: hac erit *Ulitius*: incolit *Giarratano.*

63 parilibus P: paliribus NG: palilibus V.

it, insomuch that the lamb cannot preserve the appearance of the sire so different from its dam, and yet testifies to both by varied colour.

A. No less transformable by my cunning, the tree puts on a dress of alien leaves and fruits of a diverse species. My cunning now crosses pears with apples and anon constrains engrafted peaches to supplant the early plums.

I. It is my joy to lop branches from tender willow or wild olive and carry them to the young flocks, that they may learn to nibble the leaves and crop the herbage with early bite, lest the lambs though weaned may follow their straying dams.

A. But I, when I plant tawny roots in the parched ground, drench the flower-bed with a welling flood and give it water in plenty lest haply the slips droop with the change of soil and feel the need of their former moisture.

I. Oh, if some god bring me Crocale here, him will I acknowledge sole ruler of earth and stars. Unto him will I hallow a grove and say, "Beneath this tree a divinity shall dwell. Begone, ye uninitiated, begone far hence, 'tis holy ground."

A. I burn with love for Crocale: if any of the gods hear my prayer, to him alone shall be dedicated a beechen bowl among the vine-clad elms, where the sparkling brook speeds its waters, where it flows among the lilies with its rippling stream.

I. Scorn not the cottage and a shepherd's homestead. Idas is a rustic, I allow; but he is not a savage too. Oft on the altar of smoking peat writhes the lamb offered by me, oft in death falls the ewe-lamb devoted at the festival of Pales.

A. nos quoque pomiferi laribus consuevimus horti
mittere primitias et fingere liba Priapo,
rorantesque favos damus et liquentia mella;
nec fore grata minus, quam si caper imbuat aras.
I. mille sub uberibus balantes pascimus agnas,
totque Tarentinae praestant mihi vellera matres;
per totum niveus premitur mihi caseus annum:
si venias, Crocale, totus tibi serviet hornus.
A. qui numerare velit quam multa sub arbore nostra
poma legam, tenues citius numerabit harenas.
semper holus metimus, nec bruma nec impedit aestas:
si venias, Crocale, totus tibi serviet hortus.
I. quamvis siccus ager languentes excoquat herbas,
sume tamen calathos nutanti lacte coactos:
vellera tunc dabimus, cum primum tempus apricum
surget et a tepidis fiet tonsura Kalendis.
A. at nos, quos etiam praetorrida munerat aestas,
mille renidenti dabimus tibi cortice Chias,
castaneasque nuces totidem, cum sole Decembri
maturis nucibus virides rumpentur echinni.

65 figere NGPA : fundere V : fingere *edd. ant.*
67 sunt NGP : fore *vel* fere V.
71 annus *vulgo* : hornus *cod. Titii.*, *edd. ant.*

[a] Flora, Pomona and Priapus are the "Lares" of the garden.

A. I too have been wont to offer first-fruits to the gods [a] who protect my apple-orchard and to mould for Priapus cakes of sacrifice. Dripping combs of trickling honey I present—nor think they shall be less acceptable to heaven than a goat's blood staining the altar.

I. A thousand lambs I feed which bleat beneath their mother's teats; as many Tarentine ewes yield me their fleeces.[b] Throughout the year I press the snow-white cheese: if you come, Crocale, the whole produce of this year will be at your command.

A. He who would count what multitude of apples I gather under my trees will sooner count fine sand. Ever am I plucking the green fruits of the earth—neither midwinter nor summer stays me. If you come, Crocale, the whole garden will be at your command.

I. Although the parched field is withering the drooping grass, yet accept from me pails of quivering curdled milk. Fleeces will I give in the early days of spring sunshine so soon as sheep-shearing starts with the temperate kalends.[c]

A. But I who receive gifts even from the scorching summer will give you a thousand Chian figs of glistening skin, and as many chestnuts, when the December sun ripens the nuts and their green husks burst.

[b] Sheep from the district of Tarentum in South Italy were famed for the good quality of their wool: Varro, *R.R.*, II. ii. 18; Columella, *R.R.*, VII, ii. 3; iv. 3: *cf.* Horace's reference to the valuable fleeces of sheep pasturing near the neighbouring river, the Galaesus, *Od.* II. vi. 10.

[c] The moderately warm weather in the months between the spring equinox and midsummer is recommended for shearing by Varro, *R.R.* II. xi. 6.

I. num, precor, informis videor tibi? num gravis annis?
decipiorque miser, quotiens mollissima tango
ora manu primique sequor vestigia floris
nescius et gracili digitos lanugine fallo?
A. fontibus in liquidis quotiens me conspicor, ipse
admiror totiens. etenim sic flore iuventae
induimur vultus, ut in arbore saepe notavi
cerea sub tenui lucere cydonia lana.
I. carmina poscit amor, nec fistula cedit amori.
sed fugit ecce dies revocatque crepuscula vesper.
hinc tu, Daphni, greges, illinc agat Alphesiboeus.
A. iam resonant frondes, iam cantibus obstrepit arbos:
i procul, o Doryla, plenumque reclude canalem,
et sine iam dudum sitientes irriget hortos.—
vix ea finierant, senior cum talia Thyrsis:
" este pares et ob hoc concordes vivite; nam vos
et decor et cantus et amor sociavit et aetas."

III

Iollas: Lycidas

I. Numquid in hac, Lycida, vidisti forte iuvencam
valle meam? solet ista tuis occurrere tauris,
et iam paene duas, dum quaeritur, eximit horas;
nec tamen apparet. duris ego perdita ruscis

96 hic procul P. o GV: y N: et P: i *Haupt.* primumque *codd.*: plenumque *Haupt, H. Schenkl*: rivumque *Baehrens*: pronumque *C. Schenkl.* canalem PV: canale NG: canali *Baehrens.*

I. Tell me, pray, you do not think me uncomely, do you? not laden with years? Is it my ill fortune to be deceived whenever my hand touches my tender cheeks and when unconsciously I trace the marks of my first bloom and beguile my fingers with the slender down?

A. Whenever I see my image in the clear stream I wonder at myself. For my visage clothes itself with the bloom of youth in like manner as I have oft remarked wax-like quinces glistening under the delicate down upon their tree.

I. Love calls for song; nor is the pipe unequal to the call of love; but lo! the day departs and evening brings the gloaming back. On this side, Daphnis, drive the flocks—on that let Alphesiboeus drive them home.

A. Now are the leaves a-rustling; now the forest drowns our song. Go yonder, Dorylas, go; and open full the channel. Let it water the garden-plots which have thirsted so long.

Scarce had they finished so, when Thyrsis full of years gave judgement thus: "Be equal: live therefore in amity; for beauty and song, love and youth, have made you comrades both."

ECLOGUE III

Iollas: Lycidas

I. Have you chanced, Lycidas, to see a heifer of mine in this vale? She is wont to go to meet your bulls. By now the search for her has wasted nearly two hours; and in spite of all she is not to be seen. For long have my legs been hurt by the rough

iam dudum nullus dubitavi crura rubetis
scindere, nec quicquam post tantum sanguinis egi.
L. non satis attendi: nec enim vacat. uror, Iolla,
uror, et immodice: Lycidan ingrata reliquit
Phyllis amatque novum post tot mea munera Mopsum.
I. mobilior ventis o femina! sic tua Phyllis:
quae sibi, nam memini, si quando solus abesses,
mella etiam sine te iurabat amara videri.
L. altius ista querar, si forte vacabis, Iolla.
has pete nunc salices et laevas flecte sub ulmos.
nam cum prata calent, illic requiescere noster
taurus amat gelidaque iacet spatiosus in umbra
et matutinas revocat palearibus herbas.
I. non equidem, Lycida, quamvis contemptus, abibo.
Tityre, quas dixit, salices pete solus et illinc,
si tamen invenies, deprensam verbere multo
huc age; sed fractum referas hastile memento.
nunc age dic, Lycida: quae noxam magna tulere
iurgia? quis vestro deus intervenit amori?
L. Phyllide contentus sola (tu testis, Iolla)
Callirhoen sprevi, quamvis cum dote rogaret:
en, sibi cum Mopso calamos intexere cera
incipit et puero comitata sub ilice cantat.

[5] nullus *Heinsius*: nullis *codd.*
[18] quavis NG: quamvis PV. contemptus P: contentus NG V *nonnulli*.
[22] vos tam PV: nos tam G: noxam *Baehrens*.

---

[a] *Palearia*, strictly the dewlap or skin hanging from the neck of oxen, is loosely used here for mouth and throat.

broom and yet I have nowise shrunk from letting the bramble thickets scratch them: and after so much loss of blood I have effected nothing.

L. I paid not enough heed; for I have not the time. I burn, I burn with love, Iollas—beyond all measure. Phyllis has left her Lycidas ungratefully, and after all my presents has found a new lover in Mopsus.

I. O woman more inconstant than the wind! Is it thus with your Phyllis, who, I remember, when you alone were absent, would swear that without you honey itself seemed bitter?

L. These troubles I will tell more fully, when you chance to have leisure, Iollas. Search now these willows, and turn beneath the elms on the left. For there, when 'tis hot in the meadows, my bull loves to rest, as he reclines his great bulk in the cool shade, and in his mouth chews the cud after his morning's grazing.[a]

I. No, Lycidas, I will not go away, though thus mocked by you. Tityrus,[b] by yourself make for those willows he spoke of, and if indeed you find the heifer, catch her and drive her thence with many a blow here; but remember to bring back your broken crook. Come now, Lycidas, tell me. What great quarrel has brought the mischief? What god has come to sunder the love of you two?

L. Content with only Phyllis (you are my witness, Iollas), I spurned Callirhoe although she asked my love with a dowry to offer. Then, lo! Phyllis begins to take Mopsus' aid in joining reeds with wax and she sings beneath the oak attended by the youth.

[b] Iollas bids his attendant search for the missing heifer, while he stays behind to hear about Lycidas' quarrel with his sweetheart. Similarly in Theocr. *Idyll.* III. 1 *sqq.* it is Tityrus who has to work while his master indulges in love and song.

haec ego cum vidi, fateor, sic intimus arsi,
ut nihil ulterius tulerim. nam protinus ambas
diduxi tunicas et pectora nuda cecidi.
Alcippen irata petit dixitque: " relicto,
improbe, te, Lycida, Mopsum tua Phyllis amabit."
nunc penes Alcippen manet; ac ne forte negetur,
a! vereor; nec tam nobis ego Phyllida reddi
exopto quam cum Mopso iurgetur anhelo.
I. a te coeperunt tua iurgia; tu prior illi
victas tende manus; decet indulgere puellae,
vel cum prima nocet. si quid mandare iuvabit,
sedulus iratae contingam nuntius aures.
L. iam dudum meditor, quo Phyllida carmine placem.
forsitan audito poterit mitescere cantu;
et solet illa meas ad sidera ferre Camenas.
I. dic age; nam cerasi tua cortice verba notabo
et decisa feram rutilanti carmina libro.
L. " has tibi, Phylli, preces iam pallidus, hos tibi cantus
dat Lycidas, quos nocte miser modulatur acerba,
dum flet et excluso disperdit lumina somno.
non sic destricta marcescit turdus oliva,
non lepus, extremas legulus cum sustulit uvas,
ut Lycidas domina sine Phyllide tabidus erro.
te sine, vae misero, mihi lilia nigra videntur

[30] deduxi V.
[33] negetur NGP : vagetur V.
[35] cum G : quod NPHV.
[47] excluso NGP : excusso V. disperdit NGPH : dispergit V : distergit *Scaliger*.

When I saw this, I own, such fire I felt within that I could endure no more: at once I tore open both her vests and beat her naked breast. In fury she went to Alcippe, saying as she went, "Spiteful Lycidas, your Phyllis will abandon you and give her love to Mopsus." And now in Alcippe's house she stays; and oh, I fear that entry will be refused me. But more than I desire to have Phyllis restored to me, do I pant[a] to see her quarrel with Mopsus.

I. It was with you that your quarrel began. You must be the first to stretch out to her your hands in surrender. It is fitting to show indulgence to a girl, even when she is the aggressor. If you please to send any word to her, I as your messenger will take care to win your angry mistress' ear.

L. Long have I been pondering with what song I am to pacify Phyllis. Mayhap, when she hears my lay, she can be softened: and it is her way to laud my poetry to the stars.

I. Come, speak—for I will carve your words upon the bark of the cherry-tree and then cut away the lines on the red rind and take them to her.

L. "These prayers, Phyllis, your Lycidas, now wan with grief, despatches to you, this song which in misery he plays through the painful night, weeping the while and by banishment of sleep doing despite to his eyes. No thrush grows thin so much when the olive-tree is stripped, nor hare when the gleaner has gathered the last grapes, as I, Lycidas, have pined a-wandering without Phyllis for my queen. Without you (poor wretch that I am!), lilies seem black to

[a] *anhelo* might be an adjective—"the wheezy Mopsus": *exopto* would then govern first an infinitive (*reddi*) and secondly a subjunctive (*iurgetur*).

nec sapiunt fontes et acescunt vina bibenti.
at si tu venias, et candida lilia fient
et sapient fontes et dulcia vina bibentur.
ille ego sum Lycidas, quo te cantante solebas
dicere felicem, cui dulcia saepe dedisti
oscula nec medios dubitasti rumpere cantus
atque inter calamos errantia labra petisti.
a dolor! et post haec placuit tibi torrida Mopsi
vox et carmen iners et acerbae stridor avenae?
quem sequeris? quem, Phylli, fugis? formosior illo
dicor, et hoc ipsum mihi tu iurare solebas.
sum quoque divitior: certaverit ille tot haedos
pascere quot nostri numerantur vespere tauri.
quid tibi quae nosti referam? scis, optima Phylli,
quam numerosa meis siccetur bucula mulctris
et quam multa suos suspendat ad ubera natos.
sed mihi nec gracilis sine te fiscella salicto
texitur et nullo tremuere coagula lacte.
quod si dura times etiam nunc verbera, Phylli,
tradimus ecce manus: licet illae vimine torto,
si libet, et lenta post tergum vite domentur,
ut mala nocturni religavit bracchia Mopsi
Tityrus et furem medio suspendit ovili.
accipe, ne dubites, meruit manus utraque poenas.
his tamen, his isdem manibus tibi saepe palumbes,
saepe etiam leporem decepta matre paventem
misimus in gremium; per me tibi lilia prima
contigerunt primaeque rosae: vixdum bene florem

[68] gracili *edd. ant.*

[72] scilicet *codd.*: si libet *Burman*: seu licet *H. Schenkl*: sic licet *Giarratano.*

[75] dubita PV.

me, fountains lose their taste and wine as I drink turns sour. But if you come, lilies will grow white again, fountains taste aright and wine be sweet to drink. I am that Lycidas at whose singing you used to declare your joy, to whom you gave many a tender kiss, whose strains half-sung you did not hesitate to interrupt by seeking my lips as they strayed o'er the reed-pipe. O sorrow! and, after that, have you been pleased by the harsh voice of Mopsus, his lifeless song and the shriek of his strident pipe? Whom do you follow? and whom, Phyllis, do you avoid? I am called more comely than he, and that is but what you were wont to say to me on oath. Besides, I am richer; let him vie in pasturing as many kids as there are bulls of mine counted at even-tide. Why should I rehearse to you what you know? You are aware, darling Phyllis, how many heifers are milked over my pails, and how many have calves clinging to their teats. But when you are gone, I can weave no slender basket-work out of willow-withes: no milk quivers in its curdled form. But if even now, Phyllis, you are afraid of cruel blows, see, I surrender my hands: let them, if you choose, be bound with twisted osier and the tough vine-twig behind my back, as Tityrus once bound the knavish arms of your night-prowler Mopsus, and strung the thief up inside his sheepfold. Take them, be not slow; both hands have earned their punishment. Yet with these, yes, these same hands, have I many a time put turtle-doves or a frightened hare into your lap, after snaring their mother; through me it was your luck to get the earliest lilies and the earliest roses; scarce had the bee well partaken of the

degustarat apis, tu cingebare coronis.
aurea sed forsan mendax tibi munera iactat,
qui metere occidua ferales nocte lupinos
dicitur et cocto pensare legumine panem:
qui sibi tunc felix, tunc fortunatus habetur,
vilia cum subigit manualibus hordea saxis.
quod si turpis amor precibus, quod abominor, istis
obstiterit, laqueum miseri nectemus ab illa
ilice, quae nostros primum violavit amores.
hi tamen ante mala figentur in arbore versus:
'credere, pastores, levibus nolite puellis;
Phyllida Mopsus habet, Lycidan habet ultima rerum.' "—
nunc age, si quicquam miseris succurris, Iolla,
perfer et exora modulato Phyllida cantu.
ipse procul stabo vel acuta carice tectus
vel propius latitans vicina sepe sub horti.
I. ibimus: et veniet, nisi me praesagia fallunt.
nam bonus a! dextrum fecit mihi Tityrus omen,
qui redit inventa non irritus ecce iuvenca.

[80] degustabat *codd.*: degustarat *Heinsius*.
[97] a dextrum *Baehrens*: a dextro GP V *plerique*: a dextra H V *nonnulli*.

flower when you were crowned with chaplets. But perhaps he may lyingly boast to you of golden gifts—he, who, they say, gathers the funeral lupines [a] when night is far spent, and makes up for the lack of bread with a boiling of greens, who deems himself happy and blest by fate in the very hour when he grinds inferior barley with a mill his own hand works. But if (I pray, heaven forfend!) a base passion is an obstacle to these my pleadings, I will in my misery twine a noose from yonder oak-tree which first did outrage to our affection.[b] Yet, ere all is o'er, these lines shall be affixed upon the accursed tree: 'Shepherds, put not your trust in fickle maids. Phyllis is loved by Mopsus; the end of all claims Lycidas.'"—Come now, Iollas, if you have any help for misery, take this missive to Phyllis and entreat her with harmonious song. Myself I will stand apart, perhaps concealed by prickly reed-grass or hiding nearer beneath the neighbouring garden hedge.

I. I will go: and Phyllis will come, unless the portents cheat me. For the good Tityrus has brought me an omen—ah! a favourable one! Look, he returns successful, my heifer found.

[a] Lupines were served at feasts in honour of the dead, and were sometimes carried off by the poorer guests: *cf.* Tibull. I. v. 53–54. Their main use was to feed cattle.

[b] See 26–27.

IV

Meliboeus: Corydon: Amyntas

M. Quid tacitus, Corydon, vultuque subinde minaci
quidve sub hac platano, quam garrulus adstrepit umor,
insueta statione sedes? iuvat algida forsan
ripa levatque diem vicini spiritus amnis?
C. carmina iam dudum, non quae nemorale resultent,
volvimus, o Meliboee; sed haec, quibus aurea possint
saecula cantari, quibus et deus ipse canatur,
qui populos urbesque regit pacemque togatam.
M. dulce quidem resonas, nec te diversus Apollo
despicit, o iuvenis, sed magnae numina Romae
non ita cantari debent, ut ovile Menalcae.
C. quicquid id est, silvestre licet videatur acutis
auribus et nostro tantum memorabile pago;
nunc mea rusticitas, si non valet arte polita
carminis, at certe valeat pietate probari.
rupe sub hac eadem, quam proxima pinus obumbrat,
haec eadem nobis frater meditatur Amyntas,
quem vicina meis natalibus admovet aetas.
M. iam puerum calamos et odorae vincula cerae
iungere non cohibes, levibus quem saepe cicutis
ludere conantem vetuisti fronte paterna?
dicentem, Corydon, te non semel ista notavi:

3 insueta NGH: inseta P: infesta *cod. Vat. Urb.* 353. humida *codd.*: algida *Baehrens*: herbida *H. Schenkl.*

8 urbemque V.

12 *in hoc versu desinit* P.

14 nunc NG, *Exc. Par.*: dum V: nam *Baehrens*: non *C. Schenkl.*

ECLOGUE IV

Meliboeus : Corydon : Amyntas

M. Corydon, why sit you silent with a visage that bodes something ever and anon? Why sit you in an unwonted place, beneath this plane-tree at whose roots brawl the prattling waters? Maybe you like the watery bank, where the breeze from the neighbouring stream assuages the heat of day?

C. For long, Meliboeus, have I been pondering verses, verses of no woodland ring but fit to celebrate the golden age, to praise even that very god who is sovereign over nations and cities and toga-clad peace.[a]

M. Sweet of sound are your lays and 'tis not with cold disdain that Apollo looks upon you, young Corydon: but the divinities of mighty Rome are not to be extolled in the same style as the sheepfold of Menalcas.

C. Whate'er my song, though it seem boorish to a critic's ears and worthy of record only in my own village, yet, as things are, my awkwardness, even if lacking in poetry's polish and skill, must surely win approval for its loyalty. Beneath this same rock shaded by the nearest pine-tree, kindred strains to mine are composed by my brother Amyntas, whose neighbouring years bring his time of birth near to mine.

M. Ah! do you not now stop the lad from joining his reeds in bonds of fragrant wax, as with a father-like frown you often checked him when he tried to play on slender hemlock-stems? Not once alone, Corydon, have I remarked you giving advice like this:

[a] *Cf.* I. 42 *sqq.*

"frange, puer, calamos et inanes desere Musas;
i, potius glandes rubicundaque collige corna,
duc ad mulctra greges et lac venale per urbem
non tacitus porta. quid enim tibi fistula reddet,
quo tutere famem? certe mea carmina nemo
praeter ab his scopulis ventosa remurmurat echo."
C. haec ego, confiteor, dixi, Meliboee, sed olim:
non eadem nobis sunt tempora, non deus idem.
spes magis arridet: certe ne fraga rubosque
colligerem viridique famem solarer hibisco,
tu facis et tua nos alit indulgentia farre;
tu nostras miseratus opes docilemque iuventam
hiberna prohibes ieiunia solvere fago.
ecce nihil querulum per te, Meliboee, sonamus;
per te secura saturi recubamus in umbra
et fruimur silvis Amaryllidos, ultima nuper
litora terrarum, nisi tu, Meliboee, fuisses,
ultima visuri trucibusque obnoxia Mauris
pascua Geryonis, liquidis ubi cursibus ingens
dicitur occiduas impellere Baetis harenas.
scilicet extremo nunc vilis in orbe iacerem,
a dolor! et pecudes inter conductus Iberas
irrita septena modularer sibila canna;
nec quisquam nostras inter dumeta Camenas
respiceret; non ipse daret mihi forsitan aurem,
ipse deus vacuam, longeque sonantia vota

39–40 *vocabula* litora *et* ultima *traiecit Haupt* (*opusc.* I. 362).

"Boy, break your pipes, forsake the beggarly Muses. Go, gather acorns instead and red cornel-cherries; lead herds to the milking-pails; loud in your cry through the city carry your milk for sale. What will the pipe bring you to ward off famine? Of a truth, no one repeats my lay save the wind-sped echo from yonder crags."

C. This, I confess, I did say, Meliboeus; but it was long ago; our times are not the same now, our god is changed.[a] Hope wears a more radiant smile; in sooth, it is your doing that I no more gather strawberries and brambles, or assuage hunger with green mallow. Your kindness feeds us with grain. You, in pity for our means and quick-taught youth, stop us from dispelling hunger-pangs with beech-nuts in winter. Lo! 'tis thanks to you, Meliboeus, that no complaint passes our lips: thanks to you we recline well-fed in care-free shade, and enjoy the woodland of Amaryllis.[b] But for thee, Meliboeus, we should of late have looked upon the furthest, yea, the furthest shores of earth, Geryon's meadows exposed to the Moor's fury, where mighty Baetis,[c] they say, with flowing currents strikes upon the western sands. Doubtless should I now lie an outcast at the world's end, oh, woe! and, but an hireling, among Iberian flocks should be playing on sevenfold pipe my unavailing scrannel tunes: no one would give a glance at my muses among the thorn-bushes: he himself, our divine sovereign himself, mayhap would never lend a leisured ear to me, nor hear,

[a] *i.e.* an emperor has come to the throne, who favours poetry with his patronage.

[b] The reference is to Virgil's *formosam resonare doces Amaryllida silvas, Ecl.* i. 5.

[c] The Guadalquivir in Spain.

scilicet extremo non exaudiret in orbe.
sed nisi forte tuas melior sonus advocat aures
et nostris aliena magis tibi carmina rident,
vis, hodierna tua subigatur pagina lima?
nam tibi non tantum venturos dicere nimbos
agricolis qualemque ferat sol aureus ortum
attribuere dei, sed dulcia carmina saepe
concinis, et modo te Baccheis Musa corymbis
munerat et lauro modo pulcher obumbrat Apollo.
quod si tu faveas trepido mihi, forsitan illos
experiar calamos, here quos mihi doctus Iollas
donavit dixitque: "truces haec fistula tauros
conciliat: nostroque sonat dulcissima Fauno.
Tityrus hanc habuit, cecinit qui primus in istis
montibus Hyblaea modulabile carmen avena."
M. magna petis, Corydon, si Tityrus esse laboras.
ille fuit vates sacer et qui posset avena
praesonuisse chelyn, blandae cui saepe canenti
allusere ferae, cui substitit advena quercus.
quem modo cantantem rutilo spargebat acantho
Nais et implicitos comebat pectine crines.

53 dicere ventos N: discere ventos GH: dicere nimbos N[2]: noscere nimbos V *plerique*.

63 modulabile carmen V: carmen mulamine (modulabile m^2) N: carmen modulavit G: carmen modulatus *H. Schenkl.*

---

[a] For theories identifying Meliboeus see Introduction. It has been pointed out there that some take this passage as a reference to Seneca.

[b] The reference is to tragedy (the ivy being sacred to Bacchus) and to lyric poetry (the laurel being sacred to Apollo).

in sooth, the distant sound of my prayers at earth's furthest ends. But if perchance no sweeter melody attract your ear, if the songs of others fail to charm you more than mine, will you let the page I compose to-day be corrected by your critical file? For not only have the gods given to you to tell husbandmen of coming rain-storms and of the kind of sunrise a golden sunset offers, but you are often the singer of sweet poetry,[a] and now the Muse rewards you with Bacchic ivy-clusters, now fair Apollo shades your brow with laurel.[b] But if you would show favour to my nervous attempts, perhaps I might make trial of those reeds which skilful Iollas [c] presented to me yesterday with the words, "This pipe wins over savage bulls, and makes sweetest melody to our own Faunus. It once was owned by Tityrus, who among these hills of yours was the first to sing his tuneful lay on the Hyblaean pipe." [d]

M. You aim high, Corydon, if you strive to be Tityrus. He was a bard inspired, one who could on the reed-pipe outplay the lyre. Often, while he sang, beasts of the wild fawned in frolic near, and the oak came close and halted there: did he but sing, a Naiad would adorn him with red acanthus and dress with a comb his tangled locks.

[c] *Iollas*, according to Wernsdorf, stands for a scholar or poet who had prompted the writing of the Eclogues. Some have suggested one of Calpurnius' teachers, or even Theocritus—which conflicts with the idea that Tityrus is Virgil. Cesareo wisely refuses to identify Iollas, *La Poesia di Calp. Sic.*, p. 174.

[d] Ancient authority regarded the Tityrus of Virgil's *Eclogues* as representing the poet himself. The allusion in *Hyblaea* is to the pastoral poetry of the Sicilian Theocritus, which Virgil imitated: Virg. *Ecl.* X. 51, *carmina pastoris Siculi modulabor avena.*

C. est—fateor, Meliboee,—deus: sed nec mihi Phoebus
forsitan abnuerit; tu tantum commodus audi:
scimus enim, quam te non aspernetur Apollo.
M. incipe, nam faveo; sed prospice, ne tibi forte
tinnula tam fragili respiret fistula buxo,
quam resonare solet, si quando laudat Alexin.
hos potius, magis hos calamos sectare: canales
exprime qui dignas cecinerunt consule silvas.
incipe, ne dubita. venit en et frater Amyntas:
cantibus iste tuis alterno succinet ore.
ducite, nec mora sit, vicibusque reducite carmen;
tuque prior, Corydon, tu proximus ibis, Amynta.
C. ab Iove principium, si quis canit aethera, sumat,
si quis Atlantiaci pondus molitur Olympi:
at mihi, qui nostras praesenti numine terras
perpetuamque regit iuvenili robore pacem,
laetus et augusto felix arrideat ore.
A. me quoque facundo comitatus Apolline Caesar
respiciat, montes neu dedignetur adire,
quos et Phoebus amat, quos Iuppiter ipse tuetur:
in quibus Augustos visuraque saepe triumphos
laurus fructificat vicinaque nascitur arbos.

76 hos potius V: hospicius NG. magnos calamos *Leo*: magis hos calamos NG: calamos magis hos V: magis hos calamo *Baehrens*.
77 exprime *Leo*: et preme NG: prome *vel* pro me V: per me A, *Wernsdorf*: primi *Bursian*.
80 dicite *codd.* (*fortasse recte, cf. V.* 81 *audiat aut dicat*): ducite *Barth*.
82 canit V: canat N (*corr. m*[2]) G.
90 visuraque NG: visurus V: visurae *Barth*.

[a] Virg. *Ecl.* IV. 3, *si canimus silvas, silvae sint consule dignae.* The contrast is between the amatory poetry of Virgil's second eclogue entitled "Alexis," and the loftier tone of the fourth entitled "Pollio" after the consul of

C. He is, I own, a poet divine, Meliboeus, but mayhap Phoebus will not say me nay either: do you but favourably hear me; for we know how far Apollo is from slighting you.

M. Begin, my favour is with you; but take heed lest perchance your tinkling pipe breathe from boxwood as frail as is its usual sound whene'er the praise of Alexis is the theme. Rather these reeds, these far more you must pursue: press the pipes which sang of woods worthy a consul.[a] Begin; have no doubt. See, your brother Amyntas comes too. In alternate refrain his voice will answer your verses. Draw out your lay: dally not: in turns resume the song. You first, Corydon, and you will come next, Amyntas.

C. From Jove let every bard begin,[b] whoso sings of the sky, whoso essays to describe the Olympian burden which Atlas bears. For myself, may I win a glad propitious smile from the imperial lips of him whose incarnate godhead rules our lands and whose youthful prowess rules the eternal peace.

A. On me too may Caesar, with eloquent Apollo for comrade, look with favour: nor let him disdain to approach my hills which even Phoebus loves, which Jove himself protects; where blooms the laurel, destined to see many an imperial triumph, where rises too the laurel's companion-tree.[c]

40 B.C. and prophesying a golden age of peace. Here in Calpurnius the praises of Nero as "Caesar" correspond to the higher theme of the "Pollio."

[b] A quotation from Virg. *Ecl.* III. 60, which is in turn an echo of Theocr. XVII. 1.

[c] The oak, sacred to Jupiter, especially at the oracle of Dodona. With the laurel of victory there may be associated in the poet's mind the oak garland given for saving a citizen's life in battle.

C. ipse polos etiam qui temperat igne geluque,
Iuppiter ipse parens, cui tu iam proximus ipse,
Caesar, abes, posito paulisper fulmine saepe
Cresia rura petit viridique reclinis in antro
carmina Dictaeis audit Curetica silvis.
A. adspicis, ut virides audito Caesare silvae
conticeant? memini, quamvis urgente procella
sic nemus immotis subito requiescere ramis,
et dixi: "deus hinc, certe deus expulit euros."
nec mora; Parrhasiae sonuerunt sibila cannae.
C. adspicis, ut teneros subitus vigor excitet agnos?
utque superfuso magis ubera lacte graventur
et nuper tonsis exundent vellera fetis?
hoc ego iam, memini, semel hac in valle notavi
et venisse Palen pecoris dixisse magistros.
A. scilicet omnis eum tellus, gens omnis adorat,
diligiturque deis, quem sic taciturna verentur
arbuta, cuius iners audito nomine tellus
incaluit floremque dedit; cui silva vocato
densat odore comas, stupefacta regerminat arbos.
C. illius ut primum senserunt numina terrae,
coepit et uberior sulcis fallentibus olim
luxuriare seges tandemque legumina plenis
vix resonant siliquis; nec praefocata malignum
messis habet lolium nec inertibus albet avenis.

93 *ad finem versus* ipse V: esse NG: ecce *Leo.*
94 habes NGV: abes H: ades *Burman*: aves *D'Orville*. ovas *Baehrens.*
101 Parrhasiae *Heinsius*: pharsalie N: farsalie G: pharsaliae AV *plerique.* sonuerunt AH: solverunt *codd. plerique.*

---

[a] Baehrens' allotment of stanzas is followed here. Giarratano gives 92–96 to Corydon and thinks that Amyntas' corresponding stanza has dropped out here: he also postulates transpositions later in the poem. H. Schenkl gives 87–96 to Amyntas so that he inverts Baehrens'

C. Even he, controller of the heavens in heat and cold, our father Jupiter himself, to whom you yourself, Caesar, now stand next, doth oft lay down his thunderbolt awhile to visit Cretan meads, and, in some verdant grot reclining, 'mid Dicte's forests listens to Curetic lays.[a]

A. Do you see how the green woods are hushed at the sound of Caesar's name? I remember how, despite the swoop of a storm, the grove, even as now, sank sudden into peace with boughs at rest. And I said, "A god, surely a god has driven the east winds hence." Forthwith the Parrhasian[b] reeds let their notes go free.

C. Do you see how a sudden vigour thrills the tender lambs, how the ewe's teats are more heavily laden with abundant milk, how, just after shearing, the fleeces of the dams grow in luxuriant waves? This once ere now, I mind me, I noted in this valley, and how the shepherds said, "Pales has come."

A. Yes, and him doth all the earth and every nation adore. He is beloved of the gods; as you see, the arbutus-tree pays him silent homage; at the sound of his name the sluggish earth has warmed to life and yielded flowers; invoke him, and in his honour the wood spreads thick its perfumed foliage, and the spellbound tree breaks into bud again.

C. As soon as the earth felt his divine influence, crops began to come in richer abundance, where furrows erstwhile disappointed hope; at length the beans scarce rattle in their well-filled pods: no harvest is choked with the spread of the barren tare, or whitens with unproductive oats.

allotment of stanzas from 97 to 121: he marks a missing stanza by Amyntas after verse 121.

[b] Parrhasia, in Arcadia, was one of Pan's haunts.

A. iam neque damnatos metuit iactare ligones
fossor et invento, si fors dedit, utitur auro;
nec timet, ut nuper, dum iugera versat arator,
ne sonet offenso contraria vomere massa,
iamque palam presso magis et magis instat aratro.
C. ille dat, ut primas Cereri dare cultor aristas
possit et intacto Bromium perfundere vino,
ut nudus ruptas saliat calcator in uvas
utque bono plaudat paganica turba magistro,
qui facit egregios ad pervia compita ludos.
A. ille meis pacem dat montibus: ecce per illum,
seu cantare iuvat seu ter pede lenta ferire
gramina, nullus obest: licet et cantare choreis
et cantus viridante licet mihi condere libro,
turbida nec calamos iam surdant classica nostros.
C. numine Caesareo securior ipse Lycaeus
Pan recolit silvas et amoena Faunus in umbra
securus recubat placidoque in fonte lavatur
Nais et humanum non calcatura cruorem
per iuga siccato velox pede currit Oreas.

124 saliat A *v*: psal(l)at NG*w*.
129 gramina *edd. antiq.*: carmina *codd.*
132 Lycaeas *Heinsius.*
134 placitoque *Heinsius*: placido quin *Haupt.*

---

[a] Wernsdorf takes *damnatos* as "wretched," "miserable," because involving toil ("pro infelicibus, laboriosis, ut *invisam* [*sc. fossori*] *terram*, Hor. *Od.* III. xviii. 15–16"). *Cf.* "hateful nights," *damnatae noctes*, Propert. V. xi. 15. But a more likely sense is "criminal," "condemned," as a transferred epithet: *i.e.* the spade is now innocent because, even if it unearths treasure, this no longer brings a prosecution on the digger.

A. No more does the digger dread to ply the criminal spade:[a] what treasure-trove of gold chance offers him he puts to use. Nor, as of late, does the ploughman, while turning up his acres, fear that an ingot may ring against the impact of his ploughshare;[b] now openly he pushes on more and more with plough deep-driven.

C. By his favour[c] the cultivator can give to Ceres the first corn-ears and to Bromius pour libation of wine till now unbroached; thanks to him the light-clad vintager tramples the bursting clusters and the village throng applauds their good mayor, who holds magnificent games at the meeting of the highways.[d]

A. He it is who bestows peace on my hills. See, it is through him that no one prevents me, if 'tis my pleasure to sing or to tread the sluggish grass in triple measure. In choral dance too may I sing, and I may preserve my songs on the green bark; and no more do boisterous trumpets drown our reed-pipes' note.

C. Emboldened by Caesar's divine protection, Lycean Pan himself revisits the groves and Faunus reclines untroubled in the lovely shade. The Naiad bathes in the unruffled stream and, free from the risk of treading on human gore, the Oread courses swiftly o'er mountain-ranges, her foot unstained.

[b] Treasure-trove had sometimes led to dangerous difficulties with the imperial authorities: see Juv. IV. 37 *sqq*.

[c] *i.e.* under the emperor's auspices, agriculture is in a position to honour the gods aright.

[d] The *Compitalia*, celebrated at the shrines where cross-roads met, were held at a date between the *Saturnalia* (Dec. 17) and Jan. 5. See W. Warde Fowler, *Roman Festivals*, 1899, pp. 279–80.

A. di, precor, hunc iuvenem, quem vos (neque fallor) ab ipso
aethere misistis, post longa reducite vitae
tempora vel potius mortale resolvite pensum
et date perpetuo caelestia fila metallo:
sit deus et nolit pensare palatia caelo!
C. tu quoque mutata seu Iuppiter ipse figura,
Caesar, ades seu quis superum sub imagine falsa
mortalique lates (es enim deus): hunc, precor, orbem,
hos, precor, aeternus populos rege! sit tibi caeli
vilis amor coeptamque, pater, ne desere pacem!
M. rustica credebam nemorales carmina vobis
concessisse deos et obesis auribus apta;
verum, quae paribus modo concinuistis avenis,
tam liquidum, tam dulce cadunt, ut non ego malim,
quod Paeligna solent examina lambere nectar.
C. o mihi quae tereti decurrunt carmina versu
tunc, Meliboee, sonent si quando montibus istis
dicar habere Larem, si quando nostra videre
pascua contingat! vellit nam saepius aurem
invida paupertas et dicit: " ovilia cura! "
at tu, si qua tamen non aspernanda putabis,
fer, Meliboee, deo mea carmina: nam tibi fas est

[142] tu quoque mutata *codd.*: tu commutata *Haupt*: tu modo mutata *Baehrens.*

[144] etenim NG: es enim *Glaeser.*

[150] canunt *codd.*: cadunt *Burman.*

[151] solent NGAH: sonant V: legunt *edd. antiq.*

[152] o mihi HV: olim NG. quae teriti G: quam tenero V: quae tereti *Glaeser* (*post hunc versum H. Schenkl lacunam statuit*).

[155] contingat NG: contigerit V, *Baehrens.*

A. O ye gods, I pray you, recall only after a long span of life this youth, whom ye, I know it well, have sent us from heaven itself: or rather untwine his allotted skein of mortality and grant him celestial threads of the metal of eternity. Let him be a god and yet loath to exchange his palace for the sky.[a]

C. Thou too,[b] Caesar, whether thou art Jupiter himself on earth in altered guise, or one other of the powers above concealed under an assumed mortal semblance (for thou art very God)—rule, I pray thee, this world, rule its peoples for ever! Let love of heaven count as nought with thee: abandon not, O Sire, the peace thou hast begun!

M. I used to think they were but rustic lays which the sylvan deities bestowed on you—lays fit for cloddish ears; but what you have even now sung on well-matched pipes has so clear, so sweet a fall that I would not liefer sip the nectarous honey which Pelignian swarms are wont to sip.[c]

C. Oh! the songs of mine which run in humble verse would then, my Meliboeus, resound, if ever on these hills I were called the owner of a homestead, if ever I had the fortune to see pastures of my own. Too often does malicious poverty pluck my ear and say, "The sheepfold is your task." But you, Meliboeus, if in spite of all you think that any of my poems are not to be disdained, then take them to the Emperor-God. For you have the right to visit

[a] *i.e.* let him remain a divine emperor in his residence on the Palatine Hill.

[b] *quoque* is justified, as the last stanza is addressed to all the gods and this one to Caesar, *i.e.* Nero.

[c] The allusion is to Ovid, who was born at Sulmo in the district of the Peligni.

sacra Palatini penetralia visere Phoebi.
tum mihi talis eris, qualis qui dulce sonantem
Tityron e silvis dominam deduxit in urbem
ostenditque deos et " spreto " dixit " ovili,
Tityre, rura prius, sed post cantabimus arma."
A. respiciat nostros utinam fortuna labores
pulchrior et meritae faveat deus ipse iuventae!
nos tamen interea tenerum mactabimus haedum
et pariter subitae peragemus fercula cenae.
M. nunc ad flumen oves deducite: iam fremit aestas,
iam sol contractas pedibus magis admovet umbras.

V

Micon

Forte Micon senior Canthusque, Miconis alumnus,
torrentem patula vitabant ilice solem,
cum iuveni senior praecepta daturus alumno
talia verba refert tremulis titubantia labris:
" quas errare vides inter dumeta capellas
canaque lascivo concidere gramina morsu,
Canthe puer, quos ecce greges a monte remotos

[162] deos *codd.*: deis *Heinsius.*
[168] fremit NV: premit *Heinsius*: furit *Maehly.* aestus *Ulitius.*
V. [6] canaque V: vanaque NG. gramina GV, *Giarratano*: germina NH (*corr.* m^2), *Baehrens, H. Schenkl.*

the holy inner shrine of the Palatine Phoebus.[a] Then you shall be to me such as he was who brought Tityrus[b] of tuneful song from the woods to the queen of cities, showed him the divine powers, and said, "We will scorn the sheepfold, Tityrus, and sing first the countryside but, later, the weapons of war."

A. Oh, that a fairer fortune would look upon my labours and that the God in person would show favour to deserving youth! Yet meanwhile we will slay a tender kid and prepare withal the courses of a hasty meal.

M. Take forthwith the sheep to the river. Now 'tis the raging heat of summer: now the sun curtails the shadows and brings them closer to our feet.[c]

ECLOGUE V

Micon

It fell out that the aged Micon and Canthus, Micon's foster-son, were seeking shelter from the blazing sun beneath a spreading holm-oak, when to give counsel to his fosterling the old man with shaky lips uttered these faltering words:

"The she-goats you see straying among the thickets and cropping with playful bite the dew-glistening grass, the flocks, Canthus, my boy, which lo! you see have left the mountain-side and are

[a] The emperor was already associated with Apollo in verse 87. The palace was near the famous library of Apollo on the Palatine.

[b] Tityrus means Virgil: under the patronage of Maecenas he turned from the *Eclogues* (*e silvis*, 161) to the *Georgics* (*rura*, 163) and, later, to the *Aeneid* (*arma*, 163).

[c] *i.e.* it is the noontide of a summer day.

cernis in aprico decerpere gramina campo,
hos tibi do senior iuveni pater: ipse tuendos
accipe. iam certe potes insudare labori,
iam pro me gnavam potes exercere iuventam.
adspicis ut nobis aetas iam mille querellas
afferat et baculum premat inclinata senectus?
sed qua lege regas et amantes lustra capellas
et melius pratis errantes mollibus agnas,
percipe.
vere novo, cum iam tinnire volucres
incipient nidosque reversa lutabit hirundo,
protinus hiberno pecus omne movebis ovili.
tunc etenim melior vernanti germine silva
pullat et aestivas reparabilis incohat umbras,
tunc florent saltus viridisque renascitur annus,
tunc Venus et calidi scintillat fervor amoris
lascivumque pecus salientes accipit hircos.
sed non ante greges in pascua mitte reclusos,
quam fuerit placata Pales. tum cespite vivo
pone focum geniumque loci Faunumque Laresque
salso farre voca; tepidos tunc hostia cultros
imbuat: hac etiam, dum vivit, ovilia lustra.
nec mora, tunc campos ovibus, dumeta capellis
orto sole dabis, simul hunc transcendere montem
coeperit ac primae spatium tepefecerit horae.
at si forte vaces, dum matutina relaxat

21 silvae *codd.*: tiliae *Maehly*: saltus *Baehrens*: segetes *C. et H. Schenkl.*
32 relaxet G.

browsing on the herbage in the sunny meadow, these I, your aged sire, make over to you, while you are yet young. Take them into your own charge: now truly can you sweat o'er the task, now in my stead you can ply your active youth.

Do you see how the years now bring me a thousand plaints, and how the stoop of age leans on the staff? But learn the rules for your control over the she-goats which love the copses and over the lambs which stray to better purpose in the grassy meadows.

In the fresh spring-time when birds will be already starting to twitter and the returned swallow daubing its nest with mud, you are forthwith to shift the whole flock from its winter fold. For richer then sprouts the wood with fresh-growing buds, and, as it revives, makes the beginning of summer shade. Then the glades are in blossom and the green year is born again. Then is Venus' time, when sparkles the warm glow of love and the wanton herd welcomes the leaping he-goats. But do not turn loose the flocks and send them into the meadows till Pales has been propitiated. Then build an altar of fresh sods and with salted meal invoke the genius of the place and Faunus and the Lares. Then let a victim stain the knives warm with blood: with it too, while it yet lives, purify the sheepfold.[a] Thereafter, you will, without delay, let the sheep roam the meadows and the goats the thickets, when the sun has risen, as soon as he has begun to surmount the hill here and has warmed the course of the matin hour. But if you chance to have leisure, while the sun melts the frosts

[a] A lustration-ritual could be carried out by solemnly leading round the victim before it was sacrificed.

frigora sol, tumidis spumantia mulctra papillis
implebit quod mane fluet; rursusque premetur
mane quod occiduae mulsura redegerit horae.
parce tamen fetis: ne sint compendia tanti,
destruat ut niveos venalis caseus agnos;
nam tibi praecipuo fetura coletur amore.
te quoque non pudeat, cum serus ovilia vises,
si qua iacebit ovis partu resoluta recenti,
hanc umeris portare tuis natosque tepenti
ferre sinu tremulos et nondum stare paratos.
nec tu longinquas procul a praesepibus herbas
nec nimis amotae sectabere pabula silvae,
dum peragit vernum Iovis inconstantia tempus.
veris enim dubitanda fides: modo fronte serena
blandius arrisit, modo cum caligine nimbos
intulit et miseras torrentibus abstulit agnas.
  at cum longa dies sitientes afferet aestus
nec fuerit variante deo mutabile caelum,
iam silvis committe greges, iam longius herbas
quaere; sed ante diem pecus exeat: umida dulces
efficit aura cibos, quotiens fugientibus euris
frigida nocturno tanguntur pascua rore
et matutinae lucent in gramine guttae.
at simul argutae nemus increpuere cicadae,

[33] spument tibi V *plerique*: spumantia *Barth.*
[34] implebis *codd.*: implebit *Haupt*: in tenebris *Housman.*
[38] coletur NG: colatur V, *Baehrens.*
[41] patenti V *plerique*: parenti NG: tepenti H*w.*
[49] sitientes G V *nonnulli*: sitientibus V *nonnulli.*

of dawn, the morning flow of milk will fill the pails a-frothing from the swelling dugs; and again the yield of milking at the evening hour will be pressed for cheese in the morning. Yet spare the younglings: let not thrift be of such moment that cheese for the market ruins the snow-white lambs.[a] For the young you will tend with supreme regard. And, when at night you visit the sheepfold, if any ewe lies enfeebled by recent lambing, be not ashamed to carry her on your own shoulders and to bear in your warm bosom the quivering lambs that cannot yet stand. You must not seek out grazing-ground far distant from your stalls, nor the food yielded by too remote a wood while the fickleness of the sky is carrying the spring season to its close. To be distrusted is the faith of spring: one hour she smiles coaxingly unclouded of brow; the next she brings rain-clouds with fog and bears away the luckless lambs in raging streams.

But when long days bring the thirsty summer heats, when the weather is no longer changeable under an inconstant sky, then trust your flocks to the woodland, then seek for pasture at a greater distance; yet see that the herd goes out ere daylight. The moist air sweetens their food, whenever, as the east winds fall, the chill meadows are touched with night-dew and in the morning sparkling drops are on the grass. But as soon as the chirping tree-crickets shrill through the grove, drive your

[a] *i.e.* your anxiety to sell must not divert to cheese-making the milk which the lambs need.

54 tinguuntur V *nonnulli.*

ad fontem compelle greges; nec protinus herbas
et campos permitte sequi, sed protegat illos
interea veteres quae porrigit aesculus umbras.
verum ubi declini iam nona tepescere sole
incipiet seraeque † videbitur hora merendae,
rursus pasce greges et opacos desere lucos.
nec prius aestivo pecus includatur ovili,
quam levibus nidis somnos captare volucris
cogitet et tremulo queribunda fritinniat ore.
  cum iam tempus erit maturas demere lanas,
sucida iam tereti constringere vellera iunco,
hircorumque iubas et olentes caedere barbas,
ante tamen secerne pecus gregibusque notatis
consimiles include comis, ne longa minutis,
mollia ne duris coeant, ne candida fuscis.
sed tibi cum vacuas posito velamine costas
denudavit ovis, circumspice, ne sit acuta
forpice laesa cutis, tacitum ne pustula virus
texerit occulto sub vulnere: quae nisi ferro
rumpitur, a! miserum fragili rubigine corpus
arrodet sanies et putria contrahet ossa.
providus (hoc moneo) viventia sulphura tecum
et scillae caput et virosa bitumina portes,
vulneribus laturus opem; nec Brutia desit
pix tibi: tu liquido picis unguine terga memento,

58 sed G: sine V.

60 declivi V: declivis NG: declini *Heinsius*. nona *codd.*: sera *Baehrens*: rura . . . incipient *Maehly*.

61 incipiet serique v.h. premendi NG: incipiet seraeque v.h. merendae V: incipit atque sĕri v.h. premendi *Baehrens*.

65 tremulo tremebundo fruniat ore NG: tinniat ore AH: tremulo queribunda (*vel* gemibunda) fritinniat ore *Glaeser*: tremuli tremebunda coagula lactis V (cf. III. 69).

66 maturas NGA: maternas V.

74 forfice V. pusula N: pustula GV.

81 pix tibi: tu *Baehrens*: pia tibi NG: dura tibi N²V.

flocks to the waters, and do not allow them to range over grass and open fields without a respite;[a] but for an interval let them be protected by the oak which spreads its ancient shade. When, however, 'neath a westering sun, the ninth hour already begins to mark a cooling of heat, when it seems to be time for a late luncheon, set your flocks grazing again and quit the shady groves. Do not pen your herd in the summer sheepfold until the birds in their fragile nests think of wooing sleep and twitter their plaints with tremulous note.

When the time is already come to shear the full-grown wool, the time to bind the greasy fleeces with swathes of rushes and cut the neck-tufts and rank beards of the he-goats, yet first separate the herd; brand your flocks and pen together the sheep of similar wool, lest long go with short, smooth with rough, or white with dark. But when you find a sheep has bare sides after losing the covering fleece, take heed lest the skin has been hurt by the sharp shears and lest an inflamed sore has covered a secret poison beneath the unnoticed wound; unless the sore is opened with the steel, alas! the corrupted blood will eat away the wretched body by reason of the tender ulcer and will shrivel the bones into a crumbling mass. Here is my counsel; have the foresight to take with you native sulphur and the head of a sea-leek and strong-smelling bitumen, so that you may bring relief to such wounds. Be not without Bruttian pitch; if the back is torn, forget not to smear it with the liquid ointment;

[a] *protinus* is here taken in a time sense, leading up to *interea* (*cf.* Juv. III. 140 *protinus ad censum, de moribus ultima fiet quaestio*): locally, it might mean "far and wide."

si sint rasa, linas. vivi quoque pondera melle
argenti coquito lentumque bitumen aheno,
impressurus ovi tua nomina; nam tibi lites
auferet ingentes lectus possessor in armo.

nunc etiam, dum siccus ager, dum fervida tellus,
dum rimosa palus et multo torrida limo
aestuat et fragiles nimium sol pulverat herbas,
lurida conveniet succendere galbana septis
et tua cervino lustrare mapalia fumo.
obfuit ille malis odor anguibus: ipse videbis
serpentum cecidisse minas: non stringere dentes
ulla potest uncos, sed inani debilis ore
marcet et obtuso iacet exarmata veneno.

nunc age vicinae circumspice tempora brumae
qua ratione geras. aperit cum vinea sepes
et portat lectas securus circitor uvas,
incipe falce nemus vivasque recidere frondes.
nunc opus est teneras summatim stringere virgas,
nunc hiemi servare comas, dum permanet umor,
dum viret et tremulas non excutit Africus umbras.
has tibi conveniet tepidis fenilibus olim
promere, cum pecudes extremus clauserit annus.
hac tibi nitendum est, labor hic in tempore noster,
gnavaque sedulitas redit et pastoria virtus.
ne pigeat ramos siccis miscere recentes

82 rasa V: rara NG: scabra *vel* cruda *H. Schenkl*. durae NG: vivi (*sc.* argenti) V *nonnulli*: vini H V *nonnulli*. massae NG: melle *vel* molle V: durae . . . malthae ardenti *Giarratano*.

83 argenti NG V *plerique* (ardenti G *in marg.*): arrhenici *H. Schenkl*: chalcanthi *Haupt, Baehrens*.

91 obfuit *codd.*: obvius *Burman*: obficit *Maehly*.

97 circitor NG: vinitor V.

104 hoc . . . hic NG: hac . . . hinc *Glaeser*: hac . . . hic *H. Schenkl*: huc . . . huc *Baehrens*.

steep too a heavy mass of quicksilver in honey and sticky pitch in a cauldron, when you mean to stamp your name on your sheep, for the owner's name read on the shoulder will save you from serious law-suits.

Now also, while the field is parched and earth burning hot, while the marsh is seamed with cracks, scorched and seething in its plenteous mud, and the sun too powerfully reduces the slender herbs to dust, then it will be suitable to set on fire pale yellow gum-resin in the folds and purify your huts with the fumes of burned hart's horn.[a] Such an odour is enemy to noxious snakes; with your own eyes you will see the serpents' threatening mien collapse; not one can bare its crooked fangs, but, jaw powerless, each shrivels in weakness and, with its poison blunted, lies disarmed.

Now come, take heed how to manage the season of approaching winter. When the vineyard clears its rows, and the watchman, care-free, carries home the gathered grapes, then begin to prune the wood and its unwithered leaves. Now is there need to lop the tender twigs at the top of the tree, now to conserve leaves for the winter, while the sap remains, while the wood is green and the African wind does not yet dislodge the quivering shade. These leaves you will find it serviceable to bring out from your warm haylofts later, when the end of the year has confined your cattle to the fold. Thus must you strive amain; such is our work in due season. Vigorous industry and the shepherd's manly task ever come round again. Be not slow to mingle fresh boughs with dry and to supply new sap, lest

[a] In ancient times a chief source of ammonia.

et sucos adhibere novos, ne torrida nimbis
instet hiemps nimioque gelu nivibusque coactis
incursare vetet nemus et constringere frondes ;
tu tamen aut leves hederas aut molle salictum
valle premes media. sitis est pensanda tuorum,
Canthe, gregum viridante cibo: nihil aridus illis,
ingenti positus quamvis strue, prosit acervus,
virgea si desint liquido turgentia suco
et quibus est aliquid plenae vitale medullae.
praecipue gelidum stipula cum fronde caduca
sterne solum, ne forte rigor penetrabile corpus
urat et interno vastet pecuaria morbo.
  plura quidem meminisse velim, nam plura supersunt.
sed iam sera dies cadit et iam sole fugato
frigidus aestivas impellit Noctifer horas."

VI

ASTYLUS: LYCIDAS: MNASYLLUS

A. Serus ades, Lycida: modo Nyctilus et puer Alcon
certavere sub his alterno carmine ramis
iudice me, sed non sine pignore. Nyctilus haedos

107 ne torrida NG V *plerique*: licet horrida *Martellius*: dum torr. *Haupt*: cum torr. *Giarratano*.
109 incurvare velit NG: incursare vetet *Haupt*.
112 cante G: chante N.

biting winter swoop upon you with its rain-clouds and by excessive frost and drifts of snow prevent you from raiding the forest and from making bundles of leaves;[a] but in the heart of the valley you will prune the smooth ivy or pliant willow-copse.[b] With fresh green fodder, Canthus, you must allay the thirst of your flocks. No withered heap, stacked in however huge a pile, would avail them, if you lacked fodder of sprouts which are swollen with juicy sap and have some life-giving substance of fullest pith. Above all strew the chill ground with stubble as well as fallen leaves lest frost nip the sensitive body and waste the herds with deep-set disease.

Fain would I recall more precepts; for more remain. But now the late day falls; and, now that the sun is put to flight, the chill Night-Bringer[c] drives forth the summer hours."

ECLOGUE VI

ASTYLUS: LYCIDAS: MNASYLLUS

A. You are here too late, Lycidas. Just now Nyctilus and young Alcon have been contending in alternate song beneath these branches. I was umpire: each laid a stake. Nyctilus pledged his

[a] The passage urges the need to get green stuff betimes for the flocks before winter makes it difficult to bring it in from the woods.

[b] *i.e.* if prevented by frost and snow from cutting other trees.

[c] *i.e.* Hesperus, the evening star: *cf.* note on *Eleg. in Maecen.* I. 129–132.

iuncta matre dedit; catulum dedit ille leaenae
iuravitque genus, sed sustulit omnia victor.
L. Nyctilon ut cantu rudis exsuperaverit Alcon,
Astyle, credibile est, si vincat acanthida cornix,
vocalem superet si dirus aedona bubo.
A. non potiar Petale, qua nunc ego maceror una,
si magis aut docili calamorum Nyctilus arte
aut cantu magis est quam vultu proximus illi.
L. iam non decipior: te iudice pallidus alter
venit et hirsuta spinosior hystrice barbam;
candidus alter erat levique decentior ovo
et ridens oculis crinemque simillimus auro,
qui posset dici, si non cantaret, Apollo.
A. o Lycida, si quis tibi carminis usus inesset,
tu quoque laudatum nosses Alcona probare.
L. vis igitur, quoniam nec nobis, improbe, par es,
ipse tuos iudex calamos committere nostris?
vis conferre manum? veniat licet arbiter Alcon.
A. vincere tu quemquam? vel te certamine quisquam
dignetur, qui vix stillantes, aride, voces
rumpis et expellis male singultantia verba?
L. fingas plura licet: nec enim potes, improbe, vera

[4] Laconem *vel* Lacaenae *Heinsius*.
[9] Petale *editio Ascensiana et vulgo*: Crocale GV.
[18] posses *codd.*: nosses *Haupt*.
[22] vinces NG: vincere V: vincen *Glaeser, Baehrens*.

goat-kids along with their mother; Alcon pledged a whelp from a lioness mother, affirming its breed on oath.[a] But he won and carried off all.

L. That untrained Alcon can have beaten Nyctilus in song is only believable, Astylus, if the crow can excel the goldfinch or the eerie owl surpass the tuneful nightingale.

A. May I never win Petale, for whom alone I pine, if Nyctilus can rank next him in trained skill upon the pipes or in song any more than in looks.

L. No longer am I deceived. When you were umpire, Nyctilus came pale, his beard pricklier than the bristly porcupine. But his rival was fair, sleeker than a smooth egg, with laughter in his eyes and the very gleam of gold in his hair, worthy the name " Apollo," if only he did not sing.

A. O Lycidas, if you'd any practice in song, you too would know how to applaud Alcon and award him the palm.

L. Well then, since you're not on a level even with me, you rascal, will you yourself, umpire though you've been, match your reed-pipes against mine? Will you join strife? Alcon, if you like, may come as arbiter.

A. Can *you* beat anyone? or would anyone deign to compete with you?—scarce can your dry throat jerk out its dribbling notes and squirt words forth in miserable gasps.

L. More lies you may tell; and yet, you rascal, you

[a] It was a cross similar to the *semifera proles* of Grattius *Cyneg.* 253. Pollux V. 38 mentions the Hyrcanian breed from dogs and lions (τὰς δὲ Ὑρκανὰς ἐκ κυνῶν καὶ λεόντων, καὶ κληθῆναι λεοντομιγεῖς). Alcon has offered a sort of sworn warranty of its pedigree.

exprobrare mihi, sicut tibi multa Lycotas.
sed quid opus vana consumere tempora lite?
ecce venit Mnasyllus: erit (nisi forte recusas)
arbiter inflatis non credulus, improbe, verbis.
A. malueram, fateor, vel praedamnatus abire
quam tibi certanti partem committere vocis.
ne tamen hoc impune feras: en adspicis illum,
candida qui medius cubat inter lilia, cervum?
quamvis hunc Petale mea diligat, accipe victor.
scit frenos et ferre iugum sequiturque vocantem
credulus et mensae non improba porrigit ora.
adspicis, ut fruticat late caput utque sub ipsis
cornibus et tereti pendent redimicula collo?
adspicis, ut niveo frons irretita capistro
lucet et a dorso, quae totam circuit alvum,
alternat vitreas lateralis cingula bullas?
cornua subtiles ramosaque tempora molles
implicuere rosae rutiloque monilia torque
extrema cervice natant, ubi pendulus apri
dens sedet et nivea distinguit pectora luna.
hunc, sicutque vides, pignus, Mnasylle, paciscor
pendere, dum sciat hic se non sine pignore vinci.
L. terreri, Mnasylle, suo me munere credit:
adspice, quam timeam! genus est, ut scitis, equarum

30 praedamnatus NA: predam nactus V.
42 subtiles *codd.*: summa vides *F. Leo*: sutilibus molles ramosa corollis *Heinsius*.
44 natant NH: natent G: notant V: nitent *Ulitius*.

can't bring true reproaches against me like all that Lycotas brings against you. But what need to waste our time in fruitless wrangling? See, here comes Mnasyllus. He will be (unless mayhap you shirk the challenge) an umpire undeceived, you rascal, by boastful words.

A. I own I had preferred to depart, even though condemned beforehand, rather than match a bit of my voice against your rivalry. Still, that you may not go unpunished for all this—look, do you see yonder stag that reclines in the heart of the white lilies? Though my own Petale is fond of him, take him if you win. He is trained to bear reins and yoke and follows a call with trustfulness; 'tis no glutton mouth he shoots out for his food. Do you see how his head branches wide with antlers, and how the necklet hangs beneath his very horns and shapely neck? Do you see how his forehead gleams, enmeshed with snowy frontlet, and how from his back the side girth, circling his whole belly, has amulets of glass on this side and on that? Roses twine neatly round his horns and softly round his branching temples; and a collaret with red-gold chain dangles from beneath the neck, where a boar's pendent tusk is set, showing up his breast with snow-white crescent. This stag, just as you see him, is the stake whose forfeiture I risk, Mnasyllus, to secure that this fellow may know he is not worsted in a stakeless conflict.

L. He thinks, Mnasyllus, that his wager frightens me. Look how alarmed I am! You know I have

[46] sicumque vides G: sicutque *Baehrens, Giarratano*: hunc ego qualemcumque vides in valle V.

[47] perdere NH: prodere G: pendere N²V.

non vulgare mihi; quarum de sanguine ponam
velocem Petason, qui gramina matre relicta
nunc primum teneris libavit dentibus: illi
terga sedent, micat acre caput, sine pondere cervix,
pes levis, adductum latus, excelsissima frons est,
et tornata brevi substringitur ungula cornu,
ungula, qua viridi sic exsultavit in arvo,
tangeret ut fragiles, sed non curvaret, aristas:
hunc dare, si vincar, silvestria numina iuro.
M. et vacat et vestros cantus audire iuvabit.
iudice me sane contendite, si libet: istic
protinus ecce torum fecere sub ilice Musae.
A. sed, ne vicini nobis sonus obstrepat amnis,
gramina linquamus ripamque volubilis undae.
namque sub exeso raucum mihi pumice lymphae
respondent et obest arguti glarea rivi.
L. si placet, antra magis vicinaque saxa petamus,
saxa, quibus viridis stillanti vellere muscus
dependet scopulisque cavum sinuantibus arcum
imminet exesa veluti testudine concha.
M. venimus et tacito sonitum mutavimus antro:
seu residere libet, dabit ecce sedilia tophus,
ponere seu cubitum, melior viret herba tapetis.
nunc mihi seposita reddantur carmina lite;
nam vicibus teneros malim cantetis amores:
Astyle, tu Petalen, Lycida, tu Phyllida lauda.

50 vulgare NGA: ĭŭgale V. *Post* 52 *vel post* 53 *est vulgo insertus dubius versus* 54 (*pes levis etc.*) *:* 53–57 *exstant in Exc. Par., om.* 54.
60 me sane NV: mascillo G: Mnasyllo *Baehrens.*
70 mutavimus NG: mutabimus *Burman.*

some mares of no mean breed; from their stock swift-footed Petasos I will stake: now for the first time weaned from his mother, he has cropped the grass with tender teeth. His back is firmly set, head tossing keenly, neck free from over-weight, foot light, flank thin, forehead high-poised; and below, in narrow sheath of horn, is bound his shapely hoof—the hoof which takes him prancing across the green cornland so lightly as to touch, but not bend, the slender blades. By the woodland deities I swear, him I will give, if I lose.

M. I am at leisure and 'twill be a joy to hear your songs. Compete, of course, if you so wish and I will judge. Look, yonder, straight ahead, the Muses have made a couch under the ilex-tree.

A. Nay, let us leave the meadow and the bank of the flowing stream, so that the sound of the neighbouring river may not drown our music. For under the worn porous rock the waters echo me hoarsely, and the gravel of the babbling brook spoils a song.

L. If you wish, let us seek the caves rather and the crags which neighbour them, those crags where clings green moss with dripping fleece, and a vaulted roof, as it were of tortoise-shell scooped out, overhangs the rocks which make a curving hollow arch.

M. We have arrived; we have exchanged the noise for the silent cave. If you wish to sit down, look, the tufa will afford a seat; if you wish to recline, the green grass is better than couch-coverlets. Now, away with your wrangling and render me your songs; I would rather that in turn you sang of tender love-affairs. Astylus, sing you the praises of Petale, and you, Lycidas, of Phyllis.

L. tu modo nos illis (iam nunc, Mnasylle, precamur)
auribus accipias, quibus hunc et Acanthida nuper
diceris in silva iudex audisse Thalea.
A. non equidem possum, cum provocet iste, tacere.
rumpor enim, Mnasylle: nihil nisi iurgia quaerit.
audiat aut dicat, quoniam cupit; hoc mihi certe
dulce satis fuerit, Lycidam spectare trementem,
dum te teste palam sua crimina pallidus audit.
L. me, puto, vicinus Stimicon, me proximus Aegon
hos inter frutices tacite risere volentem
oscula cum tenero simulare virilia Mopso.
A. fortior o utinam nondum Mnasyllus adesset!
efficerem, ne te quisquam tibi turpior esset.
M. quid furitis, quo vos insania tendere iussit?
si vicibus certare placet—sed non ego vobis
arbiter: hoc alius possit discernere iudex!
et venit ecce Micon, venit et vicinus Iollas:
litibus hi vestris poterunt imponere finem.

80 mnasille N: mascille G: merito V.
83 te teste GH: te stante NV.
86 mutare *Maehly*: miscere *Baehrens*: sociare *C. Schenkl.*
90 sed G: sum *Baehrens*: sic *Barth.*

---

[a] Acanthis has been guessed to be either an ordinary shepherdess or a dangerous witch, like her namesake in

L. I pray you, Mnasyllus, do you but hear us this very hour with that same ear with which, 'tis said, you heard and judged Astylus and Acanthis of late in the Thalean wood.[a]

A. I cannot keep quiet when that fellow provokes me. I am ready to burst, Mnasyllus; he is only seeking a quarrel. Let him listen or recite, since so he desires. 'Twill be joy enough for me to watch Lycidas quaking, when, blenched, he hears in your presence his evil deeds made public.

L. It was at *me*, I suppose, friend Stimicon and at *me* neighbour Aegon had their secret laugh in the shrubbery here for wanting to ape the kisses of a grown man with young Mopsus.

A. Mnasyllus is stronger than I am. Oh, I wish he were still off the scene! then I'd take good care that you (Lycidas) never saw an uglier face than your own!

M. Why do you storm at each other? To what bounds has your madness urged you to go? If you want to compete in turn—— But no, I'll not be your umpire: someone else may be the judge to settle this! Look, here come both Mycon and neighbour Iollas: they will be able to put a close to your strife.

Propertius, IV. v. 63. *Thale(i)a* may imply either "Sicilian" from association with the nymph of that name in Sicily mentioned by Macrobius, *Sat.* V. xix, or simply "bucolic," since Thalia was muse of pastoral poetry as well as of comedy (*cf.* Virg. *Ecl.* VI. 1–2, where Servius gives *Thalea* as the proper Latin form). Some think it = Latin *virens*, connecting it with the root of θάλλειν and θαλλός, a young branch. Another view is to take *Thalea* as a nominative, *i.e.* "a true bucolic muse when you acted as judge," "a Thalea come to judgement." Whatever the obscurity of allusion, however, it is certain that Astylus is annoyed, and would assault Lycidas but for the presence of Mnasyllus.

VII

Lycotas : Corydon

L. Lentus ab urbe venis, Corydon ; vicesima certe
nox fuit, ut nostrae cupiunt te cernere silvae,
ut tua maerentes exspectant iubila tauri.
C. o piger, o duro non mollior axe, Lycota,
qui veteres fagos nova quam spectacula mavis
cernere, quae patula iuvenis deus edit harena.
L. mirabar, quae tanta foret tibi causa morandi,
cur tua cessaret taciturnis fistula silvis
et solus Stimicon caneret pallente corymbo :
quem sine te maesti tenero donavimus haedo.
nam, dum lentus abes, lustravit ovilia Thyrsis,
iussit et arguta iuvenes certare cicuta.
C. sit licet invictus Stimicon et praemia dives
auferat, accepto nec solum gaudeat haedo,
verum tota ferat quae lustrat ovilia Thyrsis :
non tamen aequabit mea gaudia ; nec mihi, si quis
omnia Lucanae donet pecuaria silvae,
grata magis fuerint quam quae spectavimus urbe.
L. dic age dic, Corydon, nec nostras invidus aures
despice : non aliter certe mihi dulce loquere
quam cantare soles, quotiens ad sacra vocatur
aut fecunda Pales aut pastoralis Apollo.

[2] fuit *codd.* : ruit *Heinsius* : subit *Baehrens.*
[13] scilicet *codd. plerique* : sit licet *V nonnulli.*
[18] spectavimus AH : spettamus in G : spectamus in NV.
[20] despice *codd.* : decipe *Baehrens.*

---

[a] The emperor Nero.

[b] The *Palilia* (*Parilia*) or festival of Pales (*cf.* 22 *infra*, II. 63, V. 25) was celebrated by shepherds in April and was accompanied by musical competitions.

CALPURNIUS SICULUS

ECLOGUE VII

LYCOTAS: CORYDON

L. You are slow, Corydon, in coming back from Rome. For twenty nights past, of a truth, have our woods longed to see you, and the saddened bulls waited for your yodellings.

C. O you slow-coach, no more unbending than a tough axle, Lycotas, you prefer to see old beech-trees rather than the new sights exhibited by our youthful god [a] in the spacious arena.

L. I wondered what could be reason enough for your delay, why your pipe was idle in the silent woods, and why Stimicon, decked in pale ivy, sang alone: to him, for want of you, we have sadly awarded a tender kid. For while you tarried from home, Thyrsis purified the sheepfolds and bade the youths compete on shrill-toned reed.[b]

C. Let Stimicon be unconquered and win prizes to enrich him,—let him not only rejoice in the kid he has received, but let him carry off the whole of the folds which Thyrsis purifies, still he will not equal my joys, nor yet, if someone gave me all the herds of Lucanian forests, would they delight me more than what I have seen in Rome.

L. Tell me, come, tell me, Corydon. Be not so grudging as to disdain my ears. Truly, I shall find your words as sweet as your songs are wont to be whenever men to sacred rites invoke Pales the fertile or Apollo of the herds.[c]

[c] The Apollo of Euripides' *Alcestis* had been compelled to tend the flocks of King Admetus in Thessaly.

C. vidimus in caelum trabibus spectacula textis
surgere, Tarpeium prope despectantia culmen;
emensique gradus et clivos lene iacentes
venimus ad sedes, ubi pulla sordida veste
inter femineas spectabat turba cathedras.
nam quaecumque patent sub aperto libera caelo,
aut eques aut nivei loca densavere tribuni.
qualiter haec patulum concedit vallis in orbem
et sinuata latus resupinis undique silvis
inter continuos curvatur concava montes:
sic ibi planitiem curvae sinus ambit harenae
et geminis medium se molibus alligat ovum.
quid tibi nunc referam, quae vix suffecimus ipsi
per partes spectare suas? sic undique fulgor
percussit. stabam defixus et ore patenti
cunctaque mirabar necdum bona singula noram,
cum mihi iam senior, lateri qui forte sinistro
iunctus erat, "quid te stupefactum, rustice," dixit
"ad tantas miraris opes, qui nescius auri
sordida tecta, casas et sola mapalia nosti?
en ego iam tremulus iam vertice canus et ista
factus in urbe senex stupeo tamen omnia: certe
vilia sunt nobis, quaecumque prioribus annis
vidimus, et sordet quicquid spectavimus olim."

[25] immensosque *codd.*: emensique *Schrader*.
[43] iam NG: tam V. tremulus et NGV: tr. tam AH: tr. iam *Friesemann*.

---

[a] This is best taken as describing the wooden amphitheatre constructed by Nero in A.D. 57 (Suet. *Nero*, 12; Tac. *Ann.* xiii. 31).

[b] For the allotment of seats at Roman *spectacula* see Suet. *Aug.* 44. Keene's edition of Calpurnius has an appendix on the amphitheatre in relation to this eclogue.

[c] The first amphitheatre determined the oval shape, as it

C. I saw a theatre that rose skyward on interwoven beams and almost looked down on the summit of the Capitoline.[a] Passing up the steps and slopes of gentle incline, we came to the seats, where in dingy garments the baser sort viewed the show close to the women's benches. For the uncovered parts, exposed beneath the open sky, were thronged by knights or white-robed tribunes.[b] Just as the valley here expands into a wide circuit, and, winding at the side, with sloping forest background all around, stretches its concave curve amid the unbroken chain of hills, so there the sweep of the amphitheatre encircles the level ground, and the oval in the middle is bound by twin piles of building.[c] Why should I now relate to you things which I myself could scarcely see in their several details? So dazzling was the glitter everywhere. Rooted to the spot, I stood with mouth agape and marvelled at all, nor yet had I grasped every single attraction, when a man advanced in years, next me as it chanced on my left, said to me: "Why wonder, country-cousin, that you are spellbound in face of such magnificence? you are a stranger to gold and only know the cottages and huts which are your humble homes. Look, even I, now palsied with age, now hoary-headed, grown old in the city there, nevertheless am amazed at it all. Certes, we rate all cheap we saw in former years, and shabby every show we one day watched."

was made by C. Scribonius Curio (Plin. *N.H.* xxxvi. 15 (24), 117) of two wooden theatres revolving on pivots to face each other, and each greater than a semicircle. Pliny pictures the imperial Roman people whirled round by this invention through the air and cheering at the risk they ran (*loc. cit.* § 118).

balteus en gemmis, en illita porticus auro
certatim radiant; nec non, ubi finis harenae
proxima marmoreo praebet spectacula muro,
sternitur adiunctis ebur admirabile truncis
et coit in rotulum, tereti qui lubricus axe
impositos subita vertigine falleret ungues
excuteretque feras. auro quoque torta refulgent
retia, quae totis in harenam dentibus exstant,
dentibus aequatis; et erat (mihi crede, Lycota,
si qua fides) nostro dens longior omnis aratro.
ordine quid referam? vidi genus omne ferarum,
hic niveos lepores et non sine cornibus apros,
hic raram silvis etiam, quibus editur, alcen.
vidimus et tauros, quibus aut cervice levata
deformis scapulis torus eminet aut quibus hirtae
iactantur per colla iubae, quibus aspera mento
barba iacet tremulisque rigent palearia setis.
nec solum nobis silvestria cernere monstra
contigit: aequoreos ego cum certantibus ursis
spectavi vitulos et equorum nomine dictum,
sed deforme pecus, quod in illo nascitur amne
qui sata riparum vernantibus irrigat undis.
a! trepidi, quotiens sola discedentis harenae

[68] vernantibus NGA: venientibus V.
[69] sol discedentis N (nos *supra* sol m^2): sodiscendentis G: nos descendentis V: sola discedentis *Haupt*: se discindentis *Baehrens*: *alii alia*.

---

[a] *i.e.* the *podium* (πόδιον), a projecting parapet or balcony just above the arena for the emperor or other distinguished spectators. The *balteus* was a *praecinctio*, a wall running round the amphitheatre at intervals dividing the tiers of seats into stories.

Look, the partition-belt begemmed and the gilded arcade vie in brilliancy; and withal just where the end of the arena presents the seats closest to the marble wall,[a] wondrous ivory is inlaid on connected beams and unites into a cylinder which, gliding smoothly on well-shaped axle, could by a sudden turn balk any claws set upon it and shake off the beasts.[b] Bright too is the gleam from the nets of gold wire which project into the arena hung on solid tusks, tusks of equal size; and (believe me, Lycotas, if you have any trust in me) every tusk was longer than our plough. Why narrate each sight in order? Beasts of every kind I saw; here I saw snow-white hares and horned boars, here I saw the elk, rare even in the forests which produce it. Bulls too I saw, either those of heightened nape, with an unsightly hump rising from the shoulder-blades, or those with shaggy mane tossed across the neck, with rugged beard covering the chin, and quivering bristles upon their stiff dewlaps.[c] Nor was it my lot only to see monsters of the forest: sea calves also I beheld with bears[d] pitted against them and the unshapely herd called by the name of horses, bred in that river whose waters, with spring-like renewal, irrigate the crops upon its banks.[e] Oh, how we quaked, whenever we saw the

[b] Between the arena and the lowest tier of seats was a marble wall, in front of which the revolving cylinder was designed to keep the beasts from clambering up to the spectators.

[c] The humped bulls suggest the buffalo, and the shaggy ones the urus.

[d] This is an allusion to far northern seas, where Polar bears prey on seals.

[e] The countryman has not knowledge enough to name the Nile: the shapeless brute to which he alludes is the hippopotamus or "river-horse."

vidimus inverti, ruptaque voragine terrae
emersisse feras; et in isdem saepe cavernis
aurea cum subito creverunt arbuta nimbo.
L. o felix Corydon, quem non tremebunda senectus
impedit! o felix, quod in haec tibi saecula primos
indulgente deo demittere contigit annos!
nunc, tibi si propius venerandum cernere numen
fors dedit et praesens vultumque habitumque notasti,
dic age dic, Corydon, quae sit mihi forma deorum.
C. o utinam nobis non rustica vestis inesset:
vidissem propius mea numina! sed mihi sordes
pullaque paupertas et adunco fibula morsu
obfuerunt. utcumque tamen conspeximus ipsum
longius; ac, nisi me visus decepit, in uno
et Martis vultus et Apollinis esse putavi.

70 in partes *codd.*: inverti *Haupt.*

72 subito N: susito G: croceo V: fulvo *Baehrens.*

77 fors NG: sors V.

78 quae sit mihi *pler. codd.*: mihi quae sit *Burman, Baehrens.*

79 obesset *Haupt.*

81 putavi AH, *ed. Ven.*: putatur NGV: probatur *Burman, Baehrens*: notatur *Haupt*: putato *Leo, Giarratano.*

arena part asunder and its soil upturned and beasts plunge out from the chasm cleft in the earth;[a] yet often from those same rifts the golden arbutes sprang amid a sudden fountain spray (of saffron).[b]

L. O lucky Corydon, unhampered by palsied eld; lucky in that by the grace of heaven it was your lot to set[c] your early years in this age! Now if fortune has vouchsafed to you close sight of our worshipful Emperor-god, if there and then you marked his countenance and mien, tell me, come, tell me, Corydon, what I may deem to be the features of the gods.

C. O would that I had not been clad in peasant garb! Else should I have gained a nearer sight of my deity: but humble dress and dingy poverty and brooch with but a crooked clasp prevented me; still, in a way, I looked upon his very self some distance off, and, unless my sight played me a trick, I thought in that one face the looks of Mars and of Apollo were combined.

[a] Such arrangements for letting beasts rise from underground in the arena are well illustrated by the excavations at the Amphitheatrum Flavium (the "Colosseum").

[b] The beauty of an artificially contrived garden in the amphitheatre contrasts with the savage beasts; and the spectators are refreshed by jets of saffron water.

[c] Barth explains *demittere* as "inserere aut intro porrigere." The metaphor may be from planting.

LAUS PISONIS

INTRODUCTION

TO LAUS PISONIS

The *Panegyric on Piso*, by a young poet who pleads poverty but covets literary fame in preference to wealth, is addressed to one Calpurnius Piso, who is eulogised as eloquent in the law-courts, in the senate and in private declamation; as generous, musical, athletic, and an adept in the chess-like game of *latrunculi*. Such qualities agree with the description in Tacitus (*Ann.* XV. 48) of that Gaius Calpurnius Piso who was the ill-fated figure-head of the abortive plot in A.D. 65 against Nero: they also agree with the scholium on Juvenal's *Piso bonus* (V. 109), which mentions this particular Piso's power of drawing crowds to see him play the *ludus latrunculorum*. The identification with the noble conspirator is plausible, though we can prove neither that *Piso bonus* was the conspirator nor that Piso the conspirator had been consul, as the person addressed in *Laus Pisonis*, 70, clearly had been. This latter point decided Hubaux (*Les Thèmes Bucoliques*, p. 185) to see in the person addressed Lucius Calpurnius Piso, consul with Nero in A.D. 57.

The authorship is still more doubtful. In the now missing Lorsch manuscript the poem was erroneously assigned to Virgil. Certain similarities to Lucan's style indicate identity rather of period than of authorship, though the old ascription to Lucan has found modern support (B. L. Ullman, *C.P.* XXIV, 1929, 109 *sqq.*). The names of Ovid, Saleius Bassus and Statius have been advocated, of whom the first lived too early and the others too late to write the *Laus Pisonis*. Resemblances in style and in careful metrical technique led Haupt (*opusc.* I. 391) to argue that the work was by the pastoral poet Calpurnius Siculus. Haupt himself lost confidence in his hypothesis; and it has been opposed by G. Ferrara in *Calpurnio Siculo e il panegirico a Calpurnio Pisone*, Pavia, 1905.

EDITIONS

Editio Princeps in J. Sichard's edn. of Ovid. Vol. II. pp. 546–549. Basel, 1527.

Hadrianus Junius. *Lucani poema ad Calpurnium Pisonem ex libro Catalecton* in *Animadversorum Libri Sex*. Basel, 1556.

[Junius used a Codex Atrebatensis of which we lack subsequent record, unless Ullman is right in identifying it with the Arras *Florilegium*; see *infra* under Sigla "a."]

Jos. Scaliger. *Lucani ad Calpurn. Pisonem Paneguricum* in *Virgilii Maronis Appendix*. Lyon, 1573.

[Scaliger's text follows that of Junius, and agrees with the Paris MSS. more than with the *editio princeps*.]

J. C. Wernsdorf. *Poet. Lat. Min.* IV. pp. 236–282. *Saleii Bassi ad Calpurnium Pisonem poemation, Lucano vulgo adscriptum*. Altenburg, 1785.

J. Held. *Incerti Auctoris ad Calp. Pisonem carmen*. Breslau, 1831.

LAUS PISONIS

C. Beck. *Statii ad Pisonem poemation.* Ansbach, 1835.

C. F. Weber. *Incerti auctoris carmen panegyricum in Calpurn. Pisonem* (appar. crit. and prolegomena). Marburg, 1859.

E. Baehrens. *Poet. Lat. Min.* I. pp. 221–236, *Incerti Laus Pisonis.* Leipzig, 1879.

Gladys Martin. *Laus Pisonis* (thesis), Cornell Univ. U.S.A., 1917.

[Introduction, text, notes.]

B. L. Ullman. *The Text Tradition and Authorship of the Laus Pisonis* in *Class. Philol.* XXIV. (1929) pp. 109–132.

[As the *Florilegia* are the only existing MSS. of the *Laus,* Ullman prints a restoration of their archetype.]

RELEVANT WORKS

R. Unger. *P. Papinii Statii ad Calp. Pisonem Poemation,* Jahns Jahrb. 1836, p. 261.

M. Haupt. *De Carminibus Bucolicis Calpurnii et Nemesiani,* Berlin, 1854, and *Opusc.* i. p. 391. Leipzig, 1875.

E. Wœlfflin. *Zu dem carmen panegyricum in Calp. Pisonem,* in *Philologus* XVII. (1861) pp. 340–344.

J. Maehly. *Zur Literatur des Panegyricus in Pisonem,* Fleckeis. Jahrb. 1862, p. 286.

G. Ferrara. *Calpurnio Siculo e il panegirico a Calpurnio Pisone.* Pavia, 1905.

F. Skutsch. *T. Calpurnius Siculus,* in P. W. *Realencycl.* III. 1404.

C. Chiavola. *Della vita e dell' opera di Tito Calpurnio Siculo,* pp. 24–36. Ragusa, 1921.

J. Hubaux. *Les Thèmes Bucoliques dans la poésie latine*, esp. pp. 184–185. Bruxelles, 1930.

SIGLA

S = readings in J. Sichard's edition of Ovid, Vol. II. pp. 546 *sqq*., Basel, 1527, representing a lost manuscript of the *Laus Pisonis* in the monastery at Lorsch (*ex bibliotheca Laurissana*).

Two MSS. of *Florilegia* containing, along with excerpts from other authors, excerpts amounting to almost 200 lines of the *Laus* (the gaps represent over 60 lines) :—

p = Parisinus-Thuaneus 7647, 12th–13th century.
n = Parisinus-Nostradamensis 17903, 13th century.
P = Consensus of p and n.

B. L. Ullman, *op. cit.*, adds evidence from three other kindred *Florilegia* :—

a = one at Arras which he believes may be Junius' Atrebatensis.
e = one in the Escorial, Q. I. 14.
b = one in Berlin (Diez. B. 60 f. 29) containing a few lines and probably descended from e.

[Ullman thinks the common ancestor-manuscript of e, p, a was "a sister or cousin of n: thus the testimony of n is worth as much as that of the other three manuscripts together."]

The main variants from Baehrens' text are noted.

LAUS PISONIS

Bibliographical addendum (1982)

Laus Pisonis (text, German translation, commentary), ed. Arno Seel, Diss. Erlangen, 1969 (argues, not very plausibly, that Lucan was the author of the poem).

LAUS PISONIS

Unde prius coepti surgat mihi carminis ordo
quosve canam titulos, dubius feror. hinc tua, Piso,
nobilitas veterisque citant sublimia Calpi
nomina, Romanas inter fulgentia gentes;
hinc tua me virtus rapit et miranda per omnes
vita modos: quae, si desset tibi forte creato
nobilitas, eadem pro nobilitate fuisset.
nam quid imaginibus, quid avitis fulta triumphis
atria, quid pleni numeroso consule fasti
profuerint, cui vita labat? perit omnis in illo
gentis honos, cuius laus est in origine sola.
at tu, qui tantis animum natalibus aequas,
et partem tituli, non summam, ponis in illis,
ipse canendus eris: nam quid memorare necesse est,
ut domus a Calpo nomen Calpurnia ducat
claraque Pisonis tulerit cognomina prima,
humida callosa cum "pinseret" hordea dextra?
nec si cuncta velim breviter decurrere possim;
et prius aethereae moles circumvaga flammae
annua bissenis revocabit mensibus astra,

[12] at tu S: felix P.
[17] fumida *Scaliger*: horrida *Maehly*.

PANEGYRIC ON PISO

Uncertain are my feelings where first should start the order of the poem which I have undertaken, or what titles of honour I should chant. On the one hand, Piso, comes the summons of your noble rank with the exalted names of ancient Calpus,[a] resplendent among the clans of Rome: on the other, I am thrilled by your own merit, your life in every phase inspiring admiration—such a life as would have been equal to nobility, if nobility had perchance not been yours at birth. For what shall halls strengthened by images and triumphs ancestral,[b] what shall archives filled with many a consulate, profit the man of unstable life? In him whose only merit is birth, the whole honour of a family is lost. But you, gifted with a mind to match your high descent in which you set a part but not the whole of your renown, you will yourself be a fit theme for song. What need to record how the Calpurnian house derives its name from Calpus and won its first famous surname of Piso for pounding (*pi(n)seret*) the moist barley with hard-skinned hand? I could not, if I would, rehearse the whole in brief; the circling mass of heavenly flame[c] will in a twelvemonth recall its yearly con-

[a] Through the Calpi the *gens Calpurnia* claimed descent from Numa Pompilius. The Pisones of Hor. *A.P.* 292 are termed "Pompilius sanguis."

[b] *fulta* suggests the columns to which triumphal ornaments were attached.

[c] The sun.

quam mihi priscorum titulos operosaque bella
contigerit memorare. manus sed bellica patrum
armorumque labor veteres decuere Quirites,
atque illos cecinere sui per carmina vates.
nos quoque pacata Pisonem laude nitentem
exaequamus avis. nec enim, si bella quierunt,
occidit et virtus: licet exercere togatae
munia militiae, licet et sine sanguinis haustu
mitia legitimo sub iudice bella movere.
hinc quoque servati contingit gloria civis,
altaque victrices intexunt limina palmae.
quin age maiorum, iuvenis facunde, tuorum
scande super titulos et avitae laudis honores,
armorumque decus praecede forensibus actis.
sic etiam magno iam tunc Cicerone vigente
laurea facundis cesserunt arma togatis.
sed quae Pisonum claros visura triumphos
olim turba vias impleverat agmine denso,
ardua nunc eadem stipat fora, cum tua maestos
defensura reos vocem facundia mittit.

22 *sic* S: memorare manus. sed bellica fama *Baehrens.*

23 docuere S: decuere *correxit vir doctus saec. XVI.*

27 occidit et S: non periit P: *fortasse* interiit *in archetypo Wight Duff.*

35 vigente *Wernsdorf*: iuventae S: iubente *Weber, Baehrens.*

stellations ere it could be mine to record the titles and toilsome wars of the men of olden days. But the warlike hand of their fathers and armed emprise well beseemed the citizens of yore, who were sung by bards of their own times in their lays.[a]

We too can praise as his grandsires' peer a Piso brilliant in the glories of peace. For, if wars have sunk to rest, courage is not dead also: there is freedom to fulfil the tasks of campaigning in the gown—freedom, with no blood drawn, to conduct mild warfare before the judge ordained by law. Hence too comes the distinction of saving a fellow-citizen: and so victorious palms enwreathe the lofty portals.[b] Come now, eloquent youth, o'er-climb the titles of your forbears and the honours of ancestral fame; outstep by forensic exploits the renown of arms. So too in great Cicero's day of vigour the laurelled arms gave way to eloquence begowned.[c] The crowd which once in close array thronged the streets to see the illustrious triumphs of the Pisos now packs the laborious law-courts, when your oratory utters its accents to set unhappy defendants

[a] This, it should be observed, indicates belief in the existence of heroic lays in ancient Rome: *cf.* Cic. *Tusc. Disp.* IV. ii.; *Brutus* xix. 75; Varro *apud* Nonium Marcellum, 76; Val. Maximus, II. i. 10. For Niebuhr's ballad-theory see J. Wight Duff, *Lit. Hist. of Rome to Golden Age*, pp. 72–73.

[b] *i.e.* the advocate can save a life in the law-court, as the soldier can on the battlefield. Successful pleadings were honoured by setting up palm-branches at the pleader's house-door: *cf.* Juv. VII. 118 *scalarum gloria palmae*; Mart. VII. xxviii. 6 *excolat et geminas plurima palma fores.*

[c] An intentional echo of Cicero's own alliterative line, *cedant arma togae, concedat laurea laudi*, *De Off.* I. xxii. 77: *cf. Philipp.* II. viii. 20.

seu trepidos ad iura decem citat hasta virorum
et firmare iubet centeno iudice causas,
seu capitale nefas operosa diluis arte,
laudibus ipsa tuis resonant fora. dum rapis una
iudicis affectum possessaque pectora temptas,
victus sponte sua sequitur quocumque vocasti:
flet si flere iubes, gaudet gaudere coactus
et te dante capit iudex, quam non habet, iram.
sic auriga solet ferventia Thessalus ora
mobilibus frenis in aperto flectere campo,
qui modo non solum rapido permittit habenas
quadrupedi, sed calce citat, modo succutit alte
flexibiles rictus et nunc cervice rotata
incipit effusos in gyrum carpere cursus.
quis non attonitus iudex tua respicit ora?
quis regit ipse suam, nisi per tua pondera, mentem?
nam tu, sive libet pariter cum grandine nimbos
densaque vibrata iaculari fulmina lingua,
seu iuvat adstrictas in nodum cogere voces
et dare subtili vivacia verba catenae,
vim Laertiadae, brevitatem vincis Atridae;
dulcia seu mavis liquidoque fluentia cursu
verba nec incluso sed aperto pingere flore,

44 dura Piso: nam S: dum rapis una *Baehrens*.
45 tentas S: ducis P (*fortasse ex versu* 138 *translatum*): frenas *Maehly*.
51 rabido *Baehrens*: rapido PS.
52 succutit alte (*sive* acre) *Baehrens*: succutit arce P: *om.* S: succedit a: subripit a².

free. Whether the spear of the decemviri summons the panic-stricken to trial and ordains the establishment of cases before the centumviri,[a] or whether with busy skill you refute a capital charge, the very courts resound with your praises. As you carry along with you a judge's feelings, assailing his captured heart, vanquished he follows of his own accord wherever you call—weeps if you say "weep," rejoices if so compelled; and you are the giver from whom a judge gets an anger not his own. So the Thessalian rider is wont on the open plain to guide his horse's steaming mouth with mobile bit, now spurring his rapid steed and not merely giving him rein, now jerking high the open jaws in his control, and now starting to wheel the horse's neck round and pull its wild rush into a circle. What judge fails to watch your lips in wonderment? Who orders his own mind save by your weighty arguments? For whether it be rain along with hail and repeated thunder-bolts that you choose to hurl with whirling tongue, or whether you please to condense compact expressions in a period and lend enduring words to the graceful texture of your speech, you surpass Ulysses' force and Menelaus' brevity; or whether with no concealed but with open flowers of speech you prefer to embellish sweet words as they flow on their clear course, the famous

[a] *Decemviri* and *centumviri* took cognisance of civil lawsuits. The spear, as a symbol of magisterial power, was set in the ground to mark the holding of a centumviral court: *cf.* Mart. VII. lxiii. 7 *centum gravis hasta virorum*; Stat. *Silv.* IV. iv. 43 *centeni moderatrix iudicis hasta.* Suet. *Aug.* 36 shows that *decemviri* (*stlitibus iudicandis*) were required from Augustus' time to call together the "Court of One Hundred" (*ut centumviralem hastam . . . decemviri cogerent*).

inclita Nestorei cedit tibi gratia mellis.
nec te, Piso, tamen populo sub iudice sola
mirantur fora; sed numerosa laude senatus
excipit et meritas reddit tibi curia voces.
quis digne referat, qualis tibi luce sub illa
gloria contigerit, qua tu, reticente senatu,
cum tua bissenos numeraret purpura fasces,
Caesareum grato cecinisti pectore numen?
  quodsi iam validae mihi robur mentis inesset
et solidus primos impleret spiritus annos,
auderem voces per carmina nostra referre,
Piso, tuas: sed fessa labat mihi pondere cervix
et tremefacta cadunt succiso poplite membra.
sic nec olorinos audet Pandionis ales
parva referre sonos nec, si velit improba, possit;
sic et aedonia superantur voce cicadae,
stridula cum rapido faciunt convicia soli.
  quare age, Calliope, posita gravitate forensi,
limina Pisonis mecum pete: plura supersunt
quae laudare velis inventa penatibus ipsis.
huc etiam tota concurrit ab urbe iuventus
auditura virum, si quando iudice fesso
turbida prolatis tacuerunt iurgia rebus.

[69] retinente S: reticente *vulgo*: recinente *Unger, Baehrens*.

---

[a] *Cf.* Hom. *Il.* I. 249 *τοῦ καὶ ἀπὸ γλώσσης μέλιτος γλυκίων ῥέεν αὐδή*. For the eloquence of Ulysses and Menelaus *cf. Il.* III. 221–223 and 213–215.

[b] The passage 68–83 (*quis . . . ipsis*) is omitted here by P *i.e.* p + n; but 77–80 (*sic nec . . . soli*) are added at the close of the poem.

charm of Nestor's honied eloquence[a] yields place to you. 'Tis not only courts before a citizen jury that admire you, Piso: the senate welcomes you with manifold praise, and its assembly renders you well-earned plaudits. Who[b] may worthily recount the glory that befell you beneath the light of that day on which, when your purple counted its twelve fasces,[c] before a hushed senate you sang from grateful heart the praise of the imperial divinity?

Yet, if the strength of powerful intellect were now within me, and my early years were filled with solid force, then should I dare to recount your eloquence, Piso, in lays of mine; but my neck sways wearily beneath the load: hamstrung, my limbs drop palsied. Even so Pandion's little bird[d] dares not record the swan's notes, nor, had it the wanton will, would it have the power; even so the nightingale's song excels the grasshoppers a-chirping their noisy abuse at the scorching sun.

Wherefore come, Calliope,[e] passing over his forensic dignity, with me approach Piso's doors: there is still more abundance of what is found in his very home to tempt your praise. Hither also repair youths from all over Rome to listen to the man, whenever judges are weary, and in vacation[f] confused wrangles are

[c] When he entered on his consulate, Piso delivered a complimentary address to the emperor. Pliny's *Panegyricus* illustrates this kind of oration.

[d] Pandion's daughter, Philomela, was changed into a nightingale, or, in some accounts, a swallow, as here.

[e] The Muse particularly of heroic narrative poetry. For a summary of the provinces of the nine Muses see the lines in this volume, pp. 434–435 and pp. 634–635.

[f] Cases are said to be *prolatae* when there is a *iustitium* or cessation of legal business, particularly at times of harvest and vintage.

tunc etenim levibus veluti proludit in armis,
compositisque suas exercet litibus artes.
quin etiam facilis Romano profluit ore
Graecia, Cecropiaeque sonat gravis aemulus urbi.
testis, Acidalia quae condidit alite muros,
Euboicam referens facunda Neapolis artem.
qualis, io superi, qualis nitor oris amoenis
vocibus! hinc solido fulgore micantia verba
implevere locos, hinc exornata figuris
advolat excusso velox sententia torno.
magna quidem virtus erat, et si sola fuisset,
eloquio sanctum modo permulcere senatum,
exonerare pios modo, nunc onerare nocentes;
sed super ista movet plenus gravitate serena
vultus et insigni praestringit imagine visus.
talis inest habitus, qualem nec dicere maestum
nec fluidum, laeta sed tetricitate decorum
possumus: ingenitae stat nobilitatis in illo
pulcher honos et digna suis natalibus ora.
additur huc et iusta fides et plena pudoris
libertas animusque mala ferrugine purus,
ipsaque possesso mens est opulentior auro.
quis tua cultorum, iuvenis facunde, tuorum
limina pauper adit, quem non animosa beatum
excipit et subito iuvat indulgentia censu?
quodque magis dono fuerit pretiosius omni,

92 foecunda S: facunda *Unger*. arcem PS, *Baehrens*: artem *Maehly*.

---

[a] Especially the exercise of declamation.

[b] Or, it may be, in settling the fictitious cases of the rhetorical *controversiae*.

[c] The Acidalian fountain in Boeotia, where the Graces bathed, was sacred to Venus. Her bird (*ales*) was the dove. *Euboicam* alludes to the connexion of Cumae, on the bay of Naples, with Chalcis in Euboea: *cf*. Virg. *Aen*. vi. 2.

hushed. For then his sport seems to be with light weapons,[a] as he plies his true accomplishments after lawsuits are settled.[b] Moreover, Greek culture flows forth readily from Roman lips, and Athens meets a weighty rival in his accents. Witness, eloquent Naples that founded her walls under Acidalian auspices and repeats the skill of Euboea.[c] What lustre, ye gods above, what lustre shines on the fair language of his lips! Here words sparkling in compact splendour have filled out his choice passages; here, decked out with tropes there flies to the hearer from the freed lathe a swift epigram.[d] Great merit truly it was, even if it had been the only one, now to delight the venerable senate with his style, now to clear the innocent, anon to lay the burden upon the guilty: yet more appealing still is a countenance full of serene dignity, while his look dazzles with the stamp of eminence. The mien he wears is such as we can call neither sad nor flippant, but seemly in a joyous seriousness. The fair honour of inborn nobility stands fast in him, and lineaments worthy of his birth. Thereto is joined true loyalty, frankness full of modesty, and a nature unstained by malicious envy—his mind itself is richer than the gold he owns.

Which of your clients, eloquent youth, approaches your threshold in poverty who is not welcomed and enriched by a generous indulgence with the aid of an unexpected income? And, what may well be more precious than any gift, you esteem him as

[d] *Cf.* the sense of *excusso* (*rudenti*) in 229. The lathe, metaphorically, is made to turn out the epigram which flies to the audience; (*cf.* Hor. *A.P.* 441 *male tornatos . . . versus*). The *tornus* is "shaken free" of its epigram, as the ship in Virg. *Aen.* VI. 353 is *excussa magistro.*

diligis ex aequo, nec te fortuna colentum
natalesve movent: probitas spectatur in illis.
nulla superborum patiuntur dicta iocorum,
nullius subitos affert iniuria risus:
unus amicitiae summos tenor ambit et imos.
rara domus tenuem non aspernatur amicum
raraque non humilem calcat fastosa clientem;
illi casta licet mens et sine crimine constet
vita, tamen probitas cum paupertate iacebit;
et lateri nullus comitem circumdare quaerit,
quem dat purus amor, sed quem tulit impia merces;
nec quisquam vero pretium largitur amico,
quem regat ex aequo vicibusque regatur ab illo,
sed miserum parva stipe focilat, ut pudibundos
exercere sales inter convivia possit.
ista procul labes, procul haec fortuna refugit,
Piso, tuam, venerande, domum: tu mitis et acri
asperitate carens positoque per omnia fastu
inter ut aequales unus numeraris amicos,
obsequiumque doces et amorem quaeris amando.
cuncta domus varia cultorum personat arte,
cuncta movet studium; nec enim tibi dura clientum
turba rudisve placet, misero quae freta labore
nil nisi summoto novit praecedere vulgo;

[120] illi n: illa p e a b: illic S. licet et S *contra metrum*: licet domus P (*ex interpolatione*): licet, licet et *Baehrens*: illic casta licet mens p *mgo. m. rec.* (*quod transiit in editt.*).
[126] focilat S: *om. in lacuna* P: munerat *aliquot edd.*

[a] *fōcĭlăt*, "revives," "cherishes," the reading of S, does not agree in quantity with the usual *fŏcĭlat* or *fŏcillat*.

an equal: neither the fortune nor the pedigree of clients influence you: uprightness is the test in them. They do not wince under any witticisms of overbearing jests: no man's grievance furnishes material for sudden laughter. A uniform tenor of friendship encompasses highest and lowest. Rare the house that does not scorn a needy friend; rare the house that does not trample contemptuously on a humble dependant. Though his mind be clean and his life unimpeachable, still his probity will rank as low as his poverty; and no patron seeks to have at his side a retainer got by pure affection but one whom cursed gain has brought him: no one confers largess on a true friend in order to guide him on an equal footing and in turn be guided by him, but one hires [a] the wretched man for a trumpery wage to have the power of practising shameful witticisms at the festal board.[b] Far has such a disgrace, far has a plight of this sort fled, worshipful Piso, from your house. In your gentleness and freedom from sharp asperity, laying aside pride everywhere, you are reckoned as but one among your friendly peers: you teach obedience, as you court love by loving. The whole house rings with the varied accomplishments of its frequenters: zeal is the motive force everywhere; for you find no satisfaction in a clumsy uneducated band of clients, whose forte lies in trivial services and whose one ability is to walk before a patron when the common herd are cleared away. No, it is a wide

[b] Juvenal, writing at the beginning of the second century A.D., draws parallel pictures of the relations between patron and client: *e.g.* with 115–116 and 118–119 *cf.* Juv. III. 152–153, *nil habet infelix paupertas durius in se quam quod ridiculos homines facit,* and with 122–124 *cf.* X. 46 *defossa in loculos quos sportula fecit amicos.*

sed virtus numerosa iuvat. tu pronus in omne
pectora ducis opus, seu te graviora vocarunt
seu leviora iuvant. nec enim facundia semper
adducta cum fronte placet: nec semper in armis
bellica turba manet, nec tota classicus horror
nocte dieque gemit, nec semper Gnosius arcum
destinat, exempto sed laxat cornua nervo,
et galea miles caput et latus ense resolvit.
ipsa vices natura subit variataque cursus
ordinat, inversis et frondibus explicat annum.
non semper fluidis adopertus nubibus aether
aurea terrificis obcaecat sidera nimbis:
cessat hiemps, madidos et siccat vere capillos;
ver fugit aestates; aestatum terga lacessit
pomifer autumnus, nivibus cessurus et undis.
ignea quin etiam superum pater arma recondit
et Ganymedeae repetens convivia mensae
pocula sumit ea, qua gessit fulmina, dextra.
temporibus servire decet: qui tempora certis
ponderibus pensavit, eum si bella vocabunt,
miles erit; si pax, positis toga vestiet armis.
hunc fora pacatum, bellantem castra decebunt.
felix illa dies totumque canenda per aevum,
quae tibi, vitales cum primum traderet auras,
contulit innumeras intra tua pectora dotes.
mira subest gravitas inter fora, mirus omissa
paulisper gravitate lepos. si carmina forte

146 frondibus S: frontibus *Beck*, *Baehrens*.
151 nubibus S: nimbis P: nebulis *Wernsdorf*: nivibus *Barth*.
157 vestiet p n^2: gestiet S n^1 (*secundum Ullmanum* vestiet n, *non ex* gestiet *corr.*, *ut Baehrens dicit*).

range [a] of good qualities that pleases you. Your own keenness leads the mind to every sort of work, whether the call has come from graver pursuits, or lighter pursuits are to your fancy; for the eloquence of the serious brow does not charm at every season: not for ever does the warlike band remain under arms: nor does the trumpet's alarum blare all night and day: not for ever does the Cretan aim his bow, but, freeing its string, he relaxes its horns: and the soldier unbinds helmet from head and sword from flank. Nature herself undergoes alternations, in varied form ordering her courses, unfolding the year with the change of the leaf. Not for ever does ether, shrouded in streaming clouds, darken the golden stars with dreadful rains. Winter flags and in the springtime dries his dripping locks. Spring flees before the summer-heats: on summer's heels presses fruit-bearing autumn, destined to yield to snow and flood. Yea, the Sire of the Gods stores away his fiery weapons, and, seeking again the banquet at the table served by Ganymede, he grasps the goblet in the right hand wherewith he wielded the thunderbolt. 'Tis meet to obey the seasons: whoso has weighed the seasons [b] with sure weights, he, if war calls him, will be a soldier; if peace, he will lay down his arms and his dress will be the gown. Him the law-court in peace, the camp in war will befit. Happy that day, for all time worthy of song, which, so soon as it gave you the breath of life, conferred on you countless gifts within your breast. A wondrous dignity upholds you in court; a wondrous wit, when for the moment dignity is dropped. If

[a] *Cf.* 66 *numerosa laude.*

[b] Here *tempora* is used in the sense of "the fit times."

nectere ludenti iuvit fluitantia versu,
Aonium facilis deducit pagina carmen;
sive chelyn digitis et eburno verbere pulsas,
dulcis Apollinea sequitur testudine cantus,
et te credibile est Phoebo didicisse magistro.
ne pudeat pepulisse lyram, cum pace serena
publica securis exultent otia terris,
ne pudeat: Phoebea chelys sic creditur illis
pulsari manibus, quibus et contenditur arcus;
sic movisse fides saevus narratur Achilles,
quamvis mille rates Priameius ureret heros
et gravis obstreperet modulatis bucina nervis:
illo dulce melos Nereius extudit heros
pollice, terribilis quo Pelias ibat in hostem.
  arma tuis etiam si forte rotare lacertis
inque gradum clausis libuit consistere membris
et vitare simul, simul et captare petentem,
mobilitate pedum celeres super orbibus orbes
plectis et obliquis fugientem cursibus urges:
et nunc vivaci scrutaris pectora dextra,
nunc latus adversum necopino percutis ictu.
nec tibi mobilitas minor est, si forte volantem
aut geminare pilam iuvat aut revocare cadentem
et non sperato fugientem reddere gestu.
haeret in haec populus spectacula, totaque ludos

[171] nec S: ne *Baehrens*. si S: sic *Baehrens*.
[177] ibat in hostem PS: iverat hasta *Schrader, Baehrens*.

mayhap it is your pleasure to twine in sportive verse the unpremeditated lay, then an easy page draws out the Aonian song; or, if you smite the lyre with finger and ivory quill, sweet comes the strain on a harp worthy of Apollo: well may we believe you learned under Phoebus' tuition. Blush not to strike the lyre: mid peace serene let national tranquillity rejoice in a care-free world: blush not: so, 'tis believed, Apollo's strings are played by the hands which also stretch the bow. Even so fierce Achilles is related to have touched the lyre, albeit the hero son of Priam (Hector) burned a thousand ships, and the war-trumpet clashed harshly with the well-tuned strings. The hero sprung from Nereus [a] beat out sweet melody with the thumb 'neath which the menacing spear from Pelion [b] sped against the foe.

If moreover you have chosen mayhap to whirl weapons from the shoulder and take your stand, limbs taut in fixed position, and at the same moment both avoid and hit your adversary, then with nimbleness of foot you swiftly interlace circle upon circle; with slantwise rush you press on your retreating opponent; now your vigorous right hand lunges at his breast, now your unexpected thrust strikes his exposed flank. No less is your nimbleness, if mayhap it is your pleasure to return the flying ball [c] or recover it when falling to the ground, and by a surprising movement get it within bounds again in its flight. To watch such play the populace remains stockstill, and the

[a] Achilles, son of Thetis, and grandson of Nereus.

[b] *Pelias*, sc. *hasta*: the spear of Achilles was so called because its shaft came from Pelion. The phrase *Pelias hasta* occurs in Ovid, *Her.* iii. 126, and in Pentadius, *De Fortuna*, 29–30.

[c] Excursus X in Wernsdorf's *Poet. Lat. Min.*, iv. pp. 398–404, deals with *lusus pilae* at Rome.

turba repente suos iam sudabunda relinquit.
te si forte iuvat studiorum pondere fessum
non languere tamen lususque movere per artem,
callidiore modo tabula variatur aperta
calculus et vitreo peraguntur milite bella,
ut niveus nigros, nunc et niger alliget albos.
sed tibi quis non terga dedit? quis te duce cessit
calculus? aut quis non periturus perdidit hostem?
mille modis acies tua dimicat: ille petentem,
dum fugit, ipse rapit; longo venit ille recessu,
qui stetit in speculis; hic se committere rixae
audet et in praedam venientem decipit hostem;
ancipites subit ille moras similisque ligato
obligat ipse duos; hic ad maiora movetur,
ut citus ecfracta prorumpat in agmina mandra
clausaque deiecto populetur moenia vallo.
interea sectis quamvis acerrima surgant
proelia militibus, plena tamen ipse phalange
aut etiam pauco spoliata milite vincis,
et tibi captiva resonat manus utraque turba.
sed prius emenso Titan versetur Olympo,
quam mea tot laudes decurrere carmina possint.
felix et longa iuvenis dignissime vita

203 et fracta S: effracta *doctus quidam*: ecfracta *Baehrens.*
204 *fortasse* quassaque *Maehly.*
207 etiam S: tantum *Baehrens.*
209 versetur PS: mersetur *Wernsdorf*: vergetur *Baehrens.*

[a] Excursus XI, *ibid.*, pp. 404–419, deals with the *ludus latrunculorum*, a game with a resemblance to chess or draughts.

[b] *i.e.* instead of advancing, this "soldier" lets himself be stopped and then, when he looks penned in, suddenly breaks out. Another explanation is that one counter "undergoes a double attack" (*mora* technically meaning "check"), *i.e.* is in danger from two opposing pieces, but by a further move endangers two enemies.

whole crowd, sweating with exertion, suddenly abandons its own games. If mayhap you please, when weary with the weight of studies, to be nevertheless not inactive but to play games of skill, then on the open board [a] in more cunning fashion a piece is moved into different positions and the contest is waged to a finish with glass soldiers, so that white checks the black pieces, and black checks white. But what player has not retreated before you? What piece is lost when you are its player? Or what piece before capture has not reduced the enemy? In a thousand ways your army fights: one piece, as it retreats, itself captures its pursuer: a reserve piece, standing on the alert, comes from its distant retreat—this one dares to join the fray and cheats the enemy coming for his spoil. Another piece submits to risky delays [b] and, seemingly checked, itself checks two more: this one moves towards higher results, so that, quickly played and breaking the opponent's defensive line,[c] it may burst out on his forces and, when the rampart is down, devastate the enclosed city.[d] Meanwhile, however fierce rises the conflict among the men in their divided ranks, still you win with your phalanx intact or deprived of only a few men, and both your hands rattle with the crowd of pieces you have taken.

But the Sun-God would complete his circuit after measuring the heavens, ere my lays could traverse so many merits. Fortunate youth, most worthy of

[c] *Mandra*, a herd of cattle, was taken by Scaliger for the *equites* of the *ludus latrunculorum*. Some suggest that, as a piece, the *latro* had higher value than pieces in the *mandra*. In the sense of "enclosure," *mandra* might mean the line of less valuable pieces (like "pawns"). R. G. Austin, "Roman Board Games," *Greece and Rome*, Oct. 1934, takes *mandra* as "any solid phalanx barring the enemy's advance."

[d] The πόλις of a similar Greek game.

eximiumque tuae gentis decus, accipe nostri
certus et hoc veri complectere pignus amoris.
quod si digna tua minus est mea pagina laude,
at voluisse sat est: animum, non carmina, iacto.
tu modo laetus ades: forsan meliora canemus
et vires dabit ipse favor, dabit ipsa feracem
spes animum: dignare tuos aperire Penates,
hoc solum petimus. nec enim me divitis auri
imperiosa fames et habendi saeva libido
impulerunt, sed laudis amor. iuvat, optime, tecum
degere cumque tuis virtutibus omne per aevum
carminibus certare meis: sublimior ibo,
si famae mihi pandis iter, si detrahis umbram.
abdita quid prodest generosi vena metalli,
si cultore caret? quid inerti condita portu,
si ductoris eget, ratis efficit, omnia quamvis
armamenta gerat teretique fluentia malo
possit ab excusso dimittere vela rudenti?
  ipse per Ausonias Aeneia carmina gentes
qui sonat, ingenti qui nomine pulsat Olympum
Maeoniumque senem Romano provocat ore,
forsitan illius nemoris latuisset in umbra
quod canit, et sterili tantum cantasset avena
ignotus populis, si Maecenate careret.
qui tamen haut uni patefecit limina vati
nec sua Vergilio permisit numina soli:
Maecenas tragico quatientem pulpita gestu

[237] numina S: nomina P: carmina *Lachmann*: somnia *Baehrens*.

---

[a] *Cf.* Ennius' *Musae quae pedibus magnum pulsatis Olympum*: or the idea may be that Virgil's fame rises and "strikes" the heavens.

[b] L. Varius Rufus, who with Plotius Tucca edited the *Aeneid*, was an epic and elegiac as well as a tragic author:

long life, distinguished ornament of your clan, assured of my loyalty, accept and welcome this pledge of true affection. Yet, if my page falls short of your renown, the intent is enough. I vaunt my aspiration, not my poetry. Do you but lend your joyful presence: perchance I shall sing better lays and your very favour will give strength, the very hope will give a fertile spirit: deign to throw open your home: this is my sole request. For it is no imperious hunger for rich gold, no savage lust of possession that has prompted me, but love of praise. I fain, noble sir, would dwell with you, and through all my life hold rivalry in my songs with your excellences: more lofty will be my way, if you are now opening for me the path of fame, if you are removing the shadow (of obscurity). What profits the hidden vein of precious metal, if it lack the miner? What can a vessel do, buried in some sluggish haven, if it lack captain, though it carry all its tackle, and could loosen its flapping sails on the shapen mast from the slackened rope?

The very bard who through Italian peoples makes his poem on Aeneas resound, the bard who in his mighty renown treads [a] Olympus and in Roman accents challenges the old man Maeonian, perchance his poem might have lurked obscure in the shadow of the grove, and he might have but sung on a fruitless reed unknown to the nations, if he had lacked a Maecenas. Yet it was not to one bard only that he opened his doors, nor did he entrust his (imperial) divinities to Virgil alone: Maecenas raised to fame Varius,[b] who shook the stage with tragic mien;

Hor. *Od.* I. vi. 1 and Porphyrion *ad loc.*; *Sat.* I. x. 44; *A.P.* 55; Quintilian X. i. 98; Mart. VIII. xviii. 7; Tac. *Dial.* xii. 6.

erexit Varium, Maecenas alta tonantis
eruit et populis ostendit nomina Graiis.
carmina Romanis etiam resonantia chordis,
Ausoniamque chelyn gracilis patefecit Horati.
o decus, in totum merito venerabilis aevum,
Pierii tutela chori, quo praeside tuti
non umquam vates inopi timuere senectae.
  quod si quis nostris precibus locus, et mea vota
si mentem subiere tuam, memorabilis olim
tu mihi Maecenas tereti cantabere versu.
possumus aeternae nomen committere famae,
si tamen hoc ulli de se promittere fas est
et deus ultor abest; superest animosa voluntas
ipsaque nescio quid mens excellentius audet.
tu nanti protende manum: tu, Piso, latentem
exsere. nos humilis domus, at sincera, parentum
et tenuis fortuna sua caligine celat.
possumus impositis caput exonerare tenebris
et lucem spectare novam, si quid modo laetus
adnuis et nostris subscribis, candide, votis.
est mihi, crede, meis animus constantior annis,
quamvis nunc iuvenile decus mihi pingere malas
coeperit et nondum vicesima venerit aestas.

240 nomina Graiis S: Troica Macri *Baehrens*.

---

[a] A divine power hostile to pride is suggested, but not named; *cf.* Sen. *H.F.* 385, *sequitur superbos ultor a tergo deus*; Ovid, *Met.* XIV. 750, *quam iam deus ultor agebat.* The idea resembles that of Nemesis, and it is noteworthy that Ovid, *Met.* XIV. 693–694 mentions the *dei ultores* and, independently, the "mindful wrath" of Nemesis.

Maecenas drew out the grand style of the thundering poet and revealed famous names to the peoples of Greece. Likewise he made known to fame songs resonant on Roman strings and the Italian lyre of graceful Horace. Hail! ornament of the age, worshipful deservedly for all time, protection of the Pierian choir, beneath whose guardianship never did poet fear for an old age of beggary.

But if there is any room for entreaties of mine, if my prayers have reached your heart, then you, Piso, shall one day be chanted in polished verse, to be enshrined in memory as my Maecenas. I can consign a name to everlasting renown, if after all 'tis right for any man to promise this of himself, and if the avenging god is absent:[a] there is abundance of spirited will, and the mind itself ventures on something of surpassing quality. Do you stretch out your hand to a swimmer:[b] do you, Piso, bring to the light one who is obscure. The home of my sires, humble but true, along with its slender fortune hides me in its own darkness. I can clear my head of its enshrouding burden, I can behold fresh light, if you, my fair-souled friend, do but cheerfully approve and support my aspirations. I have, trust me, a spirit firmer than my years, though youth's comeliness has just begun to shade my cheeks and my twentieth summer is not yet at hand.

[b] The appeal of this young poet contrasts with Johnson's famous sarcasm: "Is not a patron, my lord, one who looks with unconcern on a man struggling for life in the water, and, when he has reached ground, encumbers him with help?"

EINSIEDELN ECLOGUES

INTRODUCTION

TO EINSIEDELN ECLOGUES

The Einsiedeln pastorals, so called after the tenth-century manuscript at Einsiedeln from which H. Hagen first published them in 1869, have already been touched upon in connexion with Calpurnius Siculus. These two incomplete poems date almost certainly from the early years of Nero's reign (A.D. 54–68). In the first, the emperor is an Apollo and a Jupiter and the inspired author of a poem on the taking of Troy. In the second, one of the shepherds is convinced that with the emperor's accession the Golden Age has returned. This poem, the earlier and the more artistic of the two, in its opening "*quid tacitus, Mystes?*" either echoes or is echoed by the opening of Calpurnius Siculus' fourth eclogue, "*quid tacitus, Corydon?*" On the ground of the *laudata chelys* of i. 17, it has been argued that the author's muse was already popular at court and that it might have been worth while for Calpurnius Siculus, a humbler person and a junior poet, to pay him the compliment of imitation.[a] The argument proceeds to identify the author of the Einsiedeln poems with the eminent Calpurnius Piso on the ground that, if Calpurnius Siculus' patron "Meliboeus"

[a] This is Groag's theory, P. W. *Realencycl.* III. 1379 : it is contradicted by Skutsch, P. W. *Realencycl.* V. 2115.

was really Piso,[a] then it is appropriate that he, as the speaker at *Eclogue* iv. 1, should appear to quote "*quid tacitus?*" from himself. Besides, in spite of Piso's later complicity in the conspiracy against Nero, he had been at one time on intimate terms with the emperor,[b] and might well have indulged in pastoral panegyrics upon him. This implies that the Einsiedeln poems preceded the Calpurnian eclogues. But if the *gaudete ruinae* and *laudate rogos* of Einsied. i. 40–41 could be taken to indicate composition after the fire of Rome in A.D. 64, then it is hard to picture Piso so praising Nero on the verge of his plot against him. However this may be, the eulogies upon Nero are in the manner of court literature during the opening years of his reign, as is evident from the tone of Seneca's praises in his *Apocolocyntosis* and *De Clementia*. Much learned speculation has been spent on the pieces. It has generally been felt needless to assert (as Hagen, Buecheler and Birt have done) two separate authors for them; and, while Lucan, as well as Piso, has been put forward as the writer, the balance of opinion tends to agree that there is not enough evidence on which to dogmatise. Ferrara[c] thinks it possible that the two pieces are by Calpurnius Siculus. There are, it is true, resemblances between the Einsiedeln pair and his eclogues; but the very fact that the adulation of Nero in the first piece and the restoration of the

[a] It must be remembered that a case can be made out for regarding "Meliboeus" as Seneca. Some, on the other hand, consider all such identifications to be futile (see introd. to Calpurnius Siculus).

[b] Tacitus, *Ann.* XV. 52.

[c] In *Calpurnio Siculo e il panegirico a Calpurnio*, Pavia, 1905.

Golden Age in the second are themes in common with the fourth and first Calpurnian eclogues militates rather against than for identity of authorship. At least, it is arguable that a writer with aspirations after originality would not go on harping on the same string. In one way, indeed, there is a departure from pastoral usage, which normally confines speakers to complete hexameters: the second poem has this amount of individuality in structure, that the interlocutors sometimes start speaking in the middle of a line (ii. 1; 4; 5 and 6).

EDITIONS

H. Hagen, in *Philol.* 28 (1869), pp. 338 *sqq.* (the first publication of the text).

A. Riese, in *Anthol. Latina*, Nos. 725 and 726.

E. Baehrens, in *P.L.M.* III, 60–64.

C. Giarratano, with *Bucolica* of Calpurnius and Nemesianus (Paravia ed.). Turin, 1924.

RELEVANT WORKS

R. Peiper. *Praefationis in Senecae tragoedias supplem.* Breslau, 1870. (First established the Neronian date.)

F. Buecheler. *Rh. Mus.* 26 (1871), 235.

O. Ribbeck. *Rh. Mus.* 26 (1871), 406, 491.

Th. Birt. *Ad historiam hexametri latini symbola*, p. 64. [Argues, like Hagen and Buecheler, that the two poems are by different authors.] Bonn, 1876.

E. Groag, in P. W. *Realencycl.* III. (1899) col. 1379. [Considers Calpurnius Piso the author.]

F. Skutsch, in P. W. *Realencycl.* V. (1905) col. 2115. [Considers Groag's conjecture unfounded.]
A. Maciejczyk. *De carminum Einsidlensium tempore et auctore.* Diss. Greifswald, 1907.
S. Loesch. *Die Einsiedler Gedichte: eine litterarhistorische Untersuchung* (w. text and a facsimile). Diss. Tübingen, 1909. [These last two writers argue for Lucan's authorship.]
J. Hubaux. *Les thèmes bucoliques dans la poésie latine*, Bruxelles, 1930, pp. 228 *sqq*.

For a fuller list see Schanz, *Gesch. d. röm. Lit.*

SIGLUM

E = Codex Einsiedlensis 266: saec. **x**.

Baehrens' transpositions of lines are not followed, nor all of his emendations.

Bibliographical addendum (1982)

Einsiedler Gedichte (with Calpurnius Siculus), Latin with German translation, by D. Korzeniewski, Darmstadt 1971.

INCERTI CARMINA BUCOLICA

I

THAMYRA: LADAS: MIDA

Th. Te, formose Mida, iam dudum nostra requirunt
iurgia: da vacuam pueris certantibus aurem.
Mi. haud moror; et casti nemoris secreta voluptas
invitat calamos: imponite lusibus artem.
Th. praemia si cessant, artis fiducia muta est.
La. sed nostram durare fidem duo pignora cogent:
vel caper ille, nota frontem qui pingitur alba,
vel levis haec et mobilibus circumdata bullis
fistula, silvicolae munus memorabile Fauni.
Th. sive caprum mavis vel Fauni ponere munus,
elige utrum perdas; sed erit, puto, certius omen
fistula damnato iam nunc pro pignore dempta.

THAMIRA E: THAMYRA *Hagen*: *cf.* Thamyras, 21.
3 et casti *Baehrens* (*cf.* Tac. *Germ.* 40 *castum nemus*): et cusu E: et lusu *Hagen*: excusum *Gundermann.*
5 nulla *Hagen*, *Ribbeck.*
7 nota . . . alba *Hagen*: notam . . . albam E.
8 nobilibus E, *corr. Hagen.*
9 munus venerabile *Baehrens*: munus et memorabile E.
11 set *Baehrens*: et E.
12 dempta *Baehrens*: empta est E.

EINSIEDELN ECLOGUES

I

[The personages are Thamyras and Ladas as contending shepherds, and Midas as umpire.]

Th. Long have our contests called for you, my handsome Midas; lend a leisured ear to competing swains.

Mi. I am ready: the sequestered charm of the holy wood is an invitation to pipings: lay skill upon your minstrelsy.

Th. If prizes are lacking, the confidence of skill is dumb.

La. Nay, two stakes will make our confidence endure: either yonder he-goat, whose forehead is decked with the white mark, or this light pipe set round with moveable knobs,[a] the memorable gift of Faunus, denizen of the woods.

Th. Whether you prefer to stake the he-goat or Faunus' gift, choose which of the two you are to lose; but the surer omen, I fancy, will be the pipe which, instead of being a stake, is as good as taken away from the rejected competitor.

[a] The *bullae* might control the musical notes by closing or opening the perforations; but they might merely be decorative. Hubaux (*Les thèmes bucoliques*, p. 230) thinks of " une flûte ornée de verroteries."

La. quid iuvat insanis lucem consumere verbis?
iudicis e gremio victoris gloria surgat.
Th. praeda mea est, quia Caesareas me dicere laudes
mens iubet: huic semper debetur palma labori.
La. et mi sidereo cor movit Cynthius ore
laudatamque chelyn iussit variare canendo.
Mi. pergite, io pueri, promissum reddere carmen;
sic vos cantantes deus adiuvet! incipe, Lada,
tu prior; alternus Thamyras imponet honorem.
La. maxime divorum caelique aeterna potestas,
seu tibi, Phoebe, placet temptare loquentia fila
et citharae modulis primordia iungere mundi
carmine uti virgo furit et canit ore coacto,
fas mihi sit vidisse deos, fas prodere mundum:
seu caeli mens illa fuit seu solis imago,
dignus utroque ⟨deo⟩ stetit ostro clarus et auro

17 mi s. cor movit (commovit *olim*) *Baehrens*: me s. corrumpit E, *Giarratano*.
20 cantantes E: certantes *Baehrens*.
21 imponit E: imponet *Baehrens*: imponat *Hagen*.
22 caelique *Hagen*: ceterique E.
23 temptare *Peiper*: emitare E.
24 *versum qui est* 24 *in* E *post* 31 *traiecit Baehrens*.
25 carmine uti *Baehrens*: carminibus E.
26 mundo *Hagen*, *Baehrens*: mundum E.
28 utraque *Peiper*. *post* stetit, dux *addidit Baehrens*: deus *Peiper*: *ante* stetit, deo *addidit Krickenberg*: Nero *Buecheler*.

[a] *i.e.* to Nero's merits.

La. What avails it to waste the daylight in wild words? Let the winner's fame rise from the umpire's bosom.

Th. The spoil is mine, because my mind prompts me to recount a Caesar's praises: to such a task the prize is ever due.

La. My heart too hath Apollo stirred with celestial lips and bade me sing changing strains to my lyre which has already won praise.

Mi. Proceed, my lads, to render the promised song: so may God aid you as ye sing! Ladas, begin—you first: Thamyras in turn will bring his tribute.[a]

La. Greatest of gods, eternal ruler of the sky,[b] whether, Phoebus, it is thy pleasure to make trial of the eloquent strings and set to melodies on the lyre the first principles of the world, even as in song the maiden-priestess raves and chants with lips o'er-mastered, so may I be allowed to have looked on gods, allowed to reveal the story of the universe:[c] whether that mind was the mind of the sky or likeness of the sun,[d] worthy of both divine principles Apollo took his place, brilliant in purple and gold, and

[b] Some have taken this as addressed to Jupiter; but Ladas is concerned with Phoebus alone (17–18), while Thamyras is concerned with the emperor (15–16). This seems to preclude the idea supported by some scholars that the emperor (instead of Apollo) is the subject of *stetit* in 28.

[c] Ladas prays for inspiration like that of the Pythian prophetess: *cf.* Lucan, V. 88–99, on Apollo as guardian of eternal fate at Delphi, a passage containing noticeable parallelisms of expression to the verses here given to Ladas.

[d] The reference is to Apollo as the omniscient god of divination (Lucan V. 88 *caeli . . . deus omnia cursus aeterni secreta tenens*) and as the Sun-God.

intonuitque manu. talis divina potestas
quae genuit mundum septemque intexuit oris
artificis zonas et totas miscet amore.
talis Phoebus erat, cum laetus caede draconis
docta repercusso generavit carmina plectro:
caelestes ulli si sunt, hac voce loquuntur!
venerat ad modulos doctarum turba sororum. . . .
Th. huc huc, Pierides, volucri concedite saltu:
hic Heliconis opes florent, hic vester Apollo est!
tu quoque Troia sacros cineres ad sidera tolle
atque Agamemnoniis opus hoc ostende Mycenis!
iam tanti cecidisse fuit! gaudete, ruinae,
et laudate rogos: vester vos tollit alumnus!
. . . .
⟨*venerat en et Maeonides, cui*⟩ plurima barba

30 orbis *Hagen*: oris E.
31 totas *Baehrens*: toto E: totum *Riese.*
35 *versum qui est* 35 *in* E *post* 41 *traiecit Baehrens.* sororum *Hagen*: sonarum E.
42 *hic versus totus et* 43 *ex maiore parte desunt in* E.
43 *explevit Baehrens ut supra.*

---

[a] Apollo's power, from a Stoic stand-point, was *totius pars magna Iovis* (Lucan, V. 95). The *artifex*, or contriver of the *mundus*, is the δημιουργός of Platonic philosophy. According to Plutarch, Thales and Pythagoras divided the heavens into five zones, Pythagoras dividing the earth into five corresponding zones (*De Placitis Philosophorum*, 2, 12 and 3, 14). The Stoic Poseidonius gave Parmenides as originator of the division into five zones (Strabo, *Geog.* II. ii. 2). Poseidonius himself recognized seven zones (Strabo, II. ii. 3 [C. 95]), and his influence acts directly or indirectly on this passage.

sped thunder with his hand. Such was the divine power which has begotten the world and has inwoven with the seven borders the artificer's zones [a] and blends them all with love.[b] Such was Phoebus, when, rejoicing in the slaughter of the dragon,[c] he produced learned minstrelsy to the beat of the plectrum: if there are any dwellers in heaven, they speak with voice like this. The band of the learned sisterhood had come to the sounds of the music. . . .

Th. Hither, hither, ye Pierian Muses, approach in the fleet dance! Here flourishes the wealth of Helicon; here is your own Apollo! You too, O Troy, raise your hallowed ashes to the stars,[d] and display this work to Agamemnon's Mycenae! Now has it proved of such value to have fallen! Rejoice, ye ruins; praise your funeral pyres: 'tis your nurseling that raises you again! . . . ⟨Lo! Homer too had come,

[b] The principle of attraction in the universe descended from the *Theogony* of Pherecydes to Stoic philosophy. This physical φιλία of the Greeks is echoed in Lucan, IV. 189–191, *nunc ades aeterno complectens omnia nexu, o rerum mixtique salus, Concordia, mundi, et sacer orbis amor.* The difficulties of the passage 22 *sqq.* are discussed by Loesch, *Die Einsiedler Gedichte* (1909), pp. 34–42.

[c] *i.e.* the serpent Python sent to torment Latona, *cf.* Lucan, V. 80.

[d] The reference might be, some have argued, to Nero's poem on Troy, from which according to common gossip he recited the episode of the fall of the city (Ἅλωσις Ἰλίου) on the occasion of the great fire at Rome, A.D. 64: Tac. *Ann.* xv. 39; Suet. *Ner.* 38; Dio, lxii. 18. But it would not be a tactful allusion, and there are difficulties in placing the poem so late.

albaque caesaries pleno radiabat honore.
ergo ut divinis implevit vocibus aures,
candida flaventi discinxit tempora vitta
Caesareumque caput merito velavit amictu.
haud procul Iliaco quondam non segnior ore
stabat et ipsa suas delebat Mantua cartas.

* * *

II

GLYCERANUS : MYSTES

Gl. Quid tacitus, Mystes? *My.* curae mea gaudia turbant:
cura dapes sequitur, magis inter pocula surgit,
et gravis anxietas laetis incumbere gaudet.
Gl. non satis accipio. *My.* nec me iuvat omnia fari.
Gl. forsitan imposuit pecori lupus? *My.* haud timet hostes
turba canum vigilans. *Gl.* vigiles quoque somnus adumbrat.
My. altius est, Glycerane, aliquid, non quod patet: erras.
Gl. atquin turbari sine ventis non solet aequor.
My. quod minime reris, satias mea gaudia vexat.

[45] implentur . . . aurae *Baehrens* : implevit aures E.
[46] discinxit *Hagen* : distinxit E.
[47] velavit *Peiper* : celabit E.
II. [7] non quod patet *Baehrens* : non non pat̄ E.

whose⟩ full beard and white hair shone in undimmed honour. So when he filled the poet's ears with accents divine, he undid the golden circlet from his fair brow and veiled the emperor's head with its deserved attire. Hard by stood Mantua,[a] erstwhile as forceful as the lips which sang of Ilion; but now with her own hands she began to tear her writings to shreds.

[The poem is incomplete. Probably Thamyras' verses are unfinished and certainly the judgement of Midas is lacking.]

II

A Dialogue between Glyceranus and Mystes.

Gl. Why silent, Mystes? *My.* Worries disturb my joys: worry pursues my meals: it rises even more amid my cups: a load of anxiety enjoys burdening my happy hours.

Gl. I don't quite take you. *My.* Well, I don't like to tell the whole.

Gl. Mayhap a wolf has tricked your cattle? *My.* My watchful band of dogs fears not enemies. *Gl.* Sleep can o'ershadow even the watchful.

My. 'Tis something deeper, Glyceranus—no open trouble: you are wrong.

Gl. Yet the sea is not usually disturbed without winds.

My. You may not think it, but 'tis satiety that plagues my joys.

[a] Virgil's birthplace, now eclipsed by Nero's ministrelsy! This gross sycophancy contrasts with the reverential homage shown towards Virgil both in Calp. Sic. iv. 62–63 and in *Laus Pisonis* 230 *sqq.* It suggests different authorship.

Gl. deliciae somnusque solent adamare querellas.
My. ergo si causas curarum scire laboras—
Gl. quae spargit ramos, tremula nos vestiet umbra
ulmus, et en tenero corpus summittere prato
herba iubet: tu dic, quae sit tibi causa tacendi.
My. cernis ut attrito diffusus cespite pagus
annua vota ferat sollennesque incohet aras?
spirant templa mero, resonant cava tympana palmis,
Maenalides teneras ducunt per sacra choreas,
tibia laeta canit, pendet sacer hircus ab ulmo
et iam nudatis cervicibus exuit exta.
ergo num dubio pugnant discrimine nati
et negat huic aevo stolidum pecus aurea regna?
Saturni rediere dies Astraeaque virgo
tutaque in antiquos redierunt saecula mores.
condit secura totas spe messor aristas,
languescit senio Bacchus, pecus errat in herba,
nec gladio metimus nec clausis oppida muris
bella tacenda parant; nullo iam noxia partu
femina quaecumque est hostem parit. arva iuventus

15 cespite pagus *Baehrens*: cortice fagus E.
16 inchoet *Baehrens*: imbuet E: imbuat *Hagen*: induat *Peiper*.
21 nunc *Baehrens*: num E.
24 tutaque *Baehrens*: totaque E.

[a] Maenalus in Arcadia was especially associated with Pan.
[b] *i.e.* the present generation has no handicap in the struggle of life: there is no conflict between man and nature, because the Golden Age has returned.
[c] The very cattle must own that the blessings of the Golden Age belong to the present era.

Gl. Pleasure and drowsihead are commonly in love with complaints.

My. Well then, if you are intent on knowing the reasons for my pangs——

Gl. There is an elm-tree with outspread branches which will cover us with its quivering shade, and, look! the green-sward bids us lie down on the soft meadow: *you* must tell what is your reason for silence.

My. Do you see how the villagers, outspread o'er the well-worn turf, offer their yearly vows and begin the regular altar-worship? Temples reek of wine; the hollow drums resound to the hands; the Maenalids[a] lead the youthful ring-dances amid the holy rites; joyful sounds the pipe; from the elm hangs the he-goat doomed to sacrifice, and with neck already stripped lays his vitals bare. Surely then the offspring of to-day fight with no doubtful hazard?[b] Surely the blockish herd denies not to these times the realms of gold?[c] The days of Saturn have returned with Justice the Maid:[d] the age has returned in safety to the olden ways. With hope unruffled does the harvester garner all his corn-ears; the Wine-god betrays the languor of old age; the herd wanders on the lea; we reap with no sword, nor do towns in fast-closed walls prepare unutterable war: there is not any woman who, dangerous in her motherhood, gives birth to an enemy.[e] Unarmed

[d] Line 23 imitates Virg. *Ecl.* iv. 6, *iam redit et Virgo, redeunt Saturnia regna.*

[e] No foeman can be born, as war is at an end.

nuda fodit tardoque puer domifactus aratro
miratur patriis pendentem sedibus ensem.
est procul a nobis infelix gloria Sullae
trinaque tempestas, moriens cum Roma supremas
desperavit ⟨opes⟩ et Martia vendidit arma.
nunc tellus inculta novos parit ubere fetus,
nunc ratibus tutis fera non irascitur unda;
mordent frena tigres, subeunt iuga saeva leones:
casta fave Lucina: tuus iam regnat Apollo!

32 est *Baehrens*: sed E.
34 opes *add. Peiper*: *om.* E.
37 sueta *Baehrens*: sęva E.

our youth can dig the fields, and the boy, trained to the slow-moving plough, marvels at the sword hanging in the abode of his fathers. Far from us is the luckless [a] glory of Sulla and the threefold crisis [b] when dying Rome despaired of her final resources and sold her martial arms. Now doth earth untilled yield fresh produce from the rich soil, now are the wild waves no longer angry with the unmenaced ship: tigers gnaw their curbs, lions endure the cruel yoke: be gracious, chaste Lucina: thine own Apollo now is King.[c]

[The poem thus relates the shepherd's *gaudia* but not the *curae* of verse 1.]

[a] Sulla was traditionally regarded as *felix*.

[b] The allusion seems to be to (1) the first capture of Rome by a Roman army when Sulla took the city in 88 B.C.; (2) Marius' reign of terror in 87 when slaves from the *ergastula* were armed (*Martia vendidit arma*), and (3) the occupation of Rome by Sulla in 82.

[c] This last line is taken from Virgil, *Ecl.* iv. 10. Lucina, goddess of childbirth, is here not Juno, but Diana, who as the Moon-goddess is sister to the Sun-god Apollo. He is the deity of the tenth Sibylline era which Virgil in *Ecl.* iv. identifies with the Golden Age.

PRECATIO TERRAE

AND

PRECATIO OMNIUM HERBARUM

INTRODUCTION

TO PRECATIO TERRAE AND PRECATIO OMNIUM HERBARUM

Both these prayers afford interesting glimpses into features of ancient religion much older than the poems themselves. It is characteristic of the worship of the Earth-Goddess that they should exhibit a recognition of her as the source of life and energy and nourishment, an anticipation of a final refuge in her at death,[a] and a confidence in her power to give help and healing. The divinity of the Earth-Mother was believed to be communicated to the dead, who were by inhumation absorbed into her. The words of the first *Precatio* find a full parallel in the epitaph—

mortua heic ego sum et sum cinis, is cinis terrast :
sein est terra dea, ego sum dea, mortua non sum.[b]

The return of the body to Mother Earth was a natural notion for a primitive agricultural folk, since much of the religious ritual of such peoples must be connected with the land. Earth had to be propitiated that she might grant increase to crops and cattle;

[a] With ll. 12–14 of the first *Precatio*, *cf. mater genuit materque recepit* in Buecheler, *Carmina lat. epigraphica*, No. 809 : *cf.* also the traditional sepulchral inscription *sit tibi terra levis*, and the spirit of the prayer to Tellus which ends the first elegy on Maecenas (141 *sqq.*, p. 134 *supra*).

[b] Buecheler, *op. cit.*, No. 1532 : *cf.* 974.

and at funerals the pig was sacrificed to the Corn-Goddess to secure her favour in receiving the dead. It is, then, intelligible that the Di Manes and Tellus Mater should sometimes be coupled; *e.g.* Decius in his *devotio* (Livy VIII. ix. 8) named them together. So Romans came to look on the tomb as an eternal home [a] where the spirit of the dead should abide, still a member of the old clan, still in some kind of communion with the living through the offering of sacrifice and food.

An excellent plastic illustration of the *Precatio Terrae* may be found in the allegorical relief of Tellus Mater, from the walls of the Ara Pacis Augustae decreed by the Senate to the emperor Augustus in 13 B.C. It is symbolic of peace and plenty, and characteristically representative of the fusion of Eastern with Western elements in Graeco-Roman art. Baehrens, indeed, would ascribe both the *Precationes* to the same period as the Ara Pacis (*Miscell. Crit.*, Groningen, 1878, pp. 107-113). Under the name of Antonius Musa we have a treatise " de herba betonica " in a Leyden MS. (Leidensis), a Breslau MS. (Vratislaviensis), and two Florentine MSS. (Laurentiani). These four also contain the two *Precationes* in senarii. The *Precatio Omnium Herbarum* is in one MS. (Laur. 11th cent.) ascribed to Musa: on this ground Baehrens concludes that both poems are by him. If this were convincing, it would settle their date as Augustan; but the argument is weak, and there are features in the poems suggestive of a later period. *Maiestas tua*, for instance, in lines 25 and 32 of the

[a] Buecheler, *op. cit.*, No. 59 *suae gnatae, sibeique, uxori hanc constituit domum aeternam ubei omnes pariter aevom degerent*: *cf.* 1488.

first piece, has a post-Augustan ring; and it is noteworthy that the word *maiestas* comes three times in the *Precatio Omnium Herbarum*.

SIGLA

(following Baehrens, *P.L.M.* I. pp. 137–138)

A = codex Leidensis (M.L.V.Q. 9), saec. VI.
B = codex Vratislaviensis (cod. bibl. univers. III. F. 19), saec. XI.
C = codex Laurentianus (plut. lxxiii. 41), saec. XI ineunte.
D = codex Laurentianus (plut. lxxiii. 16), saec. XIII.

PRECATIO TERRAE

Dea sancta Tellus, rerum naturae parens,
quae cuncta generas et regeneras indidem,
quod sola praestas gentibus vitalia,
caeli ac maris diva arbitra rerumque omnium,
per quam silet natura et somnos concipit,
itemque lucem reparas et noctem fugas:
tu Ditis umbras tegis et immensum chaos
ventosque et imbres tempestatesque attines
et, cum libet, dimittis et misces freta
fugasque soles et procellas concitas,
itemque, cum vis, hilarem promittis diem.
tu alimenta vitae tribuis perpetua fide,
et, cum recesserit anima, in tete refugimus:
ita, quicquid tribuis, in te cuncta recidunt.
merito vocaris Magna tu Mater deum,
pietate quia vicisti divom numina;
tuque illa vera es gentium et divom parens,
sine qua nil maturatur nec nasci potest:
tu es Magna tuque divom regina es, dea.
te, diva, adoro tuumque ego numen invoco,
facilisque praestes hoc mihi quod te rogo;
referamque grates, diva, tibi merita fide.
exaudi ⟨me⟩, quaeso, et fave coeptis meis;

[2] sidus *codd.* : indidem *Baehrens* : in dies *Buecheler*.
[3] tutela *codd.* : vitalia *Baehrens*.
[10] solem *codd.* : soles *Baehrens*.
[17] ver et BC: vere A: vero D: vera es *Baehrens*.

A LITANY TO EARTH

Goddess revered, O Earth, of all nature Mother, engendering all things and re-engendering them from the same womb, because thou only dost supply each species with living force, thou divine controller of sky and sea and of all things, through thee is nature hushed and lays hold on sleep, and thou likewise renewest the day and dost banish night. Thou coverest Pluto's shades and chaos immeasurable: winds, rains and tempests thou dost detain, and, at thy will, let loose, and so convulse the sea, banishing sunshine, stirring gales to fury, and likewise, when thou wilt, thou speedest forth the joyous day. Thou dost bestow life's nourishment with never-failing faithfulness, and, when our breath has gone, in thee we find our refuge: so, whatsoe'er thou bestowest, all falls back to thee. Deservedly art thou called Mighty Mother of Gods, since in duteous service thou hast surpassed the divinities of heaven, and thou art that true parent of living species and of gods, without which nothing is ripened or can be born. Thou art the Mighty Being and thou art queen of divinities, O Goddess. Thee, divine one, I adore and thy godhead I invoke: graciously vouchsafe me this which I ask of thee: and with due fealty, Goddess, I will repay thee thanks. Give ear to me, I pray, and favour my undertakings: this which I seek of

hoc quod peto a te, diva, mihi praesta volens.
herbas, quascumque generat maiestas tua,
salutis causa tribuis cunctis gentibus:
hanc ⟨nunc⟩ mihi permittas medicinam tuam.
veniat medicina cum tuis virtutibus:
quidque ex his fecero, habeat eventum bonum,
cuique easdem dedero quique easdem a me acceperint,
sanos eos praestes. denique nunc, diva, hoc mihi
maiestas praestet ⟨tua⟩, quod te supplex rogo.

PRECATIO OMNIUM HERBARUM

Nunc vos potentes omnes herbas deprecor.
exoro maiestatem vestram, quas parens
tellus generavit et cunctis dono dedit:
medicinam sanitatis in vos contulit
maiestatemque, ut omni generi ⟨identidem⟩
humano sitis auxilium utilissimum.
hoc supplex exposco ⟨et⟩ precor: ve⟨locius⟩
⟨huc⟩ huc adeste cum vestris virtutibus,
quia, quae creavit, ipsa permisit mihi,
ut colligam vos; favit hic etiam, cui
medicina tradita est. quantumque vestra ⟨nunc⟩
virtus potest, praestate medicinam bonam
causa salutis. gratiam, precor, mihi
praestetis per virtutem vestram, ut omnibus
in rebus, quicquid ex vobis ⟨ego⟩ fecero,

28 veni ad me cum A: veniat me cum BCD: veniat medicina cum *Baehrens*: veni veni ad me *Buecheler*.

10 favente (-tem A) hoc *codd.*: favit hic *Baehrens*.

15 viribus ACD: virtutibus B: in rebus *Baehrens*.

thee, Goddess, vouchsafe to me willingly. All herbs soever which thy majesty [a] engendereth, for health's sake thou bestowest upon every race: entrust to me now this healing virtue of thine: let healing come with thy powers: whate'er I do in consonance therewith, let it have favourable issue: to whomso I give those same powers or whoso shall receive the same from me, all such do thou make whole. Finally now, O Goddess, let thy majesty vouchsafe to me what I ask of thee in prayer.

A PRAYER TO ALL HERBS

With all you potent herbs do I now intercede; and to your majesty make my appeal: ye were engendered by Mother Earth, and given for a gift to all. On you she has conferred the healing which makes whole, on you high excellence, so that to all mankind you may be time and again an aid most serviceable. This in suppliant wise I implore and entreat: hither, hither swiftly come with all your potency, forasmuch as the very one who gave you birth has granted me leave to gather you: he also to whom the healing art is entrusted has shown his favour.[b] As far as your potency now extends, vouchsafe sound healing for health's sake. Bestow on me, I pray, favour by your potency, that in all things, whatsoever I do according to your will, or for what-

[a] *maiestas tua* (in lines 25 and 32) sounds post-Augustan: *maiestas* had already become a title of respect for an emperor in Phaedrus II. 5. 23. *Cf.* in the following poem, *maiestatem vestram* addressed to the *herbae* in line 2: *cf.* lines 5 and 18 and Juvenal's *templorum quoque maiestas praesentior*, XI. 111, for a "mystic presence" in temples.

[b] *i.e.* Paean, Apollo as deity of healing.

cuive homini dedero, habeatis eventus bonos
et effectum celerrimum. ut semper mihi
liceat favente maiestate vestra vos
colligere, ...
ponamque vobis fruges et grates agam
per nomen Matris, quae vos iussit nascier.

[21] maiestatis *codd.* : Matris *Baehrens.* nasci *codd.* : nascier *Riese.*

soever man I prescribe, ye may have favourable issues and most speedy result. That I may ever be allowed, with the favour of your majesty, to gather you . . . and I shall set forth the produce of the fields for you and return thanks through the name of the Mother who ordained your birth.

AETNA

INTRODUCTION

TO AETNA

The poem on Aetna has many claims on the attention of readers. It was placed among the minor works of Virgil by manuscript tradition, though this assignation, which came to be disputed by the time of Donatus, finds few scholars to support it now. But whatever its authorship and its date,[a] *Aetna* was written by an author who must win respect by reason of his earnest enthusiasm for the study of nature. He is in quest of a *vera causa* to explain volcanic action, and in his concentration of purpose, coupled with his disdain for mythology, there rings, notwithstanding his errors, a note half-suggestive of scientific modernity. If he despises mythology as no true explanation (though, like Lucretius, accepting it as an ornament), the author also despises sight-seers who gad about the world to the neglect of the wonders of nature near their homes. His is a call to observe: "study the colossal work of nature the artist" (*artificis naturae ingens opus adspice*, 601). Basing his observations and theories upon Aetna specially—because Vesuvius was mistakenly considered extinct (431–432)—he argues that the controlling motive force behind eruptions is air operating in the *vacua* with which the earth is honeycombed,

[a] See J. Wight Duff, *A Literary History of Rome in the Silver Age*, 1927, pp. 338–339.

and that the volcanic fire gets a nutritive material in the lava-stone (*lapis molaris*).

There are digressions from which the poem gains in attractiveness. One passage (224–273) utters a stirring proclamation of the majesty of physical research in contrast with mankind's ignoble cares. Again, towards the conclusion, the poet turns from theorising about physical phenomena to an episode (604–646) which centres in the human quality of heroic devotion shown by two brothers who rescue their parents from a sea of fire during an appalling eruption.

The difficulty of the poem itself is partly textual, partly stylistic—the former becomes evident in the *apparatus criticus*; the latter, in great measure, arises from a striving after brevity, a tendency to overload words and phrases, a fondness for metaphor and for personification, and perhaps an occasional adoption of expressions from the *sermo plebeius* of Rome.[a] These points resemble characteristics of the "Silver" Latinity of the early empire. The terseness, too, in mythological references, where details are taken for granted as well known, suggests some degree of lateness in period,[b] and is consistent with Buecheler's verdict that the poem must be later than Ovid and Manilius and with Munro's testimony regarding its versification. But it must have been composed before A.D. 63, as the terrible earthquake which devastated the towns close to Vesuvius in that year could not have been overlooked by a didactic poet who had the volcanic zone of Campania under

[a] See J. M. Stowasser, *Zur Latinität des Aetna* in *Zeitschrift für d. oesterr. Gymn.*, 51 (1900), p. 385.

[b] E. Bickel, *Rhein. Mus.* lxxix. 3 (1930).

consideration and dismissed it as inactive (431–432). Similarities to expressions in Seneca's *Naturales Quaestiones* of A.D. 65 do not prove the contention that *Aetna* came after that work; for both authors may well have used a common source. A summer visit to the volcano may have turned the poet to study Posidonian theories[a]: congruity of subject must have directed him to read Lucretius and Manilius, while in the use of the hexameter he had before him as models both Virgil and Ovid.

There is no clear way of deciding the authorship. Seneca's letter to his friend Lucilius Junior (*Epist.* lxxix. 4–7), once widely accepted as proof that Lucilius composed the work, implies nothing beyond a prediction that Lucilius was to insert a passage about Aetna in a projected poem on Sicily.

EDITIONS

J. B. Ascensius. *Virgilii Opera.* Paris, 1507.

Jos. Scaliger. In *Virgilii Appendix.* Leyden, 1573.

J. Le Clerc (Gorallus). *Aetna* c. notis et interpret. Amsterdam, 1703, 1715.

J. C. Wernsdorf. *Lucilii Junioris Aetna* in *Poetae Latini Minores.* Altenburg, 1780–1799.

F. Jacob. *Lucilii Junioris Aetna* (Latin notes; translation in German hexameters). Leipzig, 1826.

[a] *e.g.* on πνεῦμα (= *spiritus*) as a volcanic agent: cf. *Aetna*, 213, 344. Poseidonius (*c.* 130–50 B.C.), born at Apamea in Syria, was a traveller of encyclopaedic knowledge, whose works are now lost. Apart from eminent services to eclectic Stoicism, he devoted much attention to physical science. A great authority on earthquakes and volcanoes, he is constantly quoted by Strabo (*c.* B.C. 63–25 A.D.) in his *Geography* (see index to Loeb ed., vol. viii). Seneca in the *Nat. Quaest.* often cites him and his pupil Asclepiodotus. For a full account of his influence on *Aetna* see Sudhaus' ed. pp. 59–81.

H. A. J. Munro. *Aetna* revised emended and explained. Cambridge, 1867.

E. Baehrens. In *Poetae Latini Minores*, Vol. II. Leipzig, 1880.

S. Sudhaus. *Aetna* erklärt (German prose trans.). Leipzig, 1898.

Robinson Ellis. *Aetna* with textual and exegetical commentary (English prose translation). Oxford, 1901.

—— *Aetna* ("incerti auctoris carmen"): in Postgate's *Corpus Poetarum Latinorum*, Vol. II. London, 1905.

J. Vessereau. *Aetna* avec traduction et commentaire. Paris, 1905.

M. L. De Gubernatis. *Aetna carmen Vergilio adscriptum* (recens. et interpret.). Turin, 1911: also an edition in Paravia series.

F. Vollmer. In *Poetae Latini Minores*, Vol. I, ed. 2. Leipzig, 1927.

E. Schwartz. Berlin, 1933. (With a limited apparatus, which claims for the editor some emendations made earlier by others: *e.g.* Ellis' *varie*, 184; Baehrens' *moles, frustra*, 489; Vessereau's *iunctas*, 509.)

RELEVANT WORKS

A. De Rooy. *Coniecturae in Martialis libr. xiv. et Severi Aetnam*. Utrecht, 1764.

F. C. Matthiae. In *Neue Bibliothek der schönen Wissenschaften*, 59 (collation of Gyraldinian variants). 1797.

M. Haupt. In *Opuscula*. Leipzig, 1875–76. (His text of *Aetna* at end of his edition of Virgil.)

J. Maehly. *Beiträge zur Kritik des Lehrgedichts Aetna.* Basel, 1862.

B. Kruczkiewicz. *Poema de Aetna Vergilio esse tribuendum.* Cracow, 1883.

P. R. Wagler. *De Aetna poemate quaestiones criticae.* Berlin, 1884. (With index verborum.)

R. Unger. *Aetna* (suggested readings). *Journal of Philology*, xvii. 34, pp. 152–154. Cambridge, 1888.

L. Alzinger. *Studia in Aetnam collata.* Leipzig, 1896.

J. Franke. *Res metrica Aetnae carminis.* Diss. Marburg, 1898.

R. Hildebrandt. *Beiträge zur Erklärung des Gedichtes Aetna.* Leipzig, 1900.

S. Sudhaus. *Zur Ueberlieferung des Gedichtes Aetna* in *Rh. Mus.* lx. pp. 574–583. Frankfurt-a-M. 1905.

E. Herr. *De Aetnae carminis sermone et de tempore quo scriptum sit.* Marburg, 1911.

E. Bickel. *Apollon und Dodona* (ein Beitrag zur Datierung, etc.) in *Rheinisches Museum*, lxxix. 3. Frankfurt-a-M. 1930.

SIGLA

C = Cantabrigiensis: in Cambridge University Library, Kk. v. 34, 10th century (considered by Ellis the best codex). See note at end of this introduction.

S = fragmentum Stabulense, now in Paris, 17177, 10th or 11th century. (Besides about 260 fairly complete lines, it has about 86 more in a truncated form.)

Z = a lost archetype whose text is represented (see Vollmer's *stemma codicum*) by three related MSS. of the 15th century: viz.

H = Helmstadiensis 332,
A = Arundelianus 133, in British Museum,
R = Rehdigeranus, 125 in the city Library, Breslau.

V = Vaticanus 3272 (lines 1–434 *fecundius aethna*), 15th century.

Exc. = florilegia of excerpts, 11th to 13th cent.

(Two are in Paris, 7647 and 17903, and one in the Escorial, Q. 1. 14.)

G = readings of a lost codex used by Lilius Gyraldus (Giglio Giraldi) in the 16th century and represented by N. Heinsius' collation for lines 138–287, and by a copy of lines 272–287 surviving in codex Laurentianus 33. 9. [The value of the recorded Gyraldinian readings for those 150 lines has been estimated differently by critics. Some are attractive, but it is difficult to see how others, though plausible on the surface, could ever have been corrupted into what C gives. Schwartz[a] has recently suggested that alterations and errors in G may be due not to a late humanist, but to a Carolingian " corrector."]

codd. = general consensus of MSS.

A text of *Aetna*, in view of the unsatisfactory evidence of the manuscripts, must be eclectic. Some passages are frankly matter for despair, and are incurable by the licence of emendation, or rather rewriting, in which Baehrens allowed himself to indulge. But there are other passages where

[a] ed. 1933, p. 8.

AETNA

Robinson Ellis' scholarship, ingenuity, and palaeographical knowledge enabled him to make conjectures of a high degree of probability. Many of these are here adopted.

The corrupt state of the tradition has necessitated what may appear to be a considerable apparatus criticus, but it does not profess to be exhaustive.

Note on C

The text in C is neatly, though often inaccurately, written on vellum as part of a miscellaneous volume which begins with a patristic comment on the story of the prodigal son and contains extracts from Ausonius among others, with the *Culex* immediately preceding the "*Aethna*" at the end. These poems are both ascribed to Virgil in the manuscript.

Bibliographical addendum (1982)

Aetna (with German translation), ed. W. Richter, Berlin 1963.

Aetna (introduction, text, apparatus, commentary, index verborum), ed. F. R. D. Goodyear, Cambridge 1956: text and apparatus reproduced in *Appendix Vergiliana* (*OCT*) pp. 37–76, Oxford 1966.

AETNA

AETNA mihi ruptique cavis fornacibus ignes
et quae tam fortes volvant incendia causae,
quid fremat imperium, quid raucos torqueat aestus.
carmen erit. dexter venias mihi carminis auctor
seu te Cynthos habet seu Delo est gratior Hyla
seu tibi Dodone potior, tecumque faventes
in nova Pierio properent a fonte sorores
vota: per insolitum Phoebo duce tutius itur.
aurea securi quis nescit saecula regis?
cum domitis nemo cererem iactaret in arvis
venturisque malas prohiberet fructibus herbas,
annua sed saturae complerent horrea messes,
ipse suo flueret Bacchus pede mellaque lentis
penderent foliis et pinguis Pallas olivae
secretos amnes ageret: tum gratia ruris:
non cessit cuiquam melius sua tempora nosse.

[5] illa SAR *om.* H: ila C: Hyla *Munro.*

[6] dodona CSH²A: do bona H¹: do dodona R: Dodone *Ald.* 1517, *Vollmer*: Ladonis *Munro, Ellis.*

[10] lactaret CS.

[14] pingui *codd.*: pinguis H².

[15] cum V: tum *ceteri codd.*: securos omnis aleret cum gratia ruris *Baehrens*: secretos amnis ageret cum gratia ruris *Vollmer.*

AETNA

Aetna shall be my poetic theme and the fires that break from her hollow furnaces. My poem shall tell what those mighty causes are which roll conflagrations on their way, what it is that chafes at governance, or whirls the clamorous heat-currents. Come with favour to be my inspirer in song, whether Cynthos [a] be thy dwelling-place, or Hyla [b] please thee more than Delos, or Dodona [c] be thy favourite: and with thee let the sister-Muses hasten from the Pierian spring to forward my new emprise. On an unwonted track 'tis safer going if Apollo guide.

Who knows not of the Golden Age of the care-free King [d]? when no man subdued fields to his will or sowed grain in them or fended harmful weeds from the crops which were to come; when plenteous harvests filled the barns to last the year; when, with no tread but his own, Bacchus ran into wine; when honies dripped from clinging leaves, and Pallas made flow her own especial streams of rich olive-oil: then had the country graciousness. To none was it e'er vouchsafed to know more joyously his own times.

[a] *Cynthos*, the rocky hill-shrine of Apollo on Delos.

[b] *Hyla* or *Hyle*, forest-land in Cyprus, is rightly inferred from Lycophron's epithet for Apollo—Ὑλάτης.

[c] E. Bickel, *Rhein. Mus.* lxxix. 3 (1930), defends Apollo's association with Dodona, traditionally the oracle of Zeus.

[d] Saturn.

ultima quis tacuit iuvenum certamina, Colchos?
quis non Argolico deflevit Pergamon igni
impositam et tristi natorum funere matrem
aversumve diem sparsumve in semine dentem?
quis non periurae doluit mendacia puppis,
desertam vacuo Minoida litore questus?
quicquid in antiquum iactata est fabula carmen.
fortius ignotas molimur pectore curas,
qui tanto motus operi, vis quanta perennis
explicet in denso flammas et trudat ab imo
ingenti sonitu moles et proxima quaeque
ignibus irriguis urat—mens carminis haec est.
principio ne quem capiat fallacia vatum,
sedes esse dei tumidisque e faucibus ignem
Vulcani ruere et clausis resonare cavernis
festinantis opus. non est tam sordida divis
cura, neque extremas ius est demittere in artes
sidera: subducto regnant sublimia caelo
illa, neque artificum curant tractare laborem.

19 matrem H²AR : mentem CSH¹ : mensam *Schwartz*.
20 semine *codd.* : semina *Scaliger*.
25 qui tanto CSH¹ : quis tantos H²AR. operi CS : operit H : reperit AR. vis quanta *Ellis*. qu(a)e CSH : quis A : quamvis R. tanta *codd.* : causa *Ald.* 1517.

Who has not told[a] of the Colchians—mellay of warriors on farthest soil? Who but has uttered a dirge for Pergamos set on her blazing Argive pyre and the mother mourning the poignant slaying of her sons, or the day that turned its course in horror, or the dragon's tooth sown mid the sprinkling of seed? Who has not lamented the lying signal of the ship that kept not troth, or chanted the plaint of Minos' daughter forlorn on a deserted shore?—yes, every form in which legend has been thrown into ancient song.

More gallantly I set my spirit toiling on a task untried; what are the forces for this mighty working, how great the energy which releases in dense array the eternal flames, thrusts masses of rock from the lowest depth with gigantic noise and burns everything near in rills of fire—this is the burden of my lay.

First, let none be deceived by the fictions poets tell—that Aetna is the home of a god, that the fire gushing from her swollen jaws is Vulcan's fire, and that the echo in that cavernous prison comes from his restless work. No task so paltry have the gods. To meanest crafts one may not rightly lower the stars; their sway is royal, aloft in a remote heaven; they reck not to handle the toil of artisans.

[a] The mythological topics here briefly dismissed as hackneyed subjects of poetry are, in the order of mention, Jason's Argonautic expedition to Colchis; the burning of Troy by the Greeks; Hecuba's loss of her sons; the retreat of the Sun-God from the "banquet of Thyestes" on human flesh; the crop of warriors which sprang from the dragon's teeth sown by Cadmus; the fatal failure of Theseus to keep his compact with his father to hoist sails of good omen in the event of a successful return to Athens; and Theseus' desertion in Naxos of King Minos' daughter, Ariadne, who had enabled him to thread the labyrinth in Crete.

discrepat a prima facies haec altera vatum:
illis Cyclopas memorant fornacibus usos,
cum super incudem numerosa in verbera fortes
horrendum magno quaterent sub pondere fulmen
armarentque Iovem: turpe est sine pignore carmen.
proxima vivaces Aetnaei verticis ignes
impia sollicitat Phlegraeis fabula castris.
temptavere (nefas) olim detrudere mundo
sidera captivique Iovis transferre gigantes
imperium et victo leges imponere caelo.
his natura sua est alvo tenus, ima per orbes
squameus intortos sinuat vestigia serpens.
construitur magnis ad proelia montibus agger:
Pelion Ossa gravat, summus premit Ossan Olympus:
iam coacervatas nituntur scandere moles,
impius et miles metuentia comminus astra
provocat, infestus cunctos ad proelia divos
provocat, admotis per inertia sidera signis.
Iuppiter e caelo metuit dextramque coruscam
armatus flamma removet caligine mundum.
incursant vasto primum clamore Gigantes,
his magno tonat ore Pater, geminantque faventes
undique discordi sonitum simul agmine venti.

[39] flumen CSH¹: fulmen H²AR.

[49] creat *codd.*: ciet *De Gubernatis* (*Paravia ed.*): gravat *Jacob*: onerat *Baehrens*: terit *Ald.* 1517.

[52] infestus CS: infensus AR: inde Iris . . . convocat *Baehrens* (an illustration of his arbitrary changes).

[53] admotisque tertia C: admotis ad territa sidera signis *Haupt*: admotisque terit iam sidera signis *Sudhaus*: admotis per inertia *Ellis*.

[54] e caelo *codd.*: et caelo *Bormans, Sudhaus, Vollmer*.

[58] discordes comitum *codd.*: discordi sonitum *Jacob, Ellis*.

There is this second form of poetic error, different from the first. Aetna's furnaces, it is declared, are those the Cyclopes used, when, employing their strength in rhythmic strokes upon the anvil, they forged the dread thunderbolt beneath their heavy hammers and so gave Jupiter his panoply—a graceless tale with ne'er a pledge of truth.

Next, there is a sacrilegious legend which molests with Phlegra's [a] warfare the ever-living fires of Aetna's summit. In olden time the giants essayed impiously to thrust down the stars from the firmament, then capturing Jove to place his sovereignty elsewhere and impose their laws on vanquished heaven. These monsters have man's nature down to the belly; below 'tis a scaly serpent that forms the tortuous windings of their steps. Great mountains are built into a pile for waging the battle. Ossa weighs down Pelion; Olympus, topmost of the three, lies heavy on Ossa. Now they strive to climb the mountain-masses heaped in one; the sacrilegious host challenges to close fight the alarmed stars—challenges in hostile array all the gods to battle: the standards advance through constellations paralysed. From heaven Jupiter shrinks in alarm; weaponing his glittering right hand with flame, he withdraws the firmament in gloom. With mighty outcry the Giants begin their onset; hereat thunders the deep voice of the Sire, and therewithal from every quarter the supporting winds with their discordant host redouble the noise. Thick burst the

[a] It was fabled that the Earth-born brood of the Giants, in their rebellion against the gods, sought to scale heaven by piling Mount Ossa on Pelion and then Olympus on Ossa. They were discomfited by Jupiter's lightnings on the Phlegraean plain in Macedonia.

densa per attonitas rumpuntur flumina nubes,
atque in bellandum quae cuique potentia divum
in commune venit: iam patri dextera Pallas
et Mars laevus erat: iam cetera turba deorum
stant utrimque decus. validos tum Iuppiter ignes
increpat et iacto proturbat fulmine montes.
illinc devictae verterunt terga ruinae
infestae divis acies, atque impius hostis
praeceps cum castris agitur Materque iacentis
impellens victos. tum pax est reddita mundo,
tum Liber cessata venit per sidera: caelum
defensique decus mundi nunc redditur astris.
gurgite Trinacrio morientem Iuppiter Aetna
obruit Enceladon, vasto qui pondere montis
aestuat et petulans exspirat faucibus ignem.

haec est mendosae vulgata licentia famae.
vatibus ingenium est: hinc audit nobile carmen.
plurima pars scaenae rerum est fallacia: vates
sub terris nigros viderunt carmine manes
atque inter cineres Ditis pallentia regna:
mentiti vates Stygias undasque canesque.
hi Tityon poena stravere in iugera foedum;
sollicitant illi te circum, Tantale, cena
sollicitantque siti; Minos, tuaque, Aeace, in umbris

[59] flumina CS: fulmina Z, *Munro, Ellis.*

[62] s(a)evus CSHA: scaevus R: laevus *Bormans.*

[63] stant CSH^1A: stat H^2R. utrimque CS: utrumque Z. deus CZ: de . . S: tuens *Baehrens, Vessereau*: verens *Ellis*: stant ut cuique decus *Unger.*

[64] victo CSH^1: vinctos H^2: victor AR: iacto *ed. Ascens.* 1507.

[66] infert(a)e S: infest(a)e Z: infert edivis (*sic*) C.

[69] tum liber *codd.*: tunc imber *Vollmer.* cessat CS: c(a)essa H^1A: cressa H^2: celsa R: tum nimbo cessante nitet *Baehrens*: Liber cessata *Ellis, Vessereau*: cessat: lenit per sidera caelum *De Gubernatis* (*Paravia ed.*).

torrents through the astonied clouds: all the warlike prowess of one and every god joins the common cause. Already was Pallas at her father's right and Mars at his left: already the rest of the gods take their stand, a glory on either flank. Then Jupiter discharges the din of his puissant fires: he hurls his bolt and lays the mountains low. From that scene the falling throng fled vanquished, the armies embattled against heaven: headlong the godless foe is driven, his camp with him, and Mother Earth urging her prostrate sons back to the fight they have lost. Then peace is restored to the firmament: then mid stars at rest comes Bacchus: the sky and the honour of a world preserved are now restored to the stars. As in the Sicilian sea Enceladus lies dying, Jupiter whelms him under Aetna. Beneath the mountain's mighty weight he tosses feverishly, and rebellious breathes fire from his throat.

Such is the widespread licence of faulty rumour. Bards have genius: so their lay wins high renown. 'Tis well-nigh all delusion that the stage gives us. Bards have beheld in poetry dark ghosts in the underworld and the pale realm of Dis amid the ashes of the dead. Bards have sung false lays of Stygian wave and Stygian hound. Some have stretched over many an acre Tityus ugly in his punishment: others torment you, Tantalus, with a banquet spread around—torment you too with thirst. They sing of your judgements, Minos, and yours,

---

73 petulans Z : petula in se CS : patulis *edd. ant.*, *Baehrens*.
79 canentes *codd.* : canesque *Scaliger*.
81 p(o)ena CSAR : cena *Baehrens*, *Ellis*.

iura canunt, idemque rotant Ixionis orbem—
quicquid et interius; falsi sibi conscia terra est.
nec tu, terra, satis: speculantur numina divom
nec metuunt oculos alieno admittere caelo.
norunt bella deum, norunt abscondita nobis
coniugia et falsa quotiens sub imagine peccet
taurus in Europen, in Ledam candidus ales
Iuppiter, ut Danaae pretiosus fluxerit imber:
debita carminibus libertas ista; sed omnis
in vero mihi cura: canam quo fervida motu
aestuet Aetna novosque rapax sibi congerat ignes.
  quacumque immensus se terrae porrigit orbis
extremique maris curvis incingitur undis,
non totum ex solido est: ducit namque omnis hiatum,
secta est omnis humus, penitusque cavata latebris
exiles suspensa vias agit; utque animanti
per tota errantes percurrunt corpora venae
ad vitam sanguis omnis qua commeat eidem,
terra voraginibus conceptas digerit auras.
scilicet aut olim diviso corpore mundi
in maria ac terras et sidera, sors data caelo
prima, secuta maris, deseditque infima tellus
sed tortis rimosa cavis; et qualis acervus
exsilit imparibus iactis ex tempore saxis,

[84] quicquid interius *codd.*: in terris *Baehrens*. sibi conscia CS: consortia Z. terrent *codd.*: texent *De Gubernatis* (*Paravia ed.*): terra est *Ald.* 1517: quidquid et infernist, falsi consortia adhaerent *Ellis*.

[88] peccent *codd.*: peccet *Schrader*.

[96] non totum et solido desunt namque omnis hiatu CS: solidum . . . hiatus R: non totum ex solido est, ducit namque omnis hiatum *Ellis*: non totum et solido densum est *Vollmer*: solidum et densum *Gercke*.

[100] idem *codd.*: eidem *Ellis*.

Aeacus, in the world of shades: they also set Ixion's wheel revolving—and whatsoe'er is deeper hid; earth is conscious of the falsehood. Nor yet do you, O earth, suffice them: they spy on the divine powers: they are not afraid to let their eyes peer into a heaven where they have no portion. They know the wars of gods, their unions hidden from us, all the sins of Jove in deceitful guise, as a bull to trick Europa, a white swan for Leda, a streaming shower of precious ore for Danaë. Such freedom must be accorded to poetry; but with truth alone is my concern. I will sing the movement that makes fervent Aetna boil and greedily gather its own stores of fire renewed.

Wherever the earth's vast sphere extends, girt with the curving waves of farthest ocean, it is not solid all in all. Everywhere the ground has its long line of fissure, everywhere is cleft and, hollowed deeply with secret holes, hangs above narrow passages which it makes.[a] As in a living creature veins run through the whole body with wandering course, along which passes every drop of blood to feed life for the selfsame organism, so the earth by its chasms draws in and distributes currents of air. Either, I mean, when of old the body of the universe was divided into sea, earth and stars, the first portion was given to the sky, then followed that of the sea, and earth sank down lowest of the three, albeit fissured by winding hollows; and, even as a heap springs out of stones of uneven shape

[a] *suspensa*: *cf. pendeat in sese*, 108.

ut crebro introrsus spatio vacuata † charybdis
pendeat in sese, simili quoque terra figura
in tenuis laxata vias, non omnis in artum
nec stipata coit: sive illi causa vetusta est,
nec nata est facies, sed liber spiritus intrat
et fugiens molitur iter, seu lympha perenni
edit humum limo furtimque obstantia mollit;
aut etiam inclusi solidum vicere vapores,
atque igni quaesita via est; sive omnia certis
pugnavere locis; non est hic causa dolendi
dum stet opus causae. quis enim non credit inanes
esse sinus penitus, tantos emergere fontes
cum videt ac totiens imo se mergere hiatu?
non ille ex tenui quocumque agat: apta necesse est
confluvia errantes arcessant undique venas
et trahat ex pleno quod fortem contrahat amnem.
flumina quin etiam latis currentia rivis
occasus habuere suos: aut illa vorago

107 vacat acta CS: vacuata *Ald.* 1517: vacefacta *Buecheler* (cf. Lucret. vi. 1005, multusque văcēfit). charibdis C: carinis *corr. in* charims S: carambos V.

108 simili *codd.*: similis *Ellis.* futur(a)e *codd.*: futura est *Vollmer*: figura *Ald.* 1517: figurae *Ellis.*

112 nympha CS: lympha Z. perenni *codd.*: perennis *Ellis.*

114 videre *codd.*: exedere *Ald.* 1517: vicere *Sevin*: rupere *Jacob*: fudere *Munro*: solvere *Birt.*

116 dolendi *codd.*: docendi *Ald.* 1517: docenda *Clericus*: docendi, dum stet opus, causas *Munro.*

117 credit CS: credat *Ald.* 1517. (In 118–122 textual difficulties have possibly been increased by the loss of a line after 119: Munro and Ellis mark a lacuna.)

119 torrens Z: torres (n superscribed) C: totiens *Haupt.* uno CSZ: imo V, *Haupt.*

120 non Z: nam CS. vocemque *codd.*: vacuoque *Scaliger*: quocumque *Sudhaus*: nam mille ex tenui vocuoque (*sic*) agitata *Munro*: non ille ex tenui violens veget; arta *Ellis.*

thrown at random, so as to form a charybdis [a] hollowed with frequent interstices within and hanging upon itself, even so in like configuration the earth, too, loosened into tiny channels, does not all unite compactly or into narrow compass. Or maybe the cause of it is indeed ancient, though the formation is not coeval with its origin, but some air enters unchecked and works a road as it escapes: or water has eaten away the ground with the mud it perpetually makes and stealthily softens what blocks its course. Or again hot vapours cribbed and confined have overcome solidity and fire has sought a path for itself: or all these forces may have striven in their assigned places. No cause is here for mourning our ignorance, so long as the working of the true cause stands assured. Who does not believe that there are gulfs of emptiness in earth's recesses, when he sees springs so mighty emerge and so often plunge again in the depth of a chasm? That chasm could not speed it from any slender source: fit confluents must needs summon from everywhere their wandering ducts and the chasm draw from a full source the making of a mighty river. Moreover, rivers running with broad currents have found their own places of sinking. Either an abyss has snatched them headlong down

[a] No editor has found a satisfactory reading here. What is wanted is a feminine noun agreeing with *vacuata* and meaning a loosely compacted heap with hollows in it: *charybdis*, "a whirlpool," does not express this. Clericus invented *corymbis* (fem.) for this passage from κόρυμβος, "a peak" or "cluster," and Gronov suggested *corymbas* (κορυμβάς, "a string running round a net").

121 cum fluvio C: cum fluvia S: confluit AR: confluvia H[1], *and modern editors.*

122 et trahat CSH: extrahat AR: ut trahat *Munro.*

derepta in praeceps fatali condidit ore,
aut occulta fluunt, tectis adoperta cavernis,
atque inopinatos referunt procul edita cursus.
quod ni diversos emittat terra canales,
hospitium fluvio det semita, nulla profecto
fontibus et rivis constet via, pigraque tellus
conferta in solidum segni sub pondere cesset.
quod si praecipiti conduntur flumina terra,
condita si redeunt, si quaedam incondita surgunt,
haud mirum clausis etiam si libera ventis
spiramenta latent. certis tibi pignora rebus
atque oculis haesura tuis dabit ordine tellus.
immensos plerumque sinus et iugera pessum
intercepta licet densaeque abscondita nocti
prospectare: procul chaos ac sine fine ruinae.
cernis et in silvis spatiosa cubilia retro
antraque demersas penitus fodisse latebras?
incomperta via est operum; tantum effluit intra . . .
argumenta dabunt ignoti vera profundi,
tu modo subtiles animo duce percipe curas
occultique fidem manifestis abstrahe rebus.
nam quo liberior quoque est animosior ignis

128 si *codd.*: ni *Jacob*: nisi *Vollmer.*

129 fluvium CS: fluminum Z: fluviorum *Ald.* 1517: fluviis *Birt*: fluvio *Baehrens.* aut CSHA: haud *Clericus*: et det *Baehrens*: det *Ellis.*

131 conserta *codd.*: conferta *Ald.* 1517.

133 si qua etiam CSR: si quae etiam V: et iam *Scaliger*: si quaedam *Munro.*

138 densaque . . . nocte G.

139 Vollmer punctuates after *procul.*

140 spatioque *codd.*: spatiosa *Ald.* 1517.

141 demissa pedibus CZ: dimiss apedibus (*sic*) S: demersas penitus G.

142 Munro and Ellis mark a lacuna after this line. operum CSZ: aer *Jacob.* effluit intra CSZ: effugit ultra G.

and buried them in its fateful jaws, or they flow unseen, o'er-arched by closed caverns, then, coming to light far away, renew their unexpected course. If earth did not let out channels in different places, if some path did not give welcome to a river, truly no road would be assured for springs and streams, and sluggish earth, packed in a dense mass, would be rendered idle by its unmoving weight. But if rivers are buried in a sheer abyss of earth, if some which are buried come back to light and others without such burial rise from earth, no wonder is it that confined winds have liberating vents which are concealed. Proofs of this through facts indisputable, proofs which hold the eye, the earth will give you in due order. Oftentimes you may look out on vast cavities and tracts of land cut off ruinously and plunged into thick darkness; 'tis far-flung chaos and unending debris. Moreover, do you see how in forests there are lairs and caves of widely receding space which have dug far down their deep-sunk coverts? Undiscovered is the route of such working: only within there is an outflow. . . .[a] These (caves) will furnish true proofs of a depth unknown to us. Let but your mind guide you to a grasp of cunning research: from things manifest gather faith in the unseen. For as fire is always more unfettered and

[a] Some part of the argument about the hidden forces of air is lost. The reasoning seems to be that, though the process of working is unascertained, yet anyone entering such caverns will be conscious of the efflux of air.

145 occultamque *codd.*: occultique *Baehrens.*

semper in inclusis nec ventis segnior ira est,
sub terra penitusque novent hoc plura necesse est,
vincla magis solvant, magis hoc obstantia pellant.
nec tamen in rigidos exit contenta canales
vis animae flammaeve: ruit qua proxima cedunt
obliquumque secat qua visa tenerrima caula est.
hinc terrae tremor, hinc motus, ubi densus hiantes
spiritus exagitat venas cessantiaque urget.
quod si spissa foret, solido si staret in omni,
nulla daret miranda sui spectacula tellus,
pigraque et in pondus conferta immobilis esset.
sed summis si forte putas concrescere causis
tantum opus et summis alimentum viribus, ora
qua patula in promptu cernis vastosque recessus,
falleris et nondum tibi lumine certa liquet res.
namque illuc quodcumque vacans hiat impetus omnis:
at sese introitu solvunt adituque patenti
conversae languent vires animosque remittunt.

148 movent CSH: movet AR: novent *Ellis.*

151 verrit CS: ruit G.

152 causa est CSH[1]: causa (*om.* est) AR: massa est *Munro*: caula est *Clericus*: crusta est *Haupt*: secant quae causa tenerrima caussa est G (faulty enough to justify Ellis' remark "the fondest admirer of Gyr. will not claim much for it here.")

158 subitis G: summis CSZ. concrescere G: concredere CS: concedere *Ellis.*

159 et subitis G: et summis CSZ: adsumptis *Ellis*: ex subitis alimenti incursibus *Unger.* oris CSZ: ora? G, *Munro.*

160 qu(a)e CSZ: qua *Ellis.* patula G: valida CSZ. vastosque G: validosque CSAR: validosaque H.

161 falleris et G: fallere sed CSZ. certo tibi lumine res est G: tibi lumine certaque retro CSZ: tibi lumine certa liquet res *Ellis.*

162 illis G: illic H[2]: illuc CSH[1]: illud AR. quaecumque G: quodcunque CSARH[2]: quocumque H[1]. vacant hiatibus G: vacat hiat impetus CS: vagantur hiatibus *Baehrens*: vacans hiat, impetus *Ellis.*

more furious in confined spaces, and as the rage of the winds is no less vehement there, so to this extent, underground and in earth's depths, must fire and wind cause greater changes, all the more loose their bonds, all the more drive off what blocks their course. Yet 'tis not into unyielding channels that the pent-up force of air or flame escapes. It hurtles on only where the nearest barriers give way, and cuts its course sideways just where the enclosure seems most frail. Hence comes the trembling, the quaking of earth, when compressed air stirs the pores till they gape and drives sluggish matter before it. But if earth had no openings, if its frame were entirely solid, it would give the eye no marvellous visions of its inner self; inert and packed into a weighty mass, it would remain immovable. But if perhaps you think that this mighty action is a growth from causes at the surface and its nourishment a growth from surface strength[a] at the point where you perceive before you outstretched clefts and vast chasms—if so, you are wrong: the case is not yet clear to you, established in its true light. For all the onslaught of the winds makes for any open vacuum, but at their entry their forces slacken; altered by the spacious access to the chasm, they turn feeble and relax their spirit. For when the

[a] Ellis' reading *concedere* means "is a yielding to forces at the surface." Conjecturing *adsumptis* in the next line, he takes *alimentum* as gen. plur.; the meaning then would be: "when a powerful addition of materials feeding the flame has been received." In either case, provided *summis* of 158 is right, the author is opposing the theory that eruptions can be caused by agencies near the surface.

163 et CSZ: set *Ellis*: at *Vessereau*.
164 conceptae G: conversae CSZ: conruptae *Baehrens*.

quippe ubi quod teneat ventos acuatque morantes
in vacuo desit cessant, tantumque profundi
explicat errantes et in ipso limine tardant.
angustis opus est turbare in faucibus illos.
fervet opus densaque premit premiturque ruina
nunc Euri Boreaeque Notus, nunc huius uterque.
hinc venti rabies, hinc saevo quassat hiatu
fundamenta soli: trepidant urbesque caducae
inde, neque est aliud, si fas est credere, mundo
venturam antiqui faciem veracius omen.
  haec primo cum sit species naturaque terrae,
introrsus cessante solo trahit undique venas
Aetna: sui manifesta fides et proxima vero est.
non illic duce me occultas scrutabere causas,
occurrent oculis ipsae cogentque fateri.
plurima namque patent illi miracula monti.
hinc vasti terrent aditus merguntque profundo,
corrigit hinc artus penitus quos exigit ultra.
hinc spissae rupes obstant discordiaque ingens.
inter opus nectunt varie mediumque coercent
pars igni domitae, pars ignes ferre coactae,

165 qui teneat G: contineat CZ: quod teneat *Haupt.* ventosa qua quaeque CS: ventos aquasque (? qua quasque) G: ventos acuatque *Munro.*

166 defit G: desint CSHA: desinit R: desit *Ellis.*

168 turbanti G: turbant in CSH: turbare R, *Ellis.* illos CSZ: illo G.

171 quassa meatu *Wernsdorf, Maehly*: quassa boatu *Unger.*

175 immo G: primo CZ: imo *Matthiae.*

176–177 Punctuation varies according as stop is placed after *venas*, *Aetna* or *sui.*

178 caulas *Baehrens.* 180 spiracula *Baehrens.*

182 porrigit G: corrigit CZ. artus GCZ: artos *Maehly.* exaestuat G: quos exigit CS.

183 spissae CZ: scissae G.

184 aliae G: varies CH[1]: varios H[2]AR: varie *Ellis.*

vacuum contains nothing to stop the winds or spur them in their delay, they flag; all the great abyss deploys them drifting to and fro, and on the very threshold they lose their speed. It must needs be in narrow gullies that the winds work their havoc. Hot glows the work:[a] now the South Wind presses or is pressed on by the thick swoop of the East Wind and the North: now, again, both these winds by a current from the South. Hence the wind's fury: hence it can shatter the foundations of the ground with cruel cleavage. For that reason do cities totter in panic, and, if such belief be not impious, there is no truer presage that the universe will return to its primeval appearance.[b]

As this from the beginning has been the character and nature of the earth, everywhere Aetna runs channels into its interior, while the surface-soil remains inert: Aetna is the plain and truest proof of its own nature. There, with my guidance, you will not have to search for hidden causes: they will of themselves leap into your vision and force acknowledgement; for that mountain has countless marvels apparent to every eye. On this side are vast openings which terrify and plunge in an abyss, on another side the mountain rearranges its limbs projected too far. Elsewhere thick crags bar the path, and enormous is the confusion. They make a chequered weaving of their work and hem it round—some rocks quite subdued by fire, others compelled to

[a] The phrase *fervet opus* occurs twice in Virgil: *Georg.* IV. 169; *Aen.* I. 436. *Cf.* other Virgilian echoes such as *manifesta fides*, 177, *Aen.* II. 309; III. 375; *volvuntur ab imo*, 200 and *volvuntur in imo*, *Aen.* VI. 581.

[b] *i.e.* chaos: *antiqui sc. mundi.*

[ut maior species et ne succurrat inanis].
haec illi sedes tantarumque area rerum est,
[haec operis visenda sacri faciesque domusque].
  nunc opus artificem incendi causamque reposcit—
non illam parvi aut tenuis discriminis; ignes
mille sub exiguo ponent tibi tempore veram.
res oculique docent; res ipsae credere cogunt.
quin etiam tactu moneant, contingere tuto
si liceat; prohibent flammae, custodiaque ignis
illi operum est arcens aditus, divinaque rerum
cura sine arbitrio, eadem procul omnia cernes.
nec tamen est dubium penitus quid torqueat Aetnam,
aut quis mirandus tantae faber imperet arti.
pellitur exustae glomeranter nimbus harenae,
flagrantes properant moles, volvuntur ab imo
fundamenta, fragor tota nunc rumpitur Aetna,
nunc fusca pallent incendia mixta ruina.
ipse procul magnos miratur Iuppiter ignes,
neve sepulta novi surgant in bella Gigantes,
neu Ditem regni pudeat neu Tartara caelo
vertat, in occulto tacitus tremit; omniaque extra
congeries operit saxorum et putris harenae.

186 aetne C : aethne S : ethnae R. The line is repeated after 195 in CSZ.

187–188 This is the order in G : CSZ omit 188.

190 parvi aut tenuis discriminis ignes CSZ (ingens *Ellis*) : parvo aut tenui discrimine signis G (signes *Heinsius*).

191 ponent tibi Z : ibi S : ponentibus C. vera CSZ : veram *Munro*. exiguum venient tibi pignora tempus G.

192 oculique docent CZ : oculos ducent G. cogunt CSAR : cogent GH[1].

193 moneant AV : moneat CS : moneam G (?), *Munro, Ellis*.

195 operum C : operi G.

197 torqueat CSZ : torreat G.

endure fires yet [to make its look more imposing and its mental picture no unreal one]. Such is Aetna's seat, the field of phenomena so mighty: [such the enticing form and home of its hallowed activity].

Now my task demands who is the maker and what the cause of the conflagration—no cause that of slight or trivial import. A thousand fires in a moment of time will set before you the true cause. Facts and your eyes instruct you: facts unaided compel belief. Nay, they would instruct you by touch, were it safe to touch. But flames forbid it; Aetna's activity has the protection of fire which prevents approach, and the divine control over all is without witness; all such things you will descry from a distance. But there is no doubt what racks Aetna within or who is the marvellous artificer that directs handiwork so great. A cloud of burnt sand is driven in a whirl; swiftly rush the flaming masses; from the depth foundations are upheaved. Now bursts a crash from Aetna everywhere: now the flames show ghastly pale as they mingle with the dark downpour. Afar off even Jupiter marvels at the mighty fires and trembles speechless in his secret haunt, lest a fresh brood of Giants be rising to renew long-buried war or lest Pluto be growing ashamed of his kingdom and be changing hell for heaven; while outside all is covered with heap on heap of rock and crumbling

---

199 exutae CZ: exhaustae G: exustae *ed. Ascens.* 1507. glomeratur CHAV: glomerantur SR: glomeratim G: glomeranter *Ellis.*

206 tantum premit CSZ: tremit G: tacitus tremit *Baehrens, Ellis.*

quae nec sponte sua veniunt nec corporis ullis
sustentata cadunt robusti viribus: omnes
exagitant venti turbas et vortice saevo
in densum collecta rotant volvuntque profundo.
hac causa exspectata ruunt incendia montis.
spiritus inflatis nomen, languentibus aer.
nam prope nequicquam per se est violentia: semper
ingenium velox igni motusque perennis,
verum opus auxilium est ut pellat corpora: nullus
impetus est ipsi; qua spiritus imperat, audit;
hic princeps magnoque sub hoc duce militat ignis.
  nunc, quoniam in promptu est operis natura solique,
unde ipsi venti? quae res incendia pascit?
cum subito cohibentur, inest quae causa silenti?
subsequar. immensus labor est, sed fertilis idem.
digna laborantis respondent praemia curis.
non oculis solum pecudum miranda tueri
more, nec effusos in humum grave pascere corpus,
nosse fidem rerum dubiasque exquirere causas,
ingenium sacrare caputque attollere caelo,
scire quot et quae sint magno natalia mundo
principia (occasus metuunt an saecula pergunt

208 veniunt G: faciunt CSZ.
211 collecta G: coniecta CSZ.
212 expectata CSZ: expectanda G. ruunt CZ: terunt G. montis Z: mortis C (*Ellis cites* montis *in error, Proleg.* lxxviii).
213 inflat iis *Maehly*. momen *Scaliger*.
214 par est CZ: pars est G: per se est *Wagler*.
217 audit CSHR[2]: audis AR[1]: audet G.
221 cum CSZ: cur G. cohibetur inest CSZ: cohibent iners G: cohibent vires *Heinsius*. silenti CSZ: silendi G.
223 laborantis *Exc.*, CSZ: laboratis G.
227 *sic* G: sacra per ingentem capitique attollere caelum CSZ.

sand. They come not so of their own accord: unsupported by the strength of any powerful body they fall. It is the winds which arouse all these forces of havoc: the rocks which they have massed thickly together they whirl in eddying storm and roll from the abyss. For this reason the rush of fire from the mountain is no surprise. Winds when swollen are called "spirit," but "air" when sunk to rest.[a] The violence of flame unaided is almost ineffectual; true, fire has always a natural velocity and perpetual motion, but some ally is needed for the propulsion of bodies. In itself it has no motive energy: where spirit is commander, it obeys. Spirit is emperor: fire serves in the army of this great captain.[b]

Now, since the character of Aetna's activity and of the soil is manifest, whence come the winds themselves? What feeds the conflagration? When they are suddenly arrested, what is the inherent cause of the hush? I shall follow up the inquiry. Infinite is the toil, yet fruitful too. Just rewards match the worker's task. Not cattle-like to gaze on the world's marvels merely with the eye, not to lie outstretched upon the ground feeding a weight of flesh, but to grasp the proof of things and search into doubtful causes, to hallow genius, to raise the head to the sky, to know the number and character of natal elements in the mighty universe (do they dread extinction or

[a] Ellis justifiably defended this line against attack, *Jrnl. Philol.* xvi. 301, citing the parallel doctrine of Seneca, *Nat. Quaest.* II. i. 3 (*cum motus terrae fiat spiritu, spiritus autem sit aer agitatus* . . .): VI. xxi. and xxii.

[b] The imperial note in the Latin of 217–218 is unmistakable.

228 natalia *Exc.*, CS; fatalia G.

et firma aeterno religata est machina vinclo?)
solis scire modum et quanto minor orbita lunae est
(haec brevior cursu ut bis senos pervolet orbes,
annuus ille meet): quae certo sidera currant
ordine quaeve suo derrent incondita gyro:
scire vices etiam signorum et tradita iura
[sex cum nocte rapi, totidem cum luce referri],
nubila cur Phatne caelo denuntiet imbres,
quo rubeat Phoebe, quo frater palleat igni,
tempora cur varient anni (ver, prima iuventa,
cur aestate perit? cur aestas ipsa senescit
autumnoque obrepit hiemps et in orbe recurrit?);
axem scire Helices et tristem nosse cometen,
Lucifer unde micet quave Hesperus, unde Bootes,
Saturni quae stella tenax, quae Martia pugnax,
quo rapiant nautae, quo sidere lintea tendant;
scire vias maris et caeli praediscere cursus;
quo volet Orion, quo Sirius incubet index,
et quaecumque iacent tanto miracula mundo
non disiecta pati, nec acervo condita rerum,
sed manifesta notis certa disponere sede
singula, divina est animi ac iucunda voluptas.

232 pervolet *Exc.*, CSZ: pervolat G. Ellis inserts *ut*.
233 movet GHR: monet CSA: meet *Exc.*
234 suos servent G: suo errant CSZ: suo derrent *Ellis*. motus G: cura CSAR: gyris *Haupt*: gyro *Schrader*: guro (? circo) *Ellis*.
236 omitted in all MSS. except G.
237 caelo terris *Exc.*, CSZ: Panope caelo G: Phatne caelo *Matthiae*.
245 tendant *Exc.*, CSAR: pandant G.
247 volet *Exc.*, CSZ: vocet G. setius CS: secius H: serus AR: Sirius *Ald.* 1517. incubet *Exc.*, CSAR: excubet G.
249 digesta *Exc.*, CSZ: disiecta *Ellis*: congesta G.

[a] *i.e.* six zodiacal signs rise by day, six by night.

go on through the ages, and is the fabric fixed secure with everlasting chain?), to know the limit of the sun's track and the measure by which the moon's orbit falls short thereof (so that in her shorter course she flies through twelve rounds while he has a yearly path), to know what stars run in constant order and which stray irregularly from their true orbit, to know likewise the changes of the zodiac-signs and their immemorial laws [that six be sped during the night and as many return with the dawn],[a] to know why lowering Phatne [b] gives celestial warning of rain, what is the nature of the Moon-Goddess' red and her brother's pallid fire, why the year's seasons vary (why does spring, its youthful prime, die with the advent of summer? why does summer itself turn old, why does winter creep upon autumn and return in the season's cycle?), to know the axle of Helice,[c] to discern the ill-omened comet, to see on what side gleams the Morning-Star, where the Evening-Star, and whence the Bear-Keeper, and which is Saturn's steadfast star and which the warlike star of Mars, under what constellation the sailor must furl or spread his sails, to know the paths of the sea and learn betimes the courses of the heavens, whither Orion is hastening, over what land broods Sirius with warning sign; in fine, to refuse to let all the outspread marvels of this mighty universe remain unordered or buried in a mass of things, but to arrange them each clearly marked in the appointed place—all this is the mind's divine and grateful pleasure.

[b] The Manger-constellation (Φάτνη) which Aratus associates with storm. Panope, the reading in G, being a fine-weather divinity, is unsuitable here.

[c] The Great Bear.

sed prior haec hominis cura est cognoscere terram
et quae tot miranda tulit natura notare.
haec nobis magis affinis caelestibus astris.
nam quae mortali spes quaeve amentia maior
in Iovis errantem regno perquirere velle,
tantum opus ante pedes transire et perdere segnem.
torquemur miseri in parvis premimurque labore:
scrutamur rimas et vertimus omne profundum.
quaeritur argenti semen, nunc aurea vena.
torquentur flamma terrae ferroque domantur,
dum sese pretio redimant; verumque professae
tum demum vilesque tacent inopesque relictae.
noctes atque dies festinant arva coloni;
callent rure manus, glebarum expendimus usum.
fertilis haec segetique feracior, altera viti.
haec platanis humus, haec herbis dignissima tellus,
haec dura et melior pecori silvisque fidelis.
aridiora tenent oleae, sucosior ulmis
grata: leves cruciant animos et corpora causae
horrea uti saturent, tumeant et dolia musto,

[252] hominis Z (? S): dominis C: omni G.

[253] et qu(a)e nunc CSH: et quae tot *Pithou*: quaeque in ea G.

[254] magna CSZ: magis G.

[255] mortalis spes est quaeve CSH: mortali cuiquam est G.

[256] velle CSZ: divos G.

[258] premimurque *Exc.*, CSZ: terimurque G.

[263] viles taceant CSZ: tum demum humilesque iacent (*unmetrical*) G: vilesque iacent *Maehly*: vilesque tacent *Wight Duff*.

[265] expendimus usum G: expellimur usu *Exc.*, CSZ: expendimur usu *Schwartz*.

[267] platanis *Exc.*, CSZ: plantis G.

Yet this is man's more primary task—to know the earth and mark all the many wonders nature has yielded there. This is for us a task more akin than the stars of heaven. For what kind of hope is it for mortal man, what madness could be greater—that he should wish to wander and explore in Jove's domain and yet pass by the mighty fabric before his feet and lose it in his negligence? We torture ourselves wretchedly over little things: we let toil weigh us down: we peer into crannies and upturn every depth. The quest is now for a germ of silver, now for a vein of gold. Parts of the earth are tortured with flame and tamed with iron till they ransom themselves at a price[a]; and, when they have owned their secret, they are silenced[b] and abandoned to contempt and beggary. Day and night farmers hasten on the cultivation of their fields; hands grow hard with rural toil; we ponder the use of different soils. One is fertile and is more fruitful for corn, another for the vine; this is the soil for plane-trees, this the worthiest of grass crops; this other is hard and better for grazing and trusty to a tree-plantation. The drier parts are held by the olive; elms like a soil more moist. Trivial motives torture men's minds and bodies—to have their barns overflowing, their wine-casks swelling with must, and their haylofts rising

[a] In man's quest for gold and silver, regions of earth are "put to the torture" by the processes of mining and smelting until they buy themselves off by the ore they have yielded (*sese pretio redimant*).

[b] *i.e.* the rest is silence after the truth (*i.e.* where their hidden treasures lie) has been extorted from them: *tacent* gives a better contrast than *iacent*.

268 dura et *Exc.*: duro G: diviti CSZ.

plenaque desecto surgant faenilia campo:
sic avidi semper, qua visum est carius, itis.
implendus sibi quisque bonis est artibus: illae
sunt animi fruges, haec rerum maxima merces:
scire quid occulto terrae natura coercet,
nullum fallere opus, non mutum cernere sacros
Aetnaei montis fremitus animosque furentes,
non subito pallere sono, non credere subter
caelestes migrasse minas aut Tartara rumpi,
nosse quid impediat ventos, quid nutriat illos,
unde repente quies et muto foedere pax sit;
cur crescant animi, penitus seu forte cavernae
introitusque ipsi servent, seu terra minutis
rara foraminibus tenues in se abstrahat auras
(plenius hoc etiam rigido quia vertice surgens
illinc infestis atque hinc obnoxia ventis,
undique diversas admittere cogitur auras,
et coniuratis addit concordia vires);
sive introrsus agunt nubes et nubilus Auster,
seu fortes flexere caput tergoque feruntur,
praecipiti deiecta sono premit unda fugatque
torpentes auras pulsataque corpora denset.

273 avidi GCS: avidis *Matthiae.* qua visum est CSZ: quovis est G. ipsis G: istis CSZ: itis *Ellis*: sic avidi semper quaestus: est carius istis *Unger.*

277 multos CS: multo Z: mutos *Scaliger*: multum G: mutum *Haupt*: motum *Postgate.*

281 impediat CSZ: intendat G. illos C: ignes GH²: ignis AR.

282 multo *codd.*: muto *Oudin* (who also suggested *inulto*): iuncto *Mencken, Vollmer*: nullo *Unger.*

283 concrescant GCSZ: cur crescant *Scaliger, Pithou.* forte CSZ: porta G.

284 servent GCZ: fervent S: sorbent *Sudhaus.*

285 tenues G: neve CSZ: nivis in sese *Ellis.*

286 surgens G: surgit CSZ.

higher, charged with the full reapings of the field. So do ye tread the path of greed where sight reveals aught more precious.

Everyone should imbue himself with noble accomplishments. They are the mind's harvest, the greatest guerdon in the world—to know what nature encloses in earth's hidden depth, to give no false report of her work, not to gaze speechless on the mystic growls and frenzied rages of the Aetnaean mount, not to blench at the sudden din, not to believe that the wrath of the gods has passed underground to a new home, or that hell is breaking its bounds; to learn what hinders winds, what nurtures them, whence their sudden calm and the silent covenant of their truce, why their furies increase, whether it chance that caverns deep down or the very inlets conserve them or that the earth, porous by reason of its minute openings, draws off into itself thin draughts of air (and this in fuller measure because Aetna, rising with its stiff peak, is exposed on this side and on that to hostile winds and of necessity admits gales all round from different quarters and their concert brings more strength to their league), or whether they are driven inwards by clouds and the cloud-laden South Wind, or whether they have gallantly encircled the summit and sweep on behind; then the water from the clouds, streaming down with headlong noise, presses on the sluggish air-currents, drives them before it, and with its buffeting condenses

---

291 forte *codd.* : fortes *Ellis.*
292 una CSZ : ima *Birt* : unda *Scaliger, Pithou.*
293 torrentes *codd.* : torpentes *De Rooy, Munro, Ellis.*

nam veluti sonat ora diu Tritone canoro—
pellit opus collectus aquae victusque moveri
spiritus et longas emugit bucina voces;
carmineque irriguo magnis cortina theatris
imparibus numerosa modis canit arte regentis,
quae tenuem impellens animam subremigat unda:
haud aliter summota furens torrentibus aura
pugnat in angusto et magnum commurmurat Aetna.
credendum est etiam ventorum exsistere causas
sub terra similis harum quas cernimus extra;
ut, cum densa premant inter se corpora, turbam
elisa in vacuum fugiant et proxima secum
momine torta trahant tutaque in sede resistant.
quod si forte mihi quaedam discordia tecum est,

[294] ora diu H: ore diu AR: ora duc C: hora duci *Munro*: hora deo *Maehly*: hora deis *Alzinger*: hora die *Haupt*: sonituro horam *Schwartz*: urna ciens Tritona canorum *Ellis*. tritone CH: tritona AR. canoro Z: cancro C.

[304] cremant CSZ: premunt *Gronov*: premant *Baehrens*.

[306] nomina CSZ: momine *Gronov*: agmina *Sudhaus*. tota CSZ: torta *Jacob*.

---

[a] The two similes illustrate from mechanical examples the theory of the action of water and air in Aetna. In the first example, the readings suggested give a choice among a variety of contrivances. If *ora* is read, the Siren-like horn might be on the sea-shore, or on the Tiber-bank during one of Julius Caesar's *naumachiae*, or at Lake Fucinus when the emperor Claudius exhibited a naval spectacle in A.D. 53 (Suet. *Claud.* xxi). If *duci* were a certain correction and if it were then clear that only Claudius was meant, the passage would assist (as some have tried to make it assist) in dating the poem. The reading *hora* implies a hydraulic time-machine for announcing the hour to gods or men (*deo?*, *deis?*, *duci?*). Ellis' *urna* is meant to denote a hydraulic vessel fitted to work the "Triton." The second comparison is concerned with a

their elements. For just as the shore echoes for long the tuneful Triton-horn—the machinery[a] is set in motion by a volume of water and the air which is perforce moved thereby, and then the trumpet bellows forth its prolonged blare; just as in some vast theatre a water-organ, whose musical modes harmonise through their unequal pipes, sounds its water-worked music thanks to the organist's skill, which starts a small draught of air while causing a rowing movement in the water below[b]—even so the wind, dislodged by the rushing streams, raves and struggles in its narrow space and Aetna murmurs loudly with the blast.

Besides, we must believe that beneath the earth there arise causes of winds like those we see above ground; so that, whenever closely massed particles press against each other, they are forced out into a free space and escape the crush, and by their motive energy whirl and drag what is nearest along in their course, halting only when a safe position is reached.

But perhaps you may be at variance with me in

hydraulic organ of a sort known in Rome from Cicero's time (*Tusc. Disp.* III. 18 (43), *hydrauli hortabere ut audiat voces potius quam Platonis?* *i.e.* "will you advise him to listen to the notes of a water-organ rather than to the words of Plato?"). The invention is ascribed to Ctesibius, a barber of Alexandria, *circ.* 200 B.C. Nero was almost madly interested in water-organs (Suet. *Nero* xli and liv).

[b] *i.e.* probably with a pedal. A mosaic found near Trier last century gives a representation of a water-organ (Wilmowsky, *Röm. Villa zu Nennig*, Bonn, 1864–65). There the position of the organ-player is consistent with his using his hands to play and his feet on a pedal to set the water in motion. In May 1931, a handsome hydraulic organ dating from A.D. 288 was discovered at Aquincum on the Danube, the capital of Lower Pannonia (now Alt-Ofen, part of Buda Pest).

principiis aliis credas consurgere ventos:
non dubium rupes aliquas penitusque cavernas
proruere ingenti sonitu, casuque propinquas
diffugere impellique animas: hinc crescere ventos:
aut umore etiam nebulas effundere largo,
ut campis agrisque solent quos alluit amnis.
vallibus exoriens caligat nubilus aer:
flumina parva ferunt auras, vis proxima vento est:
eminus adspirat fortes et verberat umor.
atque haec in vacuo si tanta potentia rorum est,
hoc plura efficiant infra clusique necesse est.
his agitur causis extra penitusque: coactu
exagitant ventos: pugnant in faucibus: arte
pugnantis suffocat iter. velut unda profundo
terque quaterque exhausta graves ubi perbibit Euros,
ingeminant fluctus et primos ultimus urget:
haud secus, adstrictus certamine, tangitur ictu
spiritus involvensque suo sibi pondere vires
densa per ardentes exercet corpora venas,
et, quacumque iter est, properat transitque morantem,
donec confluvio veluti siponibus actus
exsilit atque furens tota vomit igneus Aetna.

310 provehere CSH : proruere *Ald.* 1517.
312 effundere CSZ : se effundere *Baehrens.*
316 fortis CSZ : fontis V. 317 rerum CZ : rorum *Jacob.*
319 coactus C: coactu *Ellis.*
326 ardentes CSZ: artantes *Jacob.* vires CZ: venas *Ald.* 1517: fauces *Sudhaus*: gyros *Ellis.*

[a] 307–329. The reasoning takes the form of an answer to a possible objector who suggests that there may be causes for winds in Aetna other than those already set forth (283–306). The argument is that you must allow that rock-falls underground generate air-currents; and, just as river vapours in valleys emit air (more perceptibly in hot climates, Munro says here; *cf.* also Lucret. VI. 476 *sqq.*), so the effect of moisture (*cf.*

your belief that winds rise from other causes.[a] It is undoubted (I claim) that there are rocks and caverns far below which fall forward with enormous crash, and that their fall disperses and sets in motion air-currents hard by: hence the gathering of winds. Again, fogs with their ample vapour pour out air, as they commonly do in plains and fields watered by a river. Rising from valleys the air makes a sombre cloud: rivulets bring gusts whose force is like the force of winds. Moisture from a distance breathes on the air-currents and whips them into strength. And, if a free space lets moisture have such power, its effects must be greater in proportion when within confined limits underground. These are the causes above and below ground which are at work. By compression they rouse the winds; they strive in narrow gorges; in that close strife their channel strangles them. As when a wave, drawn up again and again from the deep, has drunk full of the East Wind's violence, the billows redouble their number and the first are pushed on by the last, in that same way the (volcanic) wind feels the impact of the struggle which compresses it, wraps its own strength within its heavy mass and impels its close-packed particles through fiery passages. Wherever a path is found, it speeds on, ignoring any wind that would stay its course, until, driven by the confluent air-stream, as by so many forcing-pumps,[b] it leaps forth and all over Aetna discharges itself in blasts of angry fire.

the clouds of 290–293) within confined caverns underground must be far more potent. Two analogies are cited—waves under strong gales and the *siphon* forcing water on burning houses.

[b] *Sipo* (*sipho*, *sifo* = σίφων) was the tube of a fire-engine used to pump up water.

quod si forte putas isdem decurrere ventos
faucibus atque isdem pulsos remeare, notandas
res oculis locus ipse dabit cogetque negare.
quamvis caeruleo siccus Iove fulgeat aether,
purpureoque rubens surgat iubar aureus ostro,
illinc obscura semper caligine nubes
pigraque defuso circum stupet umida vultu,
prospectans sublimis opus vastosque receptus.
non illam videt Aetna nec ullo intercipit aestu;
obsequitur quacumque iubet levis aura, reditque.
placantes etiam caelestia numina ture
summo cerne iugo, vel qua liberrimus Aetnae
introspectus hiat, tantarum semina rerum,
si nihil irritet flammas stupeatque profundum.
huicne igitur credis torrens ut spiritus ille
qui rupes terramque rotat, qui fulminat ignes,
cum rexit vires et praeceps flexit habenas,
praesertim ipsa suo declinia pondere, numquam

[341] (a)ethnae AR: aethna C: etna H (? ablative).
[342] inprospectus CSZ: introspectus *Schrader*.
[344] huiṇc C: huicne *Ellis*: hinc *Scaliger*, *Baehrens*.
[345] notat CSZ: rotat *Jacob*.
[347] declivia CZ: declinia *Ellis*. All lines after 346 are missing in S.

[a] 330–358. This passage aims at disproving the idea that the wind which in an eruption issues from the crater has been constantly entering the mountain by the same avenue. Two arguments refute the notion: (1) the cloud which hangs invariably over the summit would be displaced by any wind

But if haply you imagine that the winds run down the same passage as that by which they are expelled and return, Aetna's own region will give your eyes facts for their notice and so compel denial.[a] However brilliant the atmosphere, however rainless under the blue sky, though the dawn rise with golden beams and blush with crimson tint, yet in that quarter there is always a cloud of impenetrable gloom and of slow movement that hangs lumpishly around, moist in its showery countenance, looking forth from its height on the mountain's state [b] and its vast recesses. Aetna ignores it and never dislodges it with any discharge of heat; wherever the bidding of a light breeze sends it, the cloud obeys, but then comes back. Further, look for yourself at worshippers who on the highest spur, just where there gapes open the freest view of the mountain's interior—source of such mighty upheavals—propitiate with incense the deities of heaven, provided nothing arouses the flames and the abyss remains in stupor. Do you then accept this as proving how that rushing volcanic "spirit," the whirler of crags and soil, the darter of fires, is, when once it has controlled its powers and put a sudden check on the reins, never known to pluck asunder bodies of matter or dislodge them from their strong arch, even though by their

passing down the crater; (2) the custom of worshippers to assemble at the crater and there offer incense would be impossible, if there were powerful winds blowing into the mountain. This, then, is ocular evidence of calm against any theory that winds from without cause volcanic explosions.

[b] *opus* here is not much more than "condition." It implies the activity, actual or latent, of the mountain, its "working": *cf.* 142, 188, 219, 277, 566. An alternative sense would be "fabric," "formation" as in 257.

corpora diripiat, validoque absolverit arcu?
quod si fallor, adest species: tantusque ruinis
impetus attentos oculorum transfugit ictus,
nec levis adstantes igitur ferit aura movetque
sparsa liquore manus sacros ubi ventilat ignes;
verberat ora tamen pulsataque corpora nostris
incursant: adeo in tenui vim causa repellit.
non cinerem stipulamve levem, non arida sorbet
gramina, non tenues placidissimus excit apludas:
surgit odoratis sublimis fumus ab aris:
tanta quies illi est et pax innoxia rapti.
  sive peregrinis igitur propriisve potentes
coniurant animae causis, ille impetus ignes
et montis partes atra subvectat harena,
vastaque concursu trepidantia saxa fragores
ardentesque simul flammas ac fulmina rumpunt.

348 diripiant CHA: diripiat R: deripiat *Clericus*. absolveret CZ: absolverit *Scaliger*. arcu CZ: aestu *vel* actu *Wernsdorf*.
351 nec levitas tantos CZ: nec levis astantes *Ellis* (*in note*).
354 *Ellis marks a lacuna after this line.*
356 humus excita praedas C: exit humus apredas H: exit humor † ap̄ndas AR: placidissimus excit apludas *Ellis*.
357 adoratis CAR: odoratus H: odoratis *Scaliger*.

---

[a] The passage is difficult. Taking *ut* with Birt and Sudhaus as "how," we may paraphrase it: "noting the calm on Aetna's summit, you can understand how the *spiritus*, so powerful when roused, fails to displace any part of the crater (*arcu*) when quiescent." [Sudhaus renders "von dem Felsrande des Kraters," but *arcu*, if the right reading, may mean an arched cavern and not the crater-curve.] Ellis propounds a different view, suggesting that *huicne credis ut numquam diripiat* may mean "Can you believe, on the showing of this, the impossibility of the *spiritus*, when in a milder form, tearing down masses of rock?"

[b] *Cf. ventilat ignem*, Juv. III. 253: *ventilet aurum* I. 28.

[c] *Cf.* Virg. *G.* IV. 6, *in tenui labor*. The connexion of

weight they have a natural tendency to fall?[a] Still, if I am wrong, appearance supports me: and such a great downward coursing rush eludes the eager glance of the eye. And so neither are they who stand near the crater struck and moved by the light wind, when the purified hand of the priest brandishes the sacred torches;[b] yet it strikes their faces, and bodies set in motion invade our bodies: in so slight an instance there is a cause which repels force.[c] The air in its complete calm[d] draws up no cinder or light stubble, stirs no parched grass or thin bits of chaff. Straight on high rises the smoke from the incense-perfumed[e] altars: so profound is that sleep of the air, a peace guiltless of ravin.

Whether then it is through extraneous or internal causes that the winds make their puissant alliance, that volcanic rush carries up amid black sand streams of fire and pieces of the mountain: huge rocks shiver as they clash and burst into explosions together with blazing flames and lightning flashes; as when forests

thought is not easy to follow. It has just been claimed that even powerful volcanic agencies may elude notice (349–350); and the parallel is cited of the air-current made by the priest in his lustration striking the worshippers' faces without their being aware of the impact. *Corpora* = "atoms": *nostris* = "our human bodies," which suffer the impact of atoms of air unconsciously. The extremely condensed *adeo in tenui vim causa repellit* is literally "in so slight an instance a cause repels force," *i.e.* keeps it from being felt. The "slight instance" is the priestly sprinkling of water and his waving the lustral fire: "force" may be said to be "repelled," if it is not allowed free play, and the worshippers are apparently unconscious of its operation. The proper explanation of *causa* is obscure, and Ellis may be right in suspecting a lacuna after *repellit*.

[d] *i.e.* on Aetna's summit between eruptions.

[e] *adoratis*, "venerated," the reading of C, makes quite good sense.

haud aliter quam cum prono iacuere sub Austro
aut Aquilone fremunt silvae, dant bracchia nodo
implicitae ac serpunt iunctis incendia ramis.
nec te decipiant stolidi mendacia vulgi,
exhaustos cessare sinus, dare tempora rursus
ut rapiant vires repetantque in proelia victi.
pelle nefas animi mendacemque exue famam:
non est divinis tam sordida rebus egestas
nec parvas mendicat opes nec corrogat auras.
praesto sunt operae, ventorum examina, semper:
causa latet quae rumpat iter cogatque morari.
saepe premit fauces magnis exstructa ruinis
congeries clauditque vias luctamine ab imo,
et spisso veluti tecto sub pondere praestat
haud similes, teneros cursu, cum frigida monti
desidia est tutoque licet discedere, ventos.
post, ubi conticuere, mora velocius urgent:
pellunt oppositi moles ac vincula rumpunt.
quicquid in obliquum est, frangunt iter: acrior ictu
impetus exoritur; magnis operata rapinis
flamma micat, latosque ruens exundat in agros:
sic cessata diu referunt spectacula venti.
  nunc superant quaecumque regant incendia silvae,
quae flammas alimenta vocent, quid nutriat Aetnam.
incendi poterunt illis vernacula causis
materia appositumque igni genus utile terrae.

370 animi CZ: animo *Ald.* 1517.
377 et scisso C: et spisso *Jacob.* pr(a)estat CZ: pressat *Baehrens.*
378 haud similis teneros cursu CV: haud simili strepere hos cursu *Munro*: aut simili tenet occursu *Ellis.*
380 conticuere CAR: convaluere mora, velocius *Morel.*
385 si CZ: sic *Maehly.*

[a] *Silvae,* "materials" = Greek ὕλη in the sense of "mass," "stuff." The plural here is noticeable.

have fallen beneath the swoop of the South wind or when they moan under a Northern gale, they intertwine their arms in a knot and with the union of the branches the fire creeps on. Do not let yourself be deceived by the blockish rabble's falsehood that the activity of the mountain recesses flags through loss of power, that mere time lets them capture their forces again and after subjection fetch them back into battle. Banish the disgraceful thought and spurn lying rumour. Such squalid poverty fits not things divine nor begs for mean supplies nor solicits doles of air. Ever at hand are workers, the swarming band of the winds: there is an unseen cause enough to interrupt the free passage and compel a stoppage. Often a pile heaped up with huge fallen boulders chokes the gullies: it bars the ways against the struggle below, and beneath its weight, under a massive roof as it were, shows the winds unlike their former selves, gentle in their current, while the mountain is in cold inaction and the onlooker may still depart in safety. Later, after their silent spell, they press on the swifter for the delay: they dislodge the masses of rock which they face: they burst their bonds. Whatever slants across their path, they break a way through: their fury rises fiercer for each impact. Flame glitters with widespread havoc for its work, and in its rush wells far across the country-side: so after long quiescence the winds renew their brave displays.

Now there remain to be discussed all the materials [a] which govern the conflagration, what fuels summon the flames, what is Aetna's food. There is native material capable of being kindled by these causes; also a serviceable sort of earth which fire finds

uritur adsidue calidus nunc sulphuris umor,
nunc spissus crebro praebetur alumine sucus.
pingue bitumen adest et quicquid comminus acris
irritat flammas: illius corporis Aetna est.
atque hanc materiam penitus discurrere, fontes
infectae crispantur aquae radice sub ipsa.
pars oculis manifesta iacet, quae robore dura est
ac lapis: in pingui fervent incendia suco.
quin etiam varie quaedam sine nomine saxa
toto monte liquent: illis custodia flammae
vera tenaxque data est. sed maxima causa molaris
illius incendi lapis est: is vindicat Aetnam.
quem si forte manu teneas ac robore cernas,
nec fervere putes, ignem nec spargere posse.
sed, simul ac ferro quaeras, respondet et ictu
scintillat dolor. hunc multis circum inice flammis
et patere extorquere animos atque exue robur.
fundetur ferro citius; nam mobilis illi
et metuens natura mali est, ubi cogitur igni.
sed simul atque hausit flammas, non tutior hausti
ulla domus, servans aciem duransque tenaci
saepta fide: tanta est illi patientia victo;

[395] eripiantur CH: eripiant AR: excipiantur *Vollmer*: crispantur *Ellis*: testantur *Maehly*: evincant tibi *Morel in supplem. novae editionis.*
[401] est si C: est sic R: est; is *Munro.*
[408] coritur C: cogitur V, *Munro.*
[411] tutum CZ: tanta *Scaliger*: bruta *Ellis.*

[a] The accus. and infin. construction *materiam discurrere* depends on a verb implied in *crispantur.*
[b] Springs of water at the foot of Aetna with a sulphurous or bituminous taste testify to the presence of inflammable substances in the mountain. The author proceeds (398–425) to argue that stones which liquefy, especially the lava-stone (*lapis molaris*) point to the same conclusion. Though a chief

proper to its use. At one time the hot liquid of sulphur burns continuously; at another a fluid presents itself thickened with copious alum; oily bitumen is at hand and everything that by close encounter provokes flames to violence. Of such substance is Aetna composed. And to show[a] that this fuel is scattered deep within the mountain, we find springs of tainted water rippling at its very base.[b] Some of this fuel lies obvious to the sight; in its solid part it is hard—a stone; but it contains an oily juice in which burns fire. Moreover, in divers places all over the mountain there are rocks of no specific name which liquefy. To them has been given a true and steadfast guardianship of flame. But the paramount source of that volcanic fire is the lava-stone. It above all claims Aetna for its own. If perchance you held it in your hand and tested it by its firmness, you would not think it could burn or discharge fire, but no sooner do you question it with iron than it replies, and sparks attest its pain beneath the blow. Throw it into the midst of a strong fire, and let it wrest away its proud temper: so strip it of its strength. It will fuse quicker than iron, for its nature is subject to change and afraid of hurt under pressure from fire. But once it has absorbed the flames, there is no safer home for what is absorbed; preserving its edge, it hardens with steadfast fidelity what it confines. Such is its endurance after being

cause of volcanic conflagration, the lava-stone externally does not look inflammable; if struck, however, with an iron bar, it gives off sparks, and in a powerful furnace is more quickly fusible than iron. Its great characteristic is its stubborn retention of fire: this marks it off from other substances which, once burnt out, cannot be rekindled.

vix umquam redit in vires atque evomit ignem.
totus enim denso stipatus robore carbo
per tenues admissa vias incendia nutrit
cunctanterque eadem et pigre concepta remittit.
nec tamen hoc uno quod montis plurima pars est,
vincit et incendi causam tenet ille: profecto
miranda est lapidis vivax animosaque virtus.
cetera materies quaecumque est fertilis igni,
ut semel accensa est, moritur nec restat in illa
quod repetas: tantum cinis et sine semine terra est.
hic semel atque iterum patiens ac mille perhaustis
ignibus instaurat vires, nec desinit ante
quam levis excocto defecit robore pumex
in cinerem putresque iacet dilapsus harenas.
cerne locis etiam: similes adsiste cavernas.
illic materiae nascentis copia maior.
sed genus hoc lapidis (certissima signa coloris)
quod nullas adiunxit opes, elanguit ignis.
dicitur insidiis flagrasse Aenaria quondam
nunc exstincta super, testisque Neapolin inter
et Cumas locus ex multis iam frigidus annis,
quamvis aeternum pingui scatet ubere sulphur.

413 cardo C: tardans AR: tarde H: carbo *Ellis*.
418 lapidum CZ: lapidis *De Rooy*.
425 iacet Z: iacit C. delapsus CZ: dilapsus *Scaliger*.
429 et languit CH: elanguit *Jacob*.
433 pinguescat et CH: pingui scatet *Ellis*.

---

[a] There is an apparent inconsistency between l. 412 and the statements of 418 and 422 *sqq*. The partial burning of successive eruptions (422–423) is to be contrasted with a complete burning out of the lava-stone (411–412 and 424–425); or

overpowered. Rarely does it ever go back to its old strength and belch out fire.[a] Throughout it is a carbonised block packed with a density of strength; narrow are the channels through which it receives and feeds its fires; slowly and unwillingly it releases them when collected. Yet not for this sole reason that lava forms the greatest part of the mountain does it remain triumphant and control the cause of volcanic fire. In truth the thing to marvel at is the vitality and pluck of the stone. Every other substance productive of fire dies after it has been lighted: nothing remains therein to be recovered—merely ashes and earth with not a seed of flame. But this lava-stone, submissive time and again, after absorbing a thousand fires, renews its strength and fails not till its heart is burnt out, and, now a light pumice-stone, has collapsed into cinders scattering a crumbling sand in its fall.

Judge likewise by special places; take your stand by similar volcanic hollows. These have a larger store of natural fuel. But because this species of stone—colour attests this most surely—has nowhere contributed its resources, the fire has died away. Aenaria,[b] we are told, once blazed out in sudden treachery, though to-day its summit is quenched. Another witness is the region[c] between Neapolis and Cumae, now cooled for many a year, though sulphur wells forth unceasingly in rich abundance.

it may be that 412 implies only an *immediate* return to former strength.

[b] Monte Epomeo (Latin *Epopeus*), the chief mountain of Ischia (Latin *Aenaria*) has been noted for sudden outbreaks.

[c] *locus* = Solfatara. Its character in antiquity is described by Lucretius (vi. 747–8), Strabo 246 (= V. 4. 6. *ad fin.*) and Petronius, *Satyr.* 120, line 67 *sqq*.

in mercem legitur, tanto est fecundius Aetna.
insula, cui nomen facies dedit ipsa rotunda,
sulphure non solum nec obesa bitumine terra est:
et lapis adiutat generandis ignibus aptus,
sed raro fumat qui vix si accenditur ardet,
in breve mortales flammas quod copia nutrit.
insula durat et a Vulcani nomine sacra,
pars tamen incendi maior refrixit et alto
iactatas recipit classes portuque tuetur.
quae restat minor et dives satis ubere terra est,
sed non Aetnaeo vires quae conferat illi.
atque haec ipsa tamen iam quondam exstincta fuisset,
ni furtim aggereret Siculi vicinia montis
materiam silvamque suam, pressove canali
huc illuc ageret ventos et pasceret ignes.
  sed melius res ipsa notis spectataque veris
occurrit signis nec temptat fallere testem.
nam circa latera atque imis radicibus Aetnae
candentes efflant lapides disiectaque saxa
intereunt venis, manifesto ut credere possis
pabula et ardendi causam lapidem esse molarem,
cuius defectus ieiunos colligit ignes.
ille ubi collegit flammas iacit et simul ictu

440 durata CZ: durat adhuc *Scaliger*: durat et a *Vollmer*.
444 Aetnaei *codd.*: Aetnaeo *Ellis*. illi CZ: igni *Haupt*.

---

[a] *Rotunda* is a translation of στρογγύλη, the Greek name represented by the modern Stromboli.

[b] Trachytic lava, not the *lapis molaris* of Aetna.

[c] In the Lipari islands Vulcano (Ἱερὰ Ἡφαίστου) is the southernmost, as Stromboli is the northernmost.

[d] or "to act the counterfcit witness."

It is gathered for merchandise, so much more plentiful is it here than on Aetna. The isle whose name comes from its own round shape [a] is land that waxes fat not merely in sulphur and bitumen; a stone [b] is found besides; fitted to beget fire, which aids eruption. But it rarely gives out smoke; if kindled, it burns with difficulty; for the supply feeds but for a little the short-lived flames. There survives too the island sanctified by Vulcan's name.[c] Most of its fire, however, has grown cold, and now the isle welcomes sea-tossed fleets and shelters them in its haven. What remains is the smaller portion—soil fairly rich in the abundance of its fuel, but not such as could match its power with that of Aetna's great supply. And yet this very island would long ago have been extinct had not its neighbour, the Sicilian mountain, always been secretly providing it with its own fuel and material, or through some sunken channel been driving the winds this way and that to feed the flames.

But better than any signs and tested by real proofs, true fact encounters us: it seeks not to deceive the watcher.[d] Round the sides and at the lowest base of Aetna rocks fume with white heat and scattered boulders cool down in their pores, enabling you to believe the evidence that the lava-stone is food and cause of the burning:[e] its failure gathers only starveling fires. When it has gathered flames, it discharges them and in the moment of

[e] *Cf.* Plin. *N.H.* xxxvi. 137, *molarem quidam pyriten vocant*: Grattius, *Cyn.* 404, *vivum lapidem.* The *lapis molaris* is appropriately called *pyrites*, "firestone" (πυρίτης) or *vivus lapis*, "the live stone," in virtue of its characteristic conservation of fire: *cf.* note on 395.

materiam accendit cogitque liquescere secum.
haud equidem mirum ⟨in⟩ facie quam cernimus extra;
si lenitur opus, res stat: magis uritur illic
sollicitatque magis vicina incendia saxum
certaque venturae praemittit pignora flammae.
nam simul atque movet vires turbamque minatur,
diffugit extemploque solum trahit: † ictaque ramis †. . . .
et grave sub terra murmur demonstrat et ignes.
tum pavidum fugere et sacris concedere rebus
par rere: e tuto speculaberis omnia collis.
nam subito effervent onerosa incendia raptis,
accensae subeunt moles truncaeque ruinae
provolvunt atque atra rotant examina harenae.
illinc incertae facies hominumque figurae:
pars lapidum domita, stanti pars robora pugnae
nec recipit flammas; hinc indefessus anhelat
atque aperit se hostis, decrescit spiritus illinc—
haud aliter quam cum laeto devicta tropaeo
prona iacet campis acies et castra sub ipsa.
tum si quis lapidum summo pertabuit igni,
asperior sopito et quaedam sordida faex est,
qualem purgato cernes desidere ferro:
verum ubi paulatim exsiluit sublata caducis

458 in *Vollmer*: *om.* CZ. facie que (*sic*) C: scate quod AR: scaterest *Ellis.*

459 restat *codd.*: res stat *Wight Duff.*

462 minatus C: minatur *Ulitius.*

463 exemploque C: extemploque Z. ictaque ramis CZ: actaque rima *Clericus*: undique rimans *Vessereau.*

466 parere CHR: par rere A. e *Scaliger*: et CZ. collis CZ: colli *ed. Ascens.* 1507.

469 atque atra *codd.*: adque astra *Ellis.* sonant *codd.*: rotant *Wight Duff*: volant *De Rooy.*

471 stanti C: stantis *Munro.*

impact kindles other fuel, forcing it to melt in a common blaze. No marvel is there in the appearance presented outside; if the action is abating, the upheaval is at a standstill. The more potent fire is in the crater: there the lava tempts more winningly all inflammable bodies within reach and sends sure forewarnings of the conflagration to come. For as soon as it stirs its forces, and threatens havoc, it flies in different directions, dragging at once the soil with it: smitten in its branches . . .[a] while the eruption is announced by a deep rumbling underground accompanied with fire. Then shall you think fit to flee in panic and yield place to the divine event. From the safety of a hill you will be able to observe all. For on a sudden the conflagration blazes out, loaded with its spoils; masses of burning matter advance; mutilated lumps of falling rock roll forth and whirl dark shoals of sand. They present vague shapes in human likeness—some of the stones suggest the defeated warrior, some a gallant host armed for a standing fight, unassailed by the flames; on one side pants the enemy unwearied and deploys his forces, on another the breath of fury wanes, even as when an army, vanquished in the victor's joyous triumph, lies prostrate on the field right to the gates of the camp. Then any stone that a surface fire has liquefied becomes, when the fire is quenched, more rugged—a sort of dirty slag like what you will see drop from iron when smelted. But when a heap has

[a] There may be a lacuna after *minatur* (462) as Munro thought, and there must be a lacuna after *ictaque ramis* (463), if that is the right reading.

[472] hinc defensus C: hinc indefessus *Ellis*.
[477] sopita es CH[1]: s. est H[2]AR: sopito *Maehly*.

congeries saxis, angusto vertice surgunt;
sic veluti in fornace lapis torretur et omnis
exustus penitus venis subit altius umor:
amissis opibus levis et sine pondere pumex
excutitur: liquor ille magis fervere magisque
fluminis in speciem mitis procedere tandem
incipit et pronis demittit collibus undas.
illae paulatim bis sena in milia pergunt.
quippe nihil revocat, certis nihil ignibus obstat,
nulla tenet (frustra) moles, simul omnia pugnant.
nunc silvae rupesque natant, hic terra solumque,
ipse adiutat opes facilesque sibi induit amnis.
quod si forte cavis cunctatus vallibus haesit,
utpote inaequales volvens perpascitur agros;
ingeminat fluctus et stantibus increpat undis,
sicut cum rapidum curvo mare † cernulat aestu,
ac primum tenues † undas agit, ulteriores . . .
progrediens late diffunditur et † succernens . . .
flumina consistunt ripis ac frigore durant,
paulatimque ignes coeunt ac flammea messis
exuitur facies. tum prima ut quaeque rigescit
effumat moles atque ipso pondere tracta
volvitur ingenti strepitu; praecepsque sonanti
cum solido inflixa est, pulsatos dissipat ignes,

486 primis Z: prunis C: pronis *Munro*.
488 curtis CH: certis *Wernsdorf*.
489 frustra moles CHA: moles, frustra s. obvia p. *Baehrens*.
490 notant CAR: natant *Baehrens*. haec tela *codd.*: nunc terra *Haupt*: hic terra *Ellis*: *perhaps* hinc . . . hinc.
491 ipsa *codd.*: ipse *Scaliger, Ellis*.
494 ingeminant CZ: ingeminat *ed. Ven.* 1475.
495 curvo CA: turbo *Vollmer*. cernulus *codd.*: cernimus *Munro*: cernulat *Jacob, Ellis*.
496 imas C: simas H: undas *Baehrens*: simans *Ellis*: rimas *Morel*: tenuis sinuans agit unda priores *Jacob*.

gradually sprung up raised from fallen rocks, they mount in a narrow-pointed pyramid. Just as a stone is calcined in a furnace and its moisture all burnt out inside and through the pores it steams on high, so the lava-stone loses its substance and is turned out a light pumice of inconsiderable weight: the lava-liquid begins to boil hotter and at last to advance more in the fashion of a gentle stream, as it lets its waves course down the slopes of the hills. By stages the waves advance some twice six miles. Nay, nothing can recall them: nothing checks these determined fires: no mass can hold them—'tis vain: all is war together. Now woodland and crag, here again earth and soil are in the flood. The lava-river itself aids their supplies and adjusts the compliant material to its own course. But if perhaps in some deep valley it lags and stops, its rolling volume browses leisurely over the fields uneven as they are. Then it redoubles its billows and chides the laggard waves; as when a violent sea plunges headforemost with curving swell; and first it urges on its feeble waves, others beyond . . . advancing, it spreads far and wide, and choosing (what to envelop). . . . The lava-streams come to a standstill inside their margins and harden as they cool; slowly the fires shrink and the appearance of a waving harvest of flame is lost. Each mass in turn, as it stiffens, emits fumes, and, dragged by its very weight, rolls on with enormous din; whenever it has crashed pell-mell into some solid substance which resounds with the impact, it spreads abroad the fires of the concussion and shines with

497 succernens CZ : succrescunt *Jacob* : sua certis *Schwartz*.
503 inflexa CZ : inflixa *Scaliger*.

et qua disclusa est candenti robore fulget.
emicat examen plagis, ardentia saxa
(scintillas procul ecce vides, procul ecce ruentes)
incolumi fervore cadunt: verum impetus ignes
Simaethi quondam ut ripas traiecerit amnis,
vix iunctas quisquam fixo dimoverit illas.
vicenos persaepe dies iacet obruta moles.
sed frustra certis disponere singula causis
temptamus, si firma manet tibi fabula mendax,
materiam ut credas aliam fluere igne, favillae
flumina proprietate simul concrescere, sive
commixtum lento flagrare bitumine sulphur.
nam posse exusto cretam quoque robore fundi
et figulos huic esse fidem, dein frigoris usu
duritiem revocare suam et constringere venas.
sed signum commune leve est atque irrita causa
quae trepidat: certo verum tibi pignore constat.
nam velut arguti natura est aeris, et igni
cum domitum est constans eademque et robore salvo,
utraque ut possis aeris cognoscere partem;
haud aliter lapis ille tenet seu forte madentes
effluit in flammas sive est securus ab illis

506 esse . . . esse CZ: ecce . . . ecce *Scaliger.* fides C: fide Z: vides *Haupt*: este pedes *Ellis.*

507 verum CZ: fert *Baehrens.* ignes *codd.*: ingens *Baehrens, Ellis*: igni est *Vessereau.*

509 iunctis *codd.*: uncis *Ellis*: iunctas *Vessereau.*

516 post . . . fundit CZ: posse . . . fundi *Wernsdorf.* exustam CHA: exusto *Sudhaus.*

521 ignis CZ: igni *Scaliger.*

522 constat CZ: constans *Haupt.*

523 ultraque CH: utramque AR: utraque *Munro.* portam CZ: partem *Clericus.*

white-glowing core wherever it has been opened out. A host of sparks flash forth at every blow: the glowing rocks (look, you see the flashes in the distance—look, raining down in the distance!) fall with undiminished heat. Yet, though the rush has been known to throw its fires across the banks of the river Simaethus,[a] hardly will anyone part those banks when once united by the hard-set lava. Very often for twenty days on end a mass of rock lies buried. But in vain I try to marshal each effect with its determined cause, if a lying fable remains unshaken in your mind, leading you to believe that it is a different substance which liquefies in fire, that the lava-streams harden in virtue of their cindery property, or that what burns is a mixture of sulphur and glutinous bitumen. For clay also, they assert, can fuse when its inner material is burnt out, and potters are a testimony to this: then by the process of cooling it recovers its hardness and tightens its pores. But this analogous indication is unimportant—an ineffectual reason given on hasty grounds. An unfailing token makes the truth evident to you. For as the essence of gleaming copper, both when fused with fire and when its solidity is unimpaired, remains constant and ever the same, so that in either state you may distinguish the copper portion, in no other way the lava-stone, whether dissolved into liquid flames or kept safe from them, retains and preserves

[a] The Simaethus or Symaethus in Eastern Sicily drains a considerable part of the island. The impetuosity of the lava-flood, carrying it over the bed of the river, is contrasted with the rigid immobility which marks it when solidified (507–510). The hard masses are described as lying immovable for twenty days together, blocking the river. D'Orville preferred to read *pedes* " buried twenty feet in the ground."

conservatque notas nec vultum perdidit ignis.
quin etiam externa † immotus color ipse refellit,
non odor aut levitas: putris magis ille magisque,
una operis facies eadem perque omnia terra est.
nec tamen infitior lapides ardescere certos,
interius furere accensos: haec propria virtus.
quin ipsis quaedam Siculi cognomina saxis
imposuere † rhytas et iam ipso nomine signant
fusilis esse notae: numquam tamen illa liquescunt,
quamvis materies foveat sucosior intus,
ni penitus venae fuerint commissa molari.
quod si quis lapidis miratur fusile robur,
cogitet obscuri verissima dicta libelli,
Heraclite, tui: nihil insuperabile ab igni,
omnia quo rerum natura semina iacta.
sed nimium hoc mirum? densissima corpora saepe
et solido vicina tamen compescimus igni.
non animos aeris flammis succumbere cernis?
lentitiem plumbi non exuit? ipsaque ferri
materies praedura tamen subvertitur igni.
spissaque suspensis fornacibus aurea saxa
exsudant pretium: et quaedam fortasse profundo

527 quin etiam *codd.*: quin speciem *Ellis*. externam multis *codd.*: externa immotus *A. M. Duff*.
531 propala CZ: propria *ed. Ven.* 1475.
533 fridicas C: frichas AR: chytas *or* rhytas *Scaliger*: Fρύδας (= frydas) *Ellis* (*in notes*).
539 gigni CZ: ab igni *Scaliger*.
540 quae *codd.*: cui *Jacob*: quo *Scaliger*.
544 lenitiem C: lentitiem A: lenticiem HR.

[a] The editorial *externa immotus* meets the difficulty of finding a noun to agree with *externam* (either substituted in the text for *etiam*, or understood like *materiam* or *naturam*). *Externa refellit* = "refutes the idea of alien substances," though the object of *refellere* is usually a person or such a word as *verbum*

its characteristics, and fire has not ruined its look. Moreover, the very constancy of its colour, not its smell or lightness, disproves any foreign elements.[a] The stone crumbles more and more, but its mode of working has the same look and the earth therein is unchanged throughout. I do not, however, deny that specific stones take fire and when kindled burn fiercely within. It is a quality proper to them. The Sicilians have given those very stones a name, *rhytae*, and by the title itself record that they are of a fusible character.[b] Yet although these stones have a somewhat juicy substance to preserve heat within, they never liquefy unless they have been brought deeply into touch with the pores of the lava-stone. But if anyone wonders that the core of stone can be fused, let him ponder those truest of sayings in thy mysterious book, O Heraclitus,[c] "naught is unconquerable by fire, in which all the seeds of the universe are sown." But is this too great a marvel? Bodies of thickest grain and well-nigh solid we nevertheless often subdue by fire. Do you not see how copper's sturdy spirit yields to flame? Does not fire strip away the toughness of lead? Even iron's substance, hard though it be, is yet undone by fire. Massive nuggets of gold sweat out their rich ore in vaulted furnaces; and mayhap there lie in the depths of earth undis-

or *mendacium*. *Immotus color* leads up to *una operis facies eadem* in 529; and the awkward *multis* disappears. For metrical parallel see 479.

[b] Scaliger based his suggestion of *rhytas* on ῥυτός (ῥεῖν) "flowing," "fluid," hence applicable to fusible substances.

[c] Heraclitus of Ephesus, one of the early Ionian philosophers, held that heat is the inherent principle of existence and that everything is in a perpetual flux. By the obscurity of his writings on physics he earned the name of "the dark" (σκοτεινός).

incomperta iacent similique obnoxia sorti.
nec locus ingenio est: oculi te iudice vincent.
nam lapis ille riget, praeclususque ignibus obstat,
si parvis torrere velis caeloque patenti.
candenti pressoque agedum fornace coerce;
nec sufferre potest nec saevum durat in hostem.
vincitur et solvit vires captusque liquescit.
quae maiora putas artem tormenta movere
posse manu? quae tanta putas incendia nostris
sustentare opibus quantis fornacibus Aetna
uritur, arcano numquam non fertilis igni?
sed non qui nostro fervet moderatior usu
sed caelo propior, vel quali Iuppiter ipse
armatus flamma est. his viribus additur ingens
spiritus, adstrictis elisus faucibus: ut cum
fabriles operae rudibus contendere massis
festinant, ignes quatiunt follesque trementes
exanimant, pressoque instigant agmine ventum.
haec operis forma est, sic nobilis uritur Aetna:
terra foraminibus vires trahit, urget in artum
spiritus, incendi via fit per maxima saxa.
  magnificas laudes operosaque visere templa
divitiis hominum aut arces memorare vetustas
traducti maria et taetris per proxima fatis
currimus, atque avidi veteris mendacia famae

549 ingenium CZ: ingenio *ed. Ven.* 1475.
555 autem C: aurem AR: artem *Ellis.*
558 ac sacro C: a sacro AR: arcano *Ellis.*
565 examinant CH[1]AR: exanimant H[2].
566 fama *codd.*: forma *Wolf.*
568 vivit *codd.*: via fit *Baehrens.*
570 sacras C: arcas *Ellis*: artes *vel* arces *Vessereau.*

covered minerals subject to similar ordinance. No place this for ingenuity: be you the judge and your eyes will triumph. The lava-stone is rigid; its surface barrier resists all fire, if you seek to burn it with small fires and in the open air. Well then, confine it in a narrow white-hot furnace—it cannot endure or stand firm against that fierce foe. It is vanquished: it relaxes its strength; in its captor's grip it melts. Now, what greater engines, think you, can skill apply with the hand, or what fires can it support with our human resources to compare with the mighty furnaces with which Aetna burns, ever the mother of secret fire? Yet her fire is not of the limited heat within our own experience, but more akin to that of heaven or the kind of flame with which Jupiter himself is armed. With these mighty forces is allied the gigantic volcanic spirit forced out of straitened jaws, as when mechanics hasten to pit their strength against masses of natural iron, they stir the fires and, expelling the wind from panting bellows, rouse the current in close array. Such is the manner of its working: so goes far-famed Aetna's burning. The earth draws in forces through her perforations; volcanic spirit compresses these into narrow space, and the path of conflagration lies through the mightiest rocks.

Over the paths of the sea, through all that borders on ghastly ways of death, we hasten to visit the stately glories of man's achievement and temples elaborate with human wealth or to rehearse the story of antique citadels. Keenly we unearth the false-

---

571 traducti CHA: tracti R. maria *De Rooy*: materia CZ. terris CZ: terras *De Rooy*: taetris *Scaliger*.

eruimus cunctasque libet percurrere gentes.
nunc iuvat Ogygiis circumdata moenia Thebis
cernere: quae fratres, ille impiger, ille canorus. . . .
condere, felicesque alieno intersumus aevo.
invitata piis nunc carmine saxa lyraque,
nunc gemina ex uno fumantia sacra vapore
miramur septemque duces raptumque profundo.
detinet Eurotas illic et Sparta Lycurgi
et sacer in bellum numerus, sua turba, trecenti.
nunc hic Cecropiae variis spectantur Athenae
carminibus gaudentque soli victrice Minerva.
excidit hic reduci quondam tibi, perfide Theseu,
candida sollicito praemittere vela parenti;
tu quoque Athenarum carmen, iam nobile sidus,
Erigone; sedes vestra est: Philomela canoris
evocat in silvis et tu, soror, hospita tectis

586 tam CZ: iam *Ald.* 1534.
587–8 Erigone edens questus P. canoras en volat in silvas *Maass*: Erigonae es, dequesta senem: P. canoris plorat Ityn silvis *Ellis*. evocat CZ: eiulat *Jacob*; en vocat *Munro*.

---

[a] The mythological allusions in lines 574–579 are to the miraculous building of Thebes when the stones obeyed the call of the "pious" brethren Amphion and Zethus; the never-ending hatred of Eteocles and Polynices, the sons of Oedipus, shown in the separation of even the flames on their altar; the seven champions who marched from Argos upon Thebes; the gulf in the earth which swallowed Amphiaraus.

[b] *piis*: Amphion and Zethus are called *pii*, not because they fortified Thebes, but because they avenged on Dirce her maltreatment of their mother Antiope. To furnish Thebes with walls and towers Zethus brought up the stones with his strong arms, and Amphion fitted them together by the music of his lyre.

[c] Eurotas was the river of Sparta and Lycurgus her legendary lawgiver.

hoods told by ancient legend [a] and we like to speed our course through every nation. Now 'tis our joy to see the walls which gird Ogygian Thebes, the walls reared by the brothers, the active one (Zethus) and the tuneful one (Amphion) . . . and so for a happy hour we live in a bygone age. We marvel now at the stones charmed into place by duteous sons,[b] with song and lyre, now at the sacrificial reek sundered as it rose from a single altar-steam, now at the seven chiefs and him whom the chasm snatched away. There the Eurotas and the Sparta of Lycurgus [c] arrest us and the troop consecrated to war, the Three Hundred, the band true to themselves.[d] Here again in manifold poetry is Cecropian Athens shown to us and her joy that Minerva won her soil.[e] Here once upon a day, faithless Theseus, your promise escaped your mind, to hoist, as you were nearing home, the white sail for an advance signal to your anxious father.[f] You too, Erigone, were an Athenian lay, henceforth a star of renown; Athens is the home of you and yours.[g] Philomela's call fills the groves with song and you, her sister (Procne), find a guest's

[d] The three hundred Spartans who laid down their lives fighting against the Persians in the pass at Thermopylae, 480 B.C.

[e] Athens is called "Cecropian" after her legendary king Cecrops. Athene (identified with Minerva) by her gift of the olive won the land belonging to Athens and so ousted Poseidon. The marble sculptures in the western pediment of the Parthenon recorded this rivalry.

Cf. 21–22 *supra* for another reference to Theseus' return from Crete.

[g] *Vestra* (" of you and yours ") alludes to her father Icar(i)us and the faithful hound which became Sirius. Erigone hanged herself for grief at her father's death. The theme was treated in a once celebrated poem by Eratosthenes.

acciperis, solis Tereus ferus exsulat agris.
miramur Troiae cineres et flebile victis
Pergamon exstinctosque suo Phrygas Hectore: parvum
conspicimus magni tumulum ducis: hic et Achilles
impiger et victus magni iacet Hectoris ultor.
quin etiam Graiae fixos tenuere tabellae
signave; nunc Paphiae rorantes arte capilli,
sub truce nunc parvi ludentes Colchide nati,
nunc tristes circa subiectae altaria cervae
velatusque pater, nunc gloria viva Myronis
et iam mille manus operum turbaeque morantur.
haec visenda putas terrae dubiusque marisque:
artificis naturae ingens opus aspice: nulla
tu tanta humanae plebis spectacula cernes,
praecipueque vigil fervens ubi Sirius ardet.
insequitur miranda tamen sua fabula montem

595 paflae CZ: Paphiae *Ald.* 1517. parte CZ: arte *Scaliger*: patre *Haupt*: matre *Baehrens, Ellis.*

599 turb(a)eque CHA: tabulaeque *Ellis.*

602 cum CZ: tu *Clericus.* humanis *codd.*: humanae *Ellis.* Ph(o)ebus CZ: rebus *Ald.* 1534: plebis *Ellis* ("*ex* plebeis *quod est in Rehd.* 60").

---

[a] Procne, wife of the Thracian King Tereus, avenged his violation of her sister Philomela by slaying their son Itys or Itylus and serving his flesh to Tereus as food. Legend changed Philomela into a nightingale, Procne into a swallow.

[b] *suo Hectore sc. exstincto.* Either (1) instrumental ablat., "through their Hector," he being by his death the cause of their destruction or (2) ablat. absolute, "their Hector having been destroyed": see Munro's note (which cites Cic. *Pro Mil.* 47, *iacent suis testibus,* "they are prostrated by the evidence of their own witnesses,") and Th. Maguire's discussion, *Journal of Philology,* III. (1871), pp. 232 *sqq.*

[c] The picture meant is the Venus Anadyomene by Apelles.

welcome in the home, while cruel Tereus lives an exile in the deserted fields.[a] We wonder at Troy in ashes and her citadel bewept by the vanquished, the Phrygians' doom owing to the fall of Hector.[b] We behold the humble burial-mound of a mighty leader: and here lie vanquished alike untiring Achilles and (Paris) the avenger of heroic Hector. Moreover, Greek paintings or sculptures have held us entranced. Now the Paphian's tresses dripping (so art shows them),[c] now the little boys playing at the feet of the pitiless Colchian,[d] a sad group with a father veiled around the altar of the substituted hind,[e] now the life-like glory of Myron's art,[f] yea a thousand examples of handiwork and crowds of masterpieces make us pause.

These attractions you think you must visit—wavering between land and sea. But look upon the colossal work of the artist nature. You will behold no sights so great belonging to the human rabble—(this you will find) especially if you keep watch when the Dog-star is blazing in his heat. Yet there is a wonderful story of its own which attends the mountain: it is

The traditional treatment of the tresses survives to some extent in Botticelli's " Nascita di Venere."

[d] The Medea of Timomachus (3rd cent. B.C.), a celebrated picture in which the painter represented the mother deliberating whether she should kill her children to revenge herself on Jason.

[e] The masterpiece of Timanthes (about 400 B.C.) in which he painted the sacrifice of Iphigenia, expressing woe on the faces of the bystanders, but veiling the face of the grief-stricken father, Agamemnon. The *cerva*, according to one form of the legend, was at the last moment miraculously substituted for the victim.

[f] The bronze cow by Myron, a greatly admired work (Cic. *Verr.* IV. lx. 135).

nec minus ille pio quam sonti est nobilis igni.
nam quondam ruptis excanduit Aetna cavernis,
et velut eversis penitus fornacibus ingens
evecta in longum lapidis fervoribus unda,
haud aliter quam cum saevo Iove fulgurat aether
et nitidum obscura caelum caligine torquet.
ardebant agris segetes et mollia cultu
iugera cum dominis; silvae collesque rubebant.
vixdum castra putant hostem movisse, tremebant
et iam finitimae portas evaserat urbis.
tum vero, ut cuique est animus viresque rapinae,
tutari conantur opes: gemit ille sub auro,
colligit ille arma et stulta cervice reponit,
defectum raptis illum sua carmina tardant,
hic velox minimo properat sub pondere pauper,
et quod cuique fuit cari fugit ipse sub illo.
sed non incolumis dominum sua praeda secuta est:
cunctantes vorat ignis et undique torret avaros,
consequitur fugisse ratos et praemia captis
concremat: ac nullis parsura incendia pascunt
vel solis parsura piis. namque optima proles

605 quamquam sors nobilis ignis CZ: quam quo sons, n. ignist *Baehrens*: quam sonti n. ignist *Maehly*.
607 ignes CZ: ingens *Scaliger*.
608 lapidis CH: rapidis AR.
610 c(a)elum CZ: telum *Postgate*.
611 mil(l)ia CZ: mollia *Scaliger*: mitia *Heinsius*.
612 urebant C: virebant Z: ruebant *Wagler*: rubebant *Munro*, *Ellis*.
619 nimio CZ: minimo *Auratus*, *Pithou*.
623 ratis CZ: ratos *Ald.* 1517.
624 concrepat CZ: concremat *Auratus*, *Pithou*.
625 dees CH: piis *Ald.* 1517.

[a] The eruption was historic. Aelian, quoted in Stobaeus' *Florilegium*, 79, 38, p. 456 (Gaisford), places it in Olympiad

no less famous for a fire of goodness than for one of guilt. Once Aetna burst open its caverns and glowed white-hot[a]: as though its deep-pent furnaces were shattered, a vast wave of fire gushed forth afar upborne by the heat of the lava-stone, just as when the ether lightens under the fury of Jupiter and plagues the bright sky with murky gloom. Corn-crops in the fields and acres soft-waving under cultivation were ablaze with their lords. Forests and hills gleamed red. Scarce yet can they believe the foe has struck camp; yet they were quaking and he had already passed the gates of the neighbouring city. Then every man strives to save his goods with such courage and strength as avails him to snatch at them. One groans beneath a burden of gold; another collects his arms and piles them again about his foolish neck; another, faint under what he has seized, has his flight hindered by his poems![b] Here the poverty-stricken man hastens nimbly beneath the lightest of loads: everyone makes for safety with what he held dear upon his shoulders. But his spoil did not follow each owner safe to the end: fire devours them as they linger: it envelops the greedy ones in flame. They think they have escaped, but the fire catches them: it consumes its prisoners' booty: and the conflagration feeds itself, set on sparing none or only the dutiful. Two noble sons,

81 (= 456–453 B.C.). He gives the names of the Catanaean youths who saved their parents from the flames as Philonomos and Kallias: *cf. n.* on 629 *infra.*

[b] 616–618. The satire at the expense of those who try to save their goods at the risk of life culminates in the glance at a poet struggling under a load of his own works. There is also a satiric undertone in the picture of tourists (569–600), who are curious sightseers rather than students of nature.

Amphinomus fraterque pari sub munere fortes
cum iam vicinis streperent incendia tectis,
adspiciunt pigrumque patrem matremque senecta
eheu! defessos posuisse in limine membra.
parcite, avara manus, dulces attollere praedas:
illis divitiae solae materque paterque:
hanc rapient praedam. mediumque exire per ignem
ipso dante fidem properant. o maxima rerum
et merito pietas homini tutissima virtus!
erubuere pios iuvenes attingere flammae
et quacumque ferunt illi vestigia cedunt.
felix illa dies, illa est innoxia terra.
dextra saeva tenent laevaque incendia: fertur
ille per obliquos ignes fraterque triumphans,
tutus uterque pio sub pondere sufficit: illa
et circa geminos avidus sibi temperat ignis.
incolumes abeunt tandem et sua numina secum
salva ferunt. illos mirantur carmina vatum,
illos seposuit claro sub nomine Ditis,
nec sanctos iuvenes attingunt sordida fata:
securae cessere domus et iura piorum.

626 Amphion CH: Amphinomus AR. fontis CH: fortis (*nom. plur.*) A.

628 senemque CZ: senecta *Scaliger*: sedentem *Barth*: senentem *Baehrens*: sequentem *Ellis*.

630 manduces *corr. in* manducens C: manus dites *Ald.* 1517: manus dulces *Ellis*.

632 rapies C: raperest *Munro*: rapient *Ellis*.

638 dextera CZ. tenet CH: tenent AR. fervent HR: ferunt *corr. in* fervent C: fertur *Buecheler*.

639 fratremque CZ: fraterque *ed. Ascens.* 1507.

640 sufficit *codd.*: substitit *Baehrens*.

646 sed curae C: securae *Munro, Ellis, Vessereau.*

Amphinomus and his brother, gallantly facing an equal task, when fire now roared in homes hard by, saw how their lame father and their mother had sunk down (alas!) in the weariness of age upon the threshold.[a] Forbear, ye avaricious throng, to lift the spoils ye love! For *them* a mother and a father are the only wealth: this is the spoil they will snatch from the burning. They hasten to escape through the heart of the fire, which grants safe-conduct unasked. O sense of loving duty, greatest of all goods, justly deemed the surest salvation for man among the virtues! The flames held it shame to touch those duteous youths and retired wherever they turned their steps. Blessed is that day: guiltless is that land. Cruel burnings reign to right and left. Flames slant aside as Amphinomus rushes among them and with him his brother in triumph: both hold out safely under the burden which affection laid on them. There—round the couple—the greedy fire restrains itself. Unhurt they go free at last, taking with them their gods in safety. To them the lays of bards do homage: to them under an illustrious name has Ditis[b] allotted a place apart. No mean destiny touches the sacred youths: their lot is a dwelling free from care, and the rightful rewards of the faithful.

[a] Claudian, *Carmina Minora*, XVII (L), has an elegiac poem on the statues of the two brothers, Amphinomus and Anapius at Catina now Catania. For allusions to their *pietas* *cf.* Strabo, vi. 2. 3 (C. 269), who calls the second brother Anapias; Sen. *Benef.* III. 37. 2; Martial, VII. 24. 5; Sil. Ital. XIV. 197. Hyginus, *Fab.* 254, gives them different names. Their heads appear on both Sicilian and Roman coins, *e.g.* Head, *Hist. Num.* 117; *Brit. Mus. Cat.*

[b] Ditis (more commonly Dis in the nominative) is Pluto, god of the under-world.

THE LOEB CLASSICAL LIBRARY

VOLUMES ALREADY PUBLISHED

Latin Authors

Ammianus Marcellinus. Translated by J. C. Rolfe. 3 Vols.

Apuleius: The Golden Ass (Metamorphoses). W. Adlington (1566). Revised by S. Gaselee.

St. Augustine: City of God. 7 Vols. Vol. I. G. E. McCracken. Vols. II and VII. W. M. Green. Vol. III. D. Wiesen. Vol. IV. P. Levine. Vol. V. E. M. Sanford and W. M. Green. Vol. VI. W. C. Greene.

St. Augustine, Confessions of. W. Watts (1631). 2 Vols.

St. Augustine, Select Letters. J. H. Baxter.

Ausonius. H. G. Evelyn White. 2 Vols.

Bede. J. E. King. 2 Vols.

Boethius: Tracts and De Consolatione Philosophiae. Rev. H. F. Stewart and E. K. Rand. Revised by S. J. Tester.

Caesar: Alexandrian, African and Spanish Wars. A. G. Way.

Caesar: Civil Wars. A. G. Peskett.

Caesar: Gallic War. H. J. Edwards.

Cato: De Re Rustica. Varro: De Re Rustica. H. B. Ash and W. D. Hooper.

Catullus. F. W. Cornish. Tibullus. J. B. Postgate. Pervigilium Veneris. J. W. Mackail.

Celsus: De Medicina. W. G. Spencer. 3 Vols.

Cicero: Brutus and Orator. G. L. Hendrickson and H. M. Hubbell.

[Cicero]: Ad Herennium. H. Caplan.

Cicero: De Oratore, etc. 2 Vols. Vol. I. De Oratore, Books I and II. E. W. Sutton and H. Rackham. Vol. II. De Oratore, Book III. De Fato; Paradoxa Stoicorum; De Partitione Oratoria. H. Rackham.

Cicero: De Finibus. H. Rackham.

Cicero: De Inventione, etc. H. M. Hubbell.

Cicero: De Natura Deorum and Academica. H. Rackham.

Cicero: De Officiis. Walter Miller.

Cicero: De Republica and De Legibus. Clinton W. Keyes.

Cicero: De Senectute, De Amicitia, De Divinatione. W. A. Falconer.

Cicero: In Catilinam, Pro Flacco, Pro Murena, Pro Sulla. New version by C. Macdonald.

Cicero: Letters to Atticus. E. O. Winstedt. 3 Vols.

Cicero: Letters to His Friends. W. Glynn Williams, M. Cary, M. Henderson. 4 Vols.

Cicero: Philippics. W. C. A. Ker.

Cicero: Pro Archia, Post Reditum, De Domo, De Haruspicum Responsis, Pro Plancio. N. H. Watts.

Cicero: Pro Caecina, Pro Lege Manilia, Pro Cluentio, Pro Rabirio. H. Grose Hodge.

Cicero: Pro Caelio, De Provinciis Consularibus, Pro Balbo. R. Gardner.

Cicero: Pro Milone, In Pisonem, Pro Scauro, Pro Fonteio, Pro Rabirio Postumo, Pro Marcello, Pro Ligario, Pro Rege Deiotaro. N. H. Watts.

Cicero: Pro Quinctio, Pro Roscio Amerino, Pro Roscio Comoedo, Contra Rullum. J. H. Freese.

Cicero: Pro Sestio, In Vatinium. R. Gardner.

Cicero: Tusculan Disputations. J. E. King.

Cicero: Verrine Orations. L. H. G. Greenwood. 2 Vols.

Claudian. M. Platnauer. 2 Vols.

Columella: De Re Rustica. De Arboribus. H. B. Ash, E. S. Forster and E. Heffner. 3 Vols.

Curtius, Q.: History of Alexander. J. C. Rolfe. 2 Vols.

Florus. E. S. Forster. Cornelius Nepos. J. C. Rolfe.

Frontinus: Stratagems and Aqueducts. C. E. Bennett and M. B. McElwain.

Fronto: Correspondence. C. R. Haines. 2 Vols.

Gellius. J. C. Rolfe. 3 Vols.

Horace: Odes and Epodes. C. E. Bennett.

Horace: Satires, Epistles, Ars Poetica. H. R. Fairclough.

Jerome: Selected Letters. F. A. Wright.

Juvenal and Persius. G. G. Ramsay.

Livy. B. O. Foster, F. G. Moore, Evan T. Sage, and A. C. Schlesinger and R. M. Geer (General Index). 14 Vols.

Lucan. J. D. Duff.

Lucretius. W. H. D. Rouse. Revised by M. F. Smith.

Manilius. G. P. Goold.

Martial. W. C. A. Ker. 2 Vols. Revised by E. H. Warmington.

Minor Latin poets: from Publilius Syrus to Rutilius Namatianus, including Grattius, Calpurnius Siculus, Nemesianus, Avianus and others, with "Aetna" and the "Phoenix." J. Wight Duff and Arnold M. Duff. 2 Vols.

Minucius Felix. Cf. Tertullian.

Ovid: The Art of Love and Other Poems. J. H. Mosley. Revised by G. P. Goold.

Ovid: Fasti. Sir James G. Frazer

Ovid: Heroides and Amores. Grant Showerman. Revised by G. P. Goold

Ovid: Metamorphoses. F. J. Miller. 2 Vols. Vol. 1 revised by G. P. Goold.

Ovid: Tristia and Ex Ponto. A. L. Wheeler.

Persius. Cf. Juvenal.

Pervigilium Veneris. Cf. Catullus.

Petronius. M. Heseltine. Seneca: Apocolocyntosis. W. H. D. Rouse. Revised by E. H. Warmington.

Phaedrus and Babrius (Greek). B. E. Perry.

Plautus. Paul Nixon. 5 Vols.

Pliny: Letters, Panegyricus. Betty Radice. 2 Vols.

Pliny: Natural History. 10 Vols. Vols. I–V and IX. H. Rackham. VI.–VIII. W. H. S. Jones. X. D. E. Eichholz.

Propertius. H. E. Butler.

Prudentius. H. J. Thomson. 2 Vols.

Quintilian. H. E. Butler. 4 Vols.

Remains of Old Latin. E. H. Warmington. 4 Vols. Vol. I. (Ennius and Caecilius) Vol. II. (Livius, Naevius Pacuvius, Accius) Vol. III. (Lucilius and Laws of XII Tables) Vol. IV. (Archaic Inscriptions)

Res Gestae Divi Augusti. Cf. Velleius Paterculus.

Sallust. J. C. Rolfe.

Scriptores Historiae Augustae. D. Magie. 3 Vols.

Seneca, The Elder: Controversiae, Suasoriae. M. Winterbottom. 2 Vols.

Seneca: Apocolocyntosis. Cf. Petronius.

Seneca: Epistulae Morales. R. M. Gummere. 3 Vols.

Seneca: Moral Essays. J. W. Basore. 3 Vols.

Seneca: Tragedies. F. J. Miller. 2 Vols.

Seneca: Naturales Quaestiones. T. H. Corcoran. 2 Vols.

Sidonius: Poems and Letters. W. B. Anderson. 2 Vols.

Silius Italicus. J. D. Duff. 2 Vols.

Statius. J. H. Mozley. 2 Vols.

Suetonius. J. C. Rolfe. 2 Vols.

Tacitus: Dialogus. Sir Wm. Peterson. Agricola and Germania. Maurice Hutton. Revised by M. Winterbottom, R. M. Ogilvie, E. H. Warmington.

Tacitus: Histories and Annals. C. H. Moore and J. Jackson. 4 Vols.

TERENCE. John Sargeaunt. 2 Vols.

TERTULLIAN: APOLOGIA and DE SPECTACULIS. T. R. Glover. MINUCIUS FELIX. G. H. Rendall.

TIBULLUS. Cf. CATULLUS.

VALERIUS FLACCUS. J. H. Mozley.

VARRO: DE LINGUA LATINA. R. G. Kent. 2 Vols.

VELLEIUS PATERCULUS and RES GESTAE DIVI AUGUSTI. F. W. Shipley.

VIRGIL. H. R. Fairclough. 2 Vols.

VITRUVIUS: DE ARCHITECTURA. F. Granger. 2 Vols.

Greek Authors

ACHILLES TATIUS. S. Gaselee.

AELIAN: ON THE NATURE OF ANIMALS. A. F. Scholfield. 3 Vols.

AENEAS TACTICUS. ASCLEPIODOTUS and ONASANDER. The Illinois Greek Club.

AESCHINES. C. D. Adams.

AESCHYLUS. H. Weir Smyth. 2 Vols.

ALCIPHRON, AELIAN, PHILOSTRATUS: LETTERS. A. R. Benner and F. H. Fobes.

ANDOCIDES, ANTIPHON. Cf. MINOR ATTIC ORATORS.

APOLLODORUS. Sir James G. Frazer. 2 Vols.

APOLLONIUS RHODIUS. R. C. Seaton.

APOSTOLIC FATHERS. Kirsopp Lake. 2 Vols.

APPIAN: ROMAN HISTORY. Horace White. 4 Vols.

ARATUS. Cf. CALLIMACHUS.

ARISTIDES: ORATIONS. C. A. Behr. Vol. I.

ARISTOPHANES. Benjamin Bickley Rogers. 3 Vols. Verse trans.

ARISTOTLE: ART OF RHETORIC. J. H. Freese.

ARISTOTLE: ATHENIAN CONSTITUTION, EUDEMIAN ETHICS, VICES AND VIRTUES. H. Rackham.

ARISTOTLE: GENERATION OF ANIMALS. A. L. Peck.

ARISTOTLE: HISTORIA ANIMALIUM. A. L. Peck. Vols. I.–II.

ARISTOTLE: METAPHYSICS. H. Tredennick. 2 Vols.

ARISTOTLE: METEOROLOGICA. H. D. P. Lee.

ARISTOTLE: MINOR WORKS. W. S. Hett. On Colours, On Things Heard, On Physiognomies, On Plants, On Marvellous Things Heard, Mechanical Problems, On Indivisible Lines, On Situations and Names of Winds, On Melissus, Xenophanes, and Gorgias.

ARISTOTLE: NICOMACHEAN ETHICS. H. Rackham.

Aristotle: Oeconomica and Magna Moralia. G. C. Armstrong (with Metaphysics, Vol. II).

Aristotle: On the Heavens. W. K. C. Guthrie.

Aristotle: On the Soul, Parva Naturalia, On Breath. W. S. Hett.

Aristotle: Categories, On Interpretation, Prior Analytics. H. P. Cooke and H. Tredennick.

Aristotle: Posterior Analytics, Topics. H. Tredennick and E. S. Forster.

Aristotle: On Sophistical Refutations.

On Coming to be and Passing Away, On the Cosmos. E. S. Forster and D. J. Furley.

Aristotle: Parts of Animals. A. L. Peck; Motion and Progression of Animals. E. S. Forster.

Aristotle: Physics. Rev. P. Wicksteed and F. M. Cornford. 2 Vols.

Aristotle: Poetics and Longinus. W. Hamilton Fyfe; Demetrius on Style. W. Rhys Roberts.

Aristotle: Politics. H. Rackham.

Aristotle: Problems. W. S. Hett. 2 Vols.

Aristotle: Rhetorica Ad Alexandrum (with Problems. Vol. II). H. Rackham.

Arrian: History of Alexander and Indica. Rev. E. Iliffe Robson. 2 Vols. New version P. Brunt.

Athenaeus: Deipnosophistae. C. B. Gulick. 7 Vols.

Babrius and Phaedrus (Latin). B. E. Perry.

St. Basil: Letters. R. J. Deferrari. 4 Vols.

Callimachus: Fragments. C. A. Trypanis. Musaeus: Hero and Leander. T. Gelzer and C. Whitman.

Callimachus, Hymns and Epigrams, and Lycophron. A. W. Mair; Aratus. G. R. Mair.

Clement of Alexandria. Rev. G. W. Butterworth.

Colluthus. Cf. Oppian.

Daphnis and Chloe. Thornley's Translation revised by J. M. Edmonds: and Parthenius. S. Gaselee.

Demosthenes I.: Olynthiacs, Philippics and Minor Orations I.–XVII. and XX. J. H. Vince.

Demosthenes II.: De Corona and De Falsa Legatione. C. A. Vince and J. H. Vince.

Demosthenes III.: Meidias, Androtion, Aristocrates, Timocrates and Aristogeiton I. and II. J. H. Vince.

Demosthenes IV.–VI: Private Orations and In Neaeram. A. T. Murray.

Demosthenes VII: Funeral Speech, Erotic Essay, Exordia and Letters. N. W. and N. J. DeWitt.

Dio Cassius: Roman History. E. Cary. 9 Vols.

DIO CHRYSOSTOM. J. W. Cohoon and H. Lamar Crosby. 5 Vols.

DIODORUS SICULUS. 12 Vols. Vols. I.–VI. C. H. Oldfather. Vol. VII. C. L. Sherman. Vol. VIII. C. B. Welles. Vols. IX. and X. R. M. Geer. Vol. XI. F. Walton. Vol. XII. F. Walton. General Index. R. M. Geer.

DIOGENES LAERTIUS. R. D. Hicks. 2 Vols. New Introduction by H. S. Long.

DIONYSIUS OF HALICARNASSUS: ROMAN ANTIQUITIES. Spelman's translation revised by E. Cary. 7 Vols.

DIONYSIUS OF HALICARNASSUS: CRITICAL ESSAYS. S. Usher. 2 Vols. Vol. I.

EPICTETUS. W. A. Oldfather. 2 Vols.

EURIPIDES. A. S. Way. 4 Vols. Verse trans.

EUSEBIUS: ECCLESIASTICAL HISTORY. Kirsopp Lake and J. E. L. Oulton. 2 Vols.

GALEN: ON THE NATURAL FACULTIES. A. J. Brock.

GREEK ANTHOLOGY. W. R. Paton. 5 Vols.

GREEK BUCOLIC POETS (THEOCRITUS, BION, MOSCHUS). J. M Edmonds.

GREEK ELEGY AND IAMBUS with the ANACREONTEA. J. M. Edmonds. 2 Vols.

GREEK LYRIC. D. A. Campbell. 4 Vols. Vol. I.

GREEK MATHEMATICAL WORKS. Ivor Thomas. 2 Vols.

HERODES. Cf. THEOPHRASTUS: CHARACTERS.

HERODIAN. C. R. Whittaker. 2 Vols.

HERODOTUS. A. D. Godley. 4 Vols.

HESIOD AND THE HOMERIC HYMNS. H. G. Evelyn White.

HIPPOCRATES and the FRAGMENTS OF HERACLEITUS. W. H. S. Jones and E. T. Withington. 4 Vols.

HOMER: ILIAD. A. T. Murray. 2 Vols.

HOMER: ODYSSEY. A. T. Murray. 2 Vols.

ISAEUS. E. W. Forster.

ISOCRATES. George Norlin and LaRue Van Hook. 3 Vols.

[ST. JOHN DAMASCENE]: BARLAAM AND IOASAPH. Rev. G. R. Woodward, Harold Mattingly and D. M. Lang.

JOSEPHUS. 10 Vols. Vols. I.–IV. H. Thackeray. Vol. V. H. Thackeray and R. Marcus. Vols. VI.–VII. R. Marcus. Vol. VIII. R. Marcus and Allen Wikgren. Vols. IX.–X. L. H. Feldman.

JULIAN. Wilmer Cave Wright. 3 Vols.

LIBANIUS. A. F. Norman. 3 Vols. Vols. I.–II.

LUCIAN. 8 Vols. Vols. I.–V. A. M. Harmon. Vol. VI. K. Kilburn. Vols. VII.–VIII. M. D. Macleod.

LYCOPHRON. Cf. CALLIMACHUS.

LYRA GRAECA, J. M. Edmonds. 2 Vols.

LYSIAS. W. R. M. Lamb.

MANETHO. W. G. Waddell.

MARCUS AURELIUS. C. R. Haines.

MENANDER. W. G. Arnott. 3 Vols. Vol. I.

MINOR ATTIC ORATORS (ANTIPHON, ANDOCIDES, LYCURGUS, DEMADES, DINARCHUS, HYPERIDES). K. J. Maidment and J. O. Burtt. 2 Vols.

MUSAEUS: HERO AND LEANDER. Cf. CALLIMACHUS.

NONNOS: DIONYSIACA. W. H. D. Rouse. 3 Vols.

OPPIAN, COLLUTHUS, TRYPHIODORUS. A. W. Mair.

PAPYRI. NON-LITERARY SELECTIONS. A. S. Hunt and C. C. Edgar. 2 Vols. LITERARY SELECTIONS (Poetry). D. L. Page.

PARTHENIUS. Cf. DAPHNIS and CHLOE.

PAUSANIAS: DESCRIPTION OF GREECE. W. H. S. Jones. 4 Vols. and Companion Vol. arranged by R. E. Wycherley.

PHILO. 10 Vols. Vols. I.–V. F. H. Colson and Rev. G. H. Whitaker. Vols. VI.–IX. F. H. Colson. Vol. X. F. H. Colson and the Rev. J. W. Earp.

PHILO: two supplementary Vols. (*Translation only.*) Ralph Marcus.

PHILOSTRATUS: THE LIFE OF APOLLONIUS OF TYANA. F. C. Conybeare. 2 Vols.

PHILOSTRATUS: IMAGINES; CALLISTRATUS: DESCRIPTIONS. A. Fairbanks.

PHILOSTRATUS and EUNAPIUS: LIVES OF THE SOPHISTS. Wilmer Cave Wright.

PINDAR. Sir J. E. Sandys.

PLATO: CHARMIDES, ALCIBIADES, HIPPARCHUS, THE LOVERS, THEAGES, MINOS and EPINOMIS. W. R. M. Lamb.

PLATO: CRATYLUS, PARMENIDES, GREATER HIPPIAS, LESSER HIPPIAS. H. N. Fowler.

PLATO: EUTHYPHRO, APOLOGY, CRITO, PHAEDO, PHAEDRUS, H. N. Fowler.

PLATO: LACHES, PROTAGORAS, MENO, EUTHYDEMUS. W. R. M. Lamb.

PLATO: LAWS. Rev. R. G. Bury. 2 Vols.

PLATO: LYSIS, SYMPOSIUM, GORGIAS. W. R. M. Lamb.

PLATO: Republic. Paul Shorey. 2 Vols.

PLATO: STATESMAN, PHILEBUS. H. N. Fowler; ION. W. R. M. Lamb.

PLATO: THEAETETUS and SOPHIST. H. N. Fowler.

PLATO: TIMAEUS, CRITIAS, CLITOPHO, MENEXENUS, EPISTULAE. Rev. R. G. Bury.

PLOTINUS: A. H. Armstrong. 7 Vols. Vols. I.–III.

PLUTARCH: MORALIA. 16 Vols. Vols I.–V. F. C. Babbitt. Vol. VI. W. C. Helmbold. Vols. VII. and XIV. P. H. De Lacy and B. Einarson. Vol. VIII. P. A. Clement and H. B. Hoffleit. Vol. IX. E. L. Minar, Jr., F. H. Sandbach, W. C. Helmbold. Vol. X. H. N. Fowler. Vol. XI. L. Pearson and F. H. Sandbach. Vol. XII. H. Cherniss and W. C. Helmbold. Vol. XIII 1–2. H. Cherniss. Vol. XV. F. H. Sandbach.

PLUTARCH: THE PARALLEL LIVES. B. Perrin. 11 Vols.

POLYBIUS. W. R. Paton. 6 Vols.

PROCOPIUS. H. B. Dewing. 7 Vols.

PTOLEMY: TETRABIBLOS. F. E. Robbins.

QUINTUS SMYRNAEUS. A. S. Way. Verse trans.

SEXTUS EMPIRICUS. Rev. R. G. Bury. 4 Vols.

SOPHOCLES. F. Storr. 2 Vols. Verse trans.

STRABO: GEOGRAPHY. Horace L. Jones. 8 Vols.

THEOCRITUS. Cf. GREEK BUCOLIC POETS.

THEOPHRASTUS: CHARACTERS. J. M. Edmonds. HERODES, etc. A. D. Knox.

THEOPHRASTUS: ENQUIRY INTO PLANTS. Sir Arthur Hort, Bart. 2 Vols.

THEOPHRASTUS: DE CAUSIS PLANTARUM. G. K. K. Link and B. Einarson. 3 Vols. Vol. I.

THUCYDIDES. C. F. Smith. 4 Vols.

TRYPHIODORUS. Cf. OPPIAN.

XENOPHON: CYROPAEDIA. Walter Miller. 2 Vols.

XENOPHON: HELLENCIA. C. L. Brownson. 2 Vols.

XENOPHON: ANABASIS. C. L. Brownson.

XENOPHON: MEMORABILIA AND OECONOMICUS. E. C. Marchant. SYMPOSIUM AND APOLOGY. O. J. Todd.

XENOPHON: SCRIPTA MINORA. E. C. Marchant. CONSTITUTION OF THE ATHENIANS. G. W. Bowersock.